THE 10 CHALLENGE

10 WEEKS
10 WAYS TO A JESUS-LED LIFE

ANDRÉ LESPERANCE • ANDREA JACKSON

THE EVANGELICAL CATHOLIC

Nihil obstat: Mr. Timothy Cavanaugh
                  Censor Deputatus
                  February 7, 2024

Imprimatur: + James Robert Bartylla
                  Vicar General of the Diocese of Madison
                  February 7, 2024

ISBN: 979-8-9891366-4-3

THE 10 CHALLENGE

10 WEEKS
10 WAYS TO A JESUS-LED LIFE

ANDRÉ LESPERANCE • ANDREA JACKSON
THE EVANGELICAL CATHOLIC

CONTENTS

PREFACE

You show me the path of life.
In your presence there is fullness of joy.
— Psalm 16:11, NRSV-CE

ow do we access the richness of our vast, mysteriously beautiful, and wonderful but at-times-puzzling Catholic faith?
Years of following Jesus and working in professional ministry
have convinced us of the power and importance of sure guidance
in the life of discipleship.

Through much prayer, discussion, trial, and error, we created *The
10:10 Challenge* as one such guide. It's a ten-week journey through
ten foundational and transformative practices of discipleship that
are both ever-ancient and ever-new. These practices, or ways of
life, have always marked the path of growing in friendship and
intimacy with the Author of all that is good.

We write as fellow seekers, followers, and participants in the
divine life this book points to. We write as flawed sinners who are
greatly loved by God; as disciples who continue to discover and
be saved by the Lord.

The emphasis throughout this book is on the *how* of discipleship
(the practice of faith), more than on the *what* (catechetics) or the
why (apologetics). Come along with us for ten weeks as we share
some of what we have learned about following Jesus. If Jesus
weren't absolutely faithful and generous, we would have zero
confidence that it would be worth your time. But he is faithful! He
is generous! And leaning into his presence and action is always a
life-changing adventure.

Thank you for trusting us enough to give it a shot. A huge thank-
you as well to the benefactors of the Evangelical Catholic who
made this possible, to our EC colleagues and various readers who
tested our drafts and offered valuable feedback, and to our spiritual directors and mentors who have shaped and accompanied
our following of Jesus over the years.

May God richly bless you during the next ten weeks and beyond,
André Lesperance and Andrea Jackson

Memorial of St. Ambrose
December 7, 2023

COME, FOLLOW ME

Come, follow me.
– Matthew 4:19, NIV

With three simple words, Jesus issues a life-changing invitation. This invitation first reached the disciples in Galilee over two thousand years ago. Then, through the Holy Spirit and the ministry of the Church, it proceeded to reach the ends of the earth. This same invitation, from the very same Jesus, still beckons us today—"Come, follow me."

This book, and the experience it represents, is for those who dare to trust that Jesus is who he said he was, and that a Jesus-led life is the surest path to the fulfillment of our hearts' deepest longings. It is for those who have tasted and seen something of the Lord's goodness and grace, but who long for more: more clarity, peace, joy, healing, guidance, confidence, prayerfulness, purpose, freedom, or resilience. In short, it's for those who desire to step more fully into the abundant life Jesus came to give.

Jesus, we believe as Christians, is far more than a wise historical figure. He is the living God who continues to come to his people and set them free. He is the way, the truth, and the life, the leader and perfecter of our faith, and the good shepherd who leads his flock into abundant life. He is the Alpha and the Omega, the beginning and the end who stands knocking at the door of our hearts, promising a heavenly feast to all who receive him. He comes so that our joy may be complete.[1]

Discipleship means hearing and answering Jesus' call, resounding through the ages and found in every human heart, "Come, follow me." It means choosing to learn from Jesus his way and his truth so that he might become our life. It means entering a lifelong journey with a decisive direction and an infinite horizon. This journey begins in Baptism, culminates in heaven, and in the in-between we discover, sometimes little by little, our deepest identity, our inestimable worth, and our highest calling—to become love as he is love.

In short, discipleship means saying "yes" to Jesus—for the first time or the thousandth time—with whatever amount of faith one has. And if you feel you have more doubt, distraction, or disinterest than faith these days, take heart! Jesus himself is the one who told us we don't need much to get started. A small amount—even "faith the size of a mustard seed" (Luke 17:6) will do just fine.

THE 10:10 CHALLENGE

In John 10:10, Jesus tells us why he came: "I came so that they might have life and have it more abundantly." The 10:10 Challenge walks you through an intentional season of growth in the abundant life that comes from following Jesus. You and a partner (or very small group) will devote ten weeks to practicing and discussing ten ways of life that Jesus himself lived and which make up the fundamentals of Catholic discipleship:[2]

1. **Pray from the Heart:** Draw close to God in the intimate dialogue of daily prayer.

2. **Dwell in God's Word:** Encounter God's living and active Word through meditation on Scripture.

3. **Grow in Freedom:** Seek healing in the Sacrament of Reconciliation and grow in detachment from sin.

4. **Worship the Lord:** Give praise and honor to God, especially through the celebration of the Eucharist.

5. **Love Your Neighbor:** Serve others with the compassion of Jesus.

6. **Encourage One Another:** Draw strength from a community of disciples who support each other and spur one another onward.

7. **Follow God's Lead:** Discern the Holy Spirit's promptings and respond to the Lord's guidance in your life.

8. **Call on Mary and the Saints:** Follow the saints toward a fully transformed life in Jesus.

9. **Entrust Your Life to Jesus:** Rely on God in every circumstance: big and small, joyful and sorrowful, life and death.

10. **Share the Good News:** Witness to the saving power of God in your actions and words.

HOW TO TAKE THE CHALLENGE

Follow these instructions to complete the 10:10 Challenge and grow in a Jesus-led, abundant life.

Find Your People

The 10:10 Challenge is designed to be used with one or a few others who are ready to take the challenge with you. Why?

Because forming new habits is hard! Even more importantly, Jesus promised a special outpouring of his presence and companionship "where two or three are gathered together in my name" (Matthew 18:20). No wonder, then, that we grow the most when we have people who explore, listen, encourage, pray, and model discipleship with us.

So as you get started, invite one, two, or three people to join you in the 10:10 Challenge. You'll meet weekly to discuss your experiences of each chapter with this friend or very small group using the conversation guides provided. This small setting allows each person to share deeply and be truly known. It creates an environment where God can work through authentic relationships of support, prayer, vulnerable conversation, and mutual accountability.

- Meet weekly for one hour.
- See page 335 for tips on who and how to invite.

Pray Daily with the Prayer Guides
Prayer is the most foundational discipleship practice, so the bulk of this book is material for prayer. It contains seven guided prayer sessions per week, for a total of seventy prayer times. These sessions allow your mind and heart to soak in various aspects of each topic in a balanced, Spirit-led experience. Set aside fifteen minutes per day for these prayer times. Though you might have to sacrifice to do it, giving fifteen minutes of your day (about one percent of your time) to the Lord in prayer and reflection is in itself transformative, especially if you don't already have this habit.

Take Action
You'll leave each conversation with an action plan for implementing the practice in your life that week.

In addition to the action plan, look for tips woven throughout each chapter. You don't need to use all of the tips between conversations, but if one stands out to you, give it a try!

Sign Up for Bonus Content
We want to support you as you take the 10:10 Challenge! Visit *1010challenge.org* to get helpful bonus content for your 10:10 Challenge experience. You'll receive encouragement from the authors as you make your way through the ten weeks of the challenge, a printable 10:10 checklist to track your progress, and a shareable version of this introduction to send to people you're inviting.

3

THE POWER OF HABIT

This ten-week journey is designed to kickstart your momentum toward establishing the ten ways above as *habits* of mind, heart, and body. That's why each chapter includes various tips and a closing section called "Make It a Habit." The 10:10 Challenge introduces you to these ten core discipleship practices and points you to ways you can continue them for years to come.

On a natural level, habits are uniquely powerful for shaping our lives. If you have ever played an instrument or learned to ride a bike, you know that difficult actions become easier (and more delightful) over time with repetition. When we choose the right thoughts and actions to repeat again and again, we not only come to think and do good things with more ease; we actually *become* the kind of people who do the good freely and joyfully.*

The same is true on a spiritual or supernatural level but with an added, even more incredible dimension of God's grace. We don't perform spiritual practices to gain God's attention, love, or blessing; we already have all this in abundant measure through no merit of our own. Discipleship practices, sometimes called spiritual disciplines, simply describe what it looks like when people walk in faith, hope, and love. More precisely, they are *thoughts and actions we can choose to do that put us in a position to receive from God the grace (power, ability) to do what we cannot do through effort alone.*[3]

We simply cannot, for example, love our enemies, forgive offenses willingly, or let go of our unhealthy attachments by sheer willpower. But we can choose to show up to Mass with an open mind, to read a small portion of God's Word reflectively, to tell God how we're feeling today, or to do something loving for our neighbor. When approached with the right attitude, these consciously chosen practices open us to God, whose grace then has more room to work both *in us* and *through us*. We become, over time, more patient, self-aware, courageous, etc. than we ever could have become on our own. When repeated, these thoughts and actions become the best kinds of habits. They become a lifestyle, a *way*.

---

* The opposite is also true. When we repeat selfish or unhealthy thoughts and actions time and again, those pathways too get easier to follow as we become the kind of people who enjoy what is decidedly not good for us or others. From ancient Greek philosophers, to present-day neuroscientists and mental health professionals, some of the brightest minds in human history have long explored and marveled at the incredible power of habit over human health and happiness.

Call this growing in *holiness,* or *abundant life,* or *true freedom and joy.* This is the ever-ancient, ever-new pathway and adventure of learning to follow Jesus.

BEYOND THE CHALLENGE

Share Your Experience
Once you've completed the challenge, visit *1010challenge.org* and share about your experience! Your testimony can help future 10:10 challengers overcome fears and hesitations about getting started. If you submit a testimony, you will receive a discount when purchasing another copy of this book to share with a friend.

Make Disciples
After you complete the 10:10 Challenge, if the experience blessed you, consider who else might enjoy and benefit from this same process. As the saying goes, pay it forward! Doing it a second time will further establish these ways of Jesus in your own life, and accompanying others through the process is one way to live out Jesus' Great Commission: to "go, therefore, and make disciples of all nations" (Matthew 28:19). It's one way to change the world!

Continue to Grow
The first time you use this book, complete the chapters in order as written. But since each of these weeks represents a whole area of Christian thought and practice, you can continue to dive deeply into them in the future. Come back to various tips throughout the chapters and the "Make It a Habit" sections for ideas on how you can continue to grow in the abundant life of Jesus.

The "Discipleship Practices" section at the end of each chapter provides a user-friendly collection of the various practices introduced throughout the book. Refer back to these when you want a reminder of a specific way to pray or to introduce a certain practice to a friend, family member, or student.

ARE YOU READY?

If you faithfully meet with another disciple or two for these ten weeks, pray with the seventy prayer guides, and practice the ways of life contained therein, we are confident you will experience more of the abundant life Jesus came to give you! And living the abundant life of Jesus is what the 10:10 Challenge is all about.

What do you say?

If you are ready and willing to enter this season of growth with an open mind and heart, we invite you to say or write a prayer, telling the Lord of your commitment, your desires, and your need for his help. Below is one prayer you may use or adapt as your own.

Jesus, I choose to make room in my life to prioritize my relationship with you.

I believe—and want to believe even more—that you are the way, the truth, and the life; that you see me, hear me, love me, and walk with me through my every joy and pain, success and failure.

Thank you for loving me as I am—a work in progress. I confess that I need your healing, strength, and guidance. I commit to giving you regular, focused time and attention; to learning new practices of faith; and to deepening the practices I already know.

Through prayer, action, and discussion, I seek to know you more and to become even more the person you've created me to be. I choose to put forth the effort to grow in friendship with you and with those you place in my path to walk with me.

Help me always in this quest, in the name of the Father, and of the Son, and of the Holy Spirit. Amen.

ENDNOTES

1. See Luke 1:68, John 14:6, Hebrews 12:2, John 10:10, Psalm 23:2, Revelation 22:13, Revelation 3:20, and John 16:24.

2. This list of practices, and the contents within them, intentionally draws upon the "six tasks of catechesis" outlined in the USCCB's *General Directory for Catechesis:* (1) promoting the knowledge of faith, (2) liturgical education, (3) moral formation, (4) teaching to pray, (5) education for community life, and (6) missionary initiation. For a similar list arranged around a memorable diagram, see the Discipleship Wheel on p. 338.

3. "General Introduction" to Richard J. Foster, ed., *The Life with God Bible: New Revised Standard Version with the Deuterocanonical Books* (San Francisco: HarperOne, 2009), xxxiv.

WEEK 1
PRAY FROM THE HEART

When you pray, go to your inner room, close the door,
and pray to your Father in secret. And your Father
who sees in secret will repay you.

– Matthew 6:6

CONVERSATION ONE
Pray from the Heart

WELCOME (3 MIN)
Read aloud.

Welcome to the 10:10 Challenge! To complete the next ten weeks of prayer, action, and growth, you'll need the people right here with you to encourage you and keep you going. Community is a key ingredient for intentional growth in following Jesus, therefore, this challenge is designed for use with a partner or a very small group. The discussion guides in this book allow you to accompany one another through the 10:10 Challenge. Here you put your minds and hearts together for prayer, discussion, accountability, support, and communal discovery.

Commit to meeting together over the next ten weeks. Open yourselves to God and one another. The Lord may indeed speak to you through what you share with each other. Perhaps this is part of what Jesus had in mind when he promised his followers, "Where two or three are gathered together in my name, there I am in the midst of them" (Matthew 18:20).

The first half of today's discussion allows you to get to know each other better, especially by sharing some of your experiences of faith. In the second half, you'll discuss this week's theme: Pray from the Heart.

OPENING PRAYER (2 MIN)
Select one person to open in prayer. Use the following prayer or your own words.

Father, thank you for gathering us here today. Come and dwell among us as we gather in your name. Speak your words to us and through us. We give you this time, in the name of the Father, and of the Son, and of the Holy Spirit. Amen.

GROUP INTRODUCTIONS (20 MIN)
Introduce yourselves and share about your hopes for the 10:10 Challenge using the following questions. Make sure everyone has a chance to share.

- What was your experience of faith growing up?
- What turning points have you experienced in your relationship with God throughout your life?

- What is motivating you to take the 10:10 Challenge at this point in your life?

ABOUT PRAY FROM THE HEART (15 MIN)

Read aloud.

esus said, "When you pray, go to your inner room, close the door, and pray to your Father in secret. And your Father who sees in secret will repay you" (Matthew 6:6). He practiced what he preached. Throughout the Gospels, we see Jesus withdrawing from the crowds and his disciples, finding solitary places to pray.

What is prayer? In its most basic sense, prayer means communicating with the living God. Like all genuine communication, it's a two-way street. In prayer, we talk to God, who listens to us, and we listen for God's voice in return.

Prayer is both profound and simple. Think of it: we dare speak to the maker of the universe, the God who breathed us into life! And yet, this same God walked with Adam and Eve in the paradise he created for them,[1] and, in the coming of Jesus, lowered himself to be with us even in the brokenness of our world.[2] He continues to draw close to us today, through the gift of the Holy Spirit.

But let's be honest: prayer is also mysterious, strange, and difficult. It can be boring, unnerving, and just plain unattractive—even to those of us who claim Christ as our friend and savior. Prayer is not only a place of communion with our loving God, it's also a battleground for our time, attention, and will. It's a call to "waste time" in the presence of God, who does not always make himself known and felt. And all too often it can feel just like that—a waste of time! Doubts abound (Is God really listening?), questions arise (Am I doing this right?), distractions beckon (Did I pay the credit card bill on time?), and the laundry remains unfolded. And even when we make the time, it can be a challenge to get real with God and truly pray from the heart, beyond the surface level.

This chapter won't take away the battle and struggle of prayer, but through its various reflections and prayer times you will strengthen a particular prayer muscle, one the Church calls "mental prayer." In this type of prayer, we talk to God in our own words, praying from the heart, and we listen for his voice speaking in the depths of our being.

YOUR CHALLENGE THIS WEEK

☐ Pray from the heart every day using the daily prayer guide.

Discuss a few of the following questions.

- What stands out to you from this description of prayer?
- What does prayer look like at this point in your life?
- What struggles do you most commonly face when attempting to pray?
- How do you desire to grow in your prayer life, if at all?

PRAY FROM THE HEART TOGETHER (7 MIN)
Read aloud.

The prayer guides throughout the 10:10 Challenge use a simple format for personal prayer.

- Open to God
- Pray from the Heart
- Close

This format helps us set aside time to slow down our minds and bodies and talk with God. While we can talk to God at any time of the day, even while driving or doing our daily work and chores, bracketing time each day where we concentrate solely on talking with God deepens our relationship with the Lord.

Try it now. One person reads the prompts aloud for everyone to follow. Allow time for silent prayer by pausing where indicated.

Open to God

In the name of the Father, and of the Son, and of the Holy Spirit. Amen.

Sit upright with your feet on the floor. Rest your hands comfortably on your lap. Close your eyes and take a few deep breaths. (Pause for a few seconds to allow everyone to do this.)

Come, Holy Spirit. We invite you to be here with us now. Quiet our minds and hearts. Help us be open to you in this time of prayer. Come, Holy Spirit.

(Pause briefly again.)

Pray from the Heart

Give thanks.
Bring to mind something you are thankful for today. It could be something big or something small, some insight or moment from this conversation, or anything else you are grateful for today. Take a moment to relish this gift and silently thank God for it. (Pause for about a minute to allow everyone to do this.)

Cast your cares.
Is there anything you are worried or preoccupied about? Bring it to mind and, in the silence of your heart, tell God what is troubling you. (Pause for about a minute to allow everyone to do this.)

Ask, seek, knock.
God is a good Father who wants us to ask for what we need. What graces or help do you need as you begin the 10:10 Challenge? Ask God for whatever you need. (Pause for about a minute to allow everyone to do this.)

Close
We will close with a minute of silence. In this time, focus on being receptive to any graces, insight, strength, or peace God may want to give you today. (Pause for about a minute).

Holy Spirit, thank you for being with us and for drawing us closer to yourself. Please continue to guide and strengthen us as we begin this challenge together.

In the name of the Father, and of the Son, and of the Holy Spirit. Amen.

ACTION PLAN (8 MIN)
Read aloud.

Once again, your challenge this week is to develop or strengthen a daily habit of praying from the heart using the seven days of prayer found in this chapter.

To set yourself up for success, make a plan: schedule your fifteen-minute daily appointments with God and choose a quiet place to meet him. Use the prayer guides each day (starting on page 13). If you miss a day, do two prayer times the next day to catch up. Try especially hard not to miss two days in a row, as you cannot "cram" this material. It's meant to be digested slowly and prayerfully, not skimmed.

Be as consistent as you can with where and when you pray. Schedule prayer in the morning if possible to establish it as part of your morning routine. This helps you keep your daily commitment and leaves room to pray later in the day if something urgent forces you to change plans. Morning is also a time of day when many people are fresh and not overly distracted by the day's events. If you are too groggy to pray, even after a shower or a cup of coffee, choose a different time when you can consistently meet God in prayer.

Discuss your action plan.

- When and where will each of you pray each day?

NEXT MEETING (2 MIN)

Make sure you have your next discussion on the calendar.

CLOSING PRAYER (3 MIN)

Close with the prayer below, which is slightly adapted from the introduction and changed to a communal form. Have one person read it aloud or take turns reading the different stanzas.

Jesus, we choose you. We make room in our lives for you and prioritize our relationship with you. We believe — and want to believe even more — that you are the way, the truth, and the life; that you see us, hear us, love us, and walk with us through our every joy and pain, success and failure.

Thank you for loving us as we are — works in progress. We confess that we need your healing, strength, and guidance. We commit to giving you regular, focused time and attention to learn new practices of faith and to deepen the practices we already know.

Through prayer, action, and discussion, we seek to know you more and to become even more the people you've created us to be. We choose to put forth the effort to grow in friendship with you and with those you place on our paths.

Help us always in this quest, in the name of the Father, and of the Son, and of the Holy Spirit. Amen.

PRAYER GUIDE
Pray from the Heart

Day 1. Available

Here I am.
– Isaiah 6:8

"Are you available?" You might hear this from a friend, a co-worker, a child, or a telemarketer. If you are available, it means you have some capacity and willingness to give your time and attention to that person. You're ready to listen, talk, or do something with them.

If you're not available, it means you're not willing or able to give the other person your attention at that moment. It's common enough for two people to be in the same room and not be available to one another. Maybe they're paying attention to their phones or one is busy cleaning the kitchen and listening to a podcast. Physical proximity to someone is one thing; availability is another.

One way to understand prayer is by thinking about availability. Though God is always present with us, prayer makes us *available* to him. Prayer says, "Here I am," (Isaiah 6:8). "I'm here with you. I'm present."

No single definition fully captures the mystery of prayer. Various saints, bishops, and theologians describe it differently. Taken together, their depictions help us explore the dynamic reality of prayer. Consider:

"Prayer is the raising of one's mind and heart to God."
– St. John Damascene[3]

"Prayer in my opinion is nothing else than a close sharing between friends; it means taking time frequently to be alone with him who we know loves us." – St. Teresa of Avila[4]

"Prayer is the encounter of God's thirst with ours. God thirsts that we may thirst for him." – *Catechism of the Catholic Church*[5]

"Prayer is putting oneself in the hands of God, at His disposition, and listening to his voice in the depth of our hearts." – St. Teresa of Calcutta[6]

13

No matter how we define it, prayer begins by opening to God, by choosing to become *available*. When we give God that space and attention, we begin to know him not just as "the God of the universe somewhere up there," but as "my Lord and my God" (John 20:28).

As you transition into this time of prayer,* get into a comfortable, receptive position. Sitting upright works for most people but if you start nodding off, try walking around slowly as you pray.

If you have trouble concentrating or formulating your thoughts, try praying aloud or writing your prayers in a journal.

OPEN TO GOD

In the name of the Father, and of the Son, and of the Holy Spirit. Amen.

Take a few deep breaths, slowing yourself down, and becoming aware of yourself and God.

Here I am, Lord. I believe you are here with me, that you are always available to me. Help me make myself—my heart, my mind, my body—available to you now. Come, Holy Spirit, and meet me here in this time of prayer.

PRAY FROM THE HEART

- Which definition of prayer on page 13 stands out to you? What is prayer for you?
- What does it mean for you to be available to God? Talk to God about how available or unavailable you've been to him recently.

---

* Hey there, it's André and Andrea. We've both been there: you come to that part in a book that tells you to pause, to reflect, or to pray. But you don't feel like it in that moment, or you're running late, so you skim the questions and just keep reading to get to the end of the section quickly. If you approach the prayer guides this way, you simply won't have the fundamental experience this book is guiding you through. These are prayer times with some reading, not reading times with some optional ideas for prayer. Only you can place yourself in the presence of God and open your heart and mind to these daily encounters with him. We can't do that for you, and reading the material won't substitute for the work that only God can do in you. Please make the Lord the center of these prayer times, and not our words. Our words are merely pointers and guides to cultivating a deeper intimacy with Jesus. Seek the Lord and you will find him and all the gifts he has to give.

Philippians 4:6-7, NRSV-CE
Do not worry about anything, but in everything by prayer and supplication with thanksgiving let your requests be made known to God. And the peace of God, which surpasses all understanding, will guard your hearts and your minds in Christ Jesus.

- God invites us to bring everything to him in prayer. Be honest with God about whatever you're bringing with you to prayer today.

CLOSE

As you bring your prayer time to a close, spend one to two minutes in silent attentiveness to God. Close your eyes and make yourself available to God's quiet work within you. Perhaps imagine the peace of God that guards your heart and mind coming to rest upon you in the silence.

Jesus, thank you for your love and your promise to be with me always. Help me stay aware of and available to you throughout my day today.

In the name of the Father, and of the Son, and of the Holy Spirit. Amen.

Day 2. Three Expressions of Prayer

He was praying in a certain place, and when he had finished, one of his disciples said to him, "Lord, teach us to pray."
– Luke 11:1

While there are endless ways to pray, the Church articulates three basic "expressions" of prayer: vocal, meditative, and contemplative.[7]

Learning even a little about each one can deepen our understanding and experience of prayer.

Vocal prayer means speaking to God. It is often the first expression of prayer we learn, whether as children or adults. The term refers to prayers written by others who came before us, which we read or recite by memory, such as the Our Father, Hail Mary, Glory Be, and meal prayers. But vocal prayer also extends to spontaneous prayers we speak to God from our hearts.

In meditative prayer (or meditation) the mind is active, reflecting on the meaning of what God has revealed. "Meditation is above all a quest. The mind seeks to understand the why and the how of the Christian life, in order to adhere and respond to what the Lord is asking."[8]

This differs somewhat from non-Christian or contemporary spiritualities' use of the term "meditation," often aimed at emptying the mind. Meditation in the Christian tradition means employing the mind in prayerful pondering of truth in dialogue with the living God within. Scripture, writings of the saints, liturgical texts, religious art, and the beauty of creation all aid Christian meditation.

Finally, contemplative prayer moves beyond words, mental ponderings, and active dialogue with God. In this prayer of silence, we simply dwell in God's presence, trusting him to hold us in love and work deeply in our soul—even without us noticing. "Contemplative prayer is a gaze of faith fixed on Jesus," the *Catechism of the Catholic Church* describes, before quoting a parishioner of St. John Vianney: "I look at him and he looks at me" (2715). Contemplative prayer is "the simplest expression of the mystery of prayer" (2713), "a silent love."[9]

Speak. Quest. Gaze. These three expressions of prayer may overlap and blend into one another within the course of a given prayer time or method. Together they describe the dynamic relationship with God we're privileged to experience in prayer.

For today's prayer time, you'll pray with the ultimate vocal prayer: the Our Father. Instead of marching through it, however, use its distinct phrases to draw you deeper into meditative prayer.

OPEN TO GOD

In the name of the Father, and of the Son, and of the Holy Spirit. Amen.

Take a few deep breaths as you open yourself to God.

Jesus, thank you for teaching us how to pray. As I pray today with the prayer you taught us, help me to slow down, using each phrase to enter into deeper communion with you and the Father. Amen.

PRAY FROM THE HEART

Pray the Lord's Prayer slowly, pausing to meditate (reflect) on the meaning of each phrase. Add your own words to some of the phrases as you pray from the heart.

Here are a few examples to give you an idea of how to add your own words:

Our Father... God, it's so amazing and sometimes hard for me to believe that you made me your own child who you love and care about.

Thank you for your love for me and for making me part of your family...

...Give us this day our daily bread...Jesus, thank you for promising to supply all that I need. Today I need your peace about my upcoming presentation. Help me be myself, do my best, and entrust the results to you...

...And forgive us our trespasses... I'm sorry Lord for letting my frustrations with my brother drive me into gossip and rumination this week. Grant me your compassion for him and show me a better way to respond...

Our Father...

Who art in heaven...

Hallowed be thy name...

Thy Kingdom come...

Thy will be done on earth as it is in heaven...

Give us this day our daily bread...

And forgive us our trespasses...

As we forgive those who trespass against us...

And lead us not into temptation...

But deliver us from evil...

Amen...

CLOSE

Before wrapping up, spend a minute or two in a silent, contemplative gaze with Jesus, who authored this great prayer. Trust that as you do this, the Holy Spirit is interceding for you and holding you in love.

God, thank you for hearing my prayers. I trust you to provide for my needs today, Lord. Keep me and those I love safe and protect us from all evil. Amen.

TIP: POSTURES IN PRAYER

Our bodies play an important and necessary role in our spiritual lives. By God's design, the physical and non-physical aspects of creation are intimately connected. Therefore, the various postures at Mass (standing, sitting, kneeling) and the physical gestures (bowing, making the Sign of the Cross, extending a sign of peace, etc.) are meant to lead us into deep communal worship and prayer. Which of these postures and movements do you use in your personal prayer times? Are there others (like pacing or raising your hands) that appeal to you? Experiment to find what helps draw you into a prayerful interior space.

Day 3. Our Identity: Beloved

We love because he first loved us.
– 1 John 4:19

As Jesus began his public ministry, he visited John the Baptist on the Jordan River. When John baptized Jesus, the heavens broke open and God the Father spoke of Jesus as "my beloved Son, with whom I am well pleased" (Matthew 3:17). Through our own baptisms we take on that same identity: we are adopted into God's family, receiving by grace what Jesus is by nature. We are made sons and daughters of God, heirs to the Kingdom, children with whom he is well pleased.

Parents talk about the wave of love that comes over them the first time they hold their child in their arms. The baby didn't do anything to deserve their parents' love. They were beloved in that moment just for existing. God's love is infinitely like that moment. He looks upon us with great love and joy just because we are his children.

Prayer is a relationship of genuine love between us and God. In order to pray from the heart, we have to remind ourselves that God truly loves us. If we think God doesn't care about us, or is just waiting for us to mess up, or is removed and uninvolved, or angry with us, it's going to be pretty difficult for us to open our hearts to him. But the Scriptures remind us, "God proves his love for us in that while we were still sinners Christ died for us" (Romans 5:8). There's nothing you can do to earn (or to lose) God's love, but you can grow in your capacity to accept and respond to this great gift.

If you have been rejected, criticized, or trained to please others to receive love, it can be hard to accept the unconditional love God wants to give you. But he knows you better than you know yourself. And he loves you. He loved you into being. You are his beloved child. Sit in that truth. Let God love you today and every day.

OPEN TO GOD

In the name of the Father, and of the Son, and of the Holy Spirit. Amen.

Take a few deep breaths to slow yourself down. Perhaps open your hands receptively in your lap.

God, I believe you are here with me. You are always with me, and you love me completely. Please, Holy Spirit, guide me in this time of prayer.

PRAY FROM THE HEART

Matthew 3:16-17, NRSV-CE

And when Jesus had been baptized, just as he came up from the water, suddenly the heavens were opened to him and he saw the Spirit of God descending like a dove and alighting on him. And a voice from heaven said, "This is my Son, the Beloved, with whom I am well pleased."

Through Baptism, we share in Jesus' identity as God's beloved child. Take a moment to sit in God's love. Imagine him looking at you with joy, cherishing you, being well pleased with you.

- What is this like for you? Is it beautiful and reassuring? Emotional? Difficult? Boring?
- If you were to live without fear, in total confidence in God, what would that be like? How would you be different?
- Tell God about any anxieties or doubts you have about your belovedness or anything else. Ask him to give you more confidence in his love and care for you.

CLOSE

Spend a minute or two in silent prayer. In this brief time, simply rest in God's unending love for you, his beloved child.

Good Father, thank you for loving me completely. You love me better than anyone, even than I do myself. Give me the grace to approach life with your gifts of peace, perseverance, and thanksgiving. Whenever I doubt myself or your love, remind me that I am your beloved child, with whom you are well pleased.

In the name of the Father, and of the Son, and of the Holy Spirit. Amen.

TIP: REMEMBER WHO(SE) YOU ARE

Write the truth of your baptismal identity on a sticky note or note-card. Put it somewhere you'll see every day to remind you of God's love for you.

"You are my beloved [son/daughter]; with you I am well pleased" (Mark 1:11).

Day 4. Notice, Tell, Invite

God does not see as a mortal, who sees the appearance. The Lord looks into the heart.
— 1 Samuel 16:7

"How are you doing today…really?"

True friends genuinely want to know how we're doing. They are not satisfied with the generic "fine" answer that might work for others.

This is true in our friendship with Jesus. He already knows us better than we know ourselves, but he wants us to be honest (with ourselves and with him) about what's *really* going on.

Sometimes, it can take us a moment to even *notice* what's happening within. Perhaps our lives are so full and fast-paced that we rarely stop to ponder our inner world. Or maybe we're afraid to admit that we're not as "fine" as we want others (and ourselves) to believe. But ignoring our deeper feelings or hidden emotions doesn't make them go away. In fact, they usually build up until we reach a breaking point and they pour out whether we want them to or not.

One way to pray (and open a release valve on that inner pressure cooker) is to notice what we're feeling, tell Jesus about it, and invite him into that space. There's nothing we need to hide from God. He's capable of receiving our every emotion—the pleasant and the unpleasant ones.

During his time on earth, Jesus experienced the full breadth of human emotions: from sadness and grief to joy and satisfaction. We know he wept at the death of his friend Lazarus, he celebrated the marriage of a couple in Cana, expressed anger at the religious establishment's abuses, and rejoiced in the disciples' triumphs. When we notice, tell, and invite God into what we're feeling, we allow God to heal and elevate our inner lives. Through prayer, we can experience these emotions in the light of God's care. He can

help us work through difficult emotions and grow to truly appreciate the beautiful moments in our lives.

OPEN TO GOD

In the name of the Father, and of the Son, and of the Holy Spirit. Amen.

Take a few deep breaths as you open yourself to God.

Come, Holy Spirit. Help me see what is going on inside of me, especially my emotions. Please highlight anything that you want me to bring to you in prayer right now.

PRAY FROM THE HEART

Breathe in a calm, unhurried way, becoming aware of your inner life. Notice any emotions that are hovering just beneath the surface. They may be pleasant or unpleasant. Try not to push them away but allow them to surface.

Notice: Identify an emotion you're feeling. Use the lists below to help you. It's common to feel multiple things at once. For example, you could feel gratitude for your job at the same time that you feel anxious about a project you're working on.

Notice the emotion. What does it feel like in your mind/heart? In your body? Is it pleasant? Unpleasant?

• *Grateful*	• *Jealous*	• *Creative*
• *Frustrated*	• *Confident*	• *Playful*
• *Bold*	• *Hopeful*	• *Ashamed*
• *Bored*	• *Angry*	• *Understood*
• *Annoyed*	• *Worthless*	• *Accepted*
• *Satisfied*	• *Loving*	• *Embarrassed*
• *Lonely*	• *Joyful*	• *Refreshed*
• *Stressed*	• *Depressed*	• *Patient*
• *Comforted*	• *Excited*	• *Hopeless*
• *Disappointed*	• *Peaceful*	• *Guilty*
• *Tired*	• *Overwhelmed*	• *Relieved*

Tell: Tell Jesus about the emotion and what it's like. Open up to him about any situations surrounding the emotion. Share openly about whatever comes to mind: the good and the bad. Feel free to elaborate a bit. He already knows, but it's good to take note of our inner worlds and to express ourselves to God.

Jesus, I feel _____ *about* _____ .

Invite: Invite Jesus into this part of your inner life, being honest about your experience and open to his companionship and guidance.

Jesus, I invite you into my feelings of _____.
What do you want to show me here?

Linger a bit and listen. Pay attention to any shifts or changes within, such as new thoughts, clarifications, or additional emotions that surface.

CLOSE

End your time of prayer with a minute or two of silence. In this brief time, rest in his care for you: body, mind, and spirit.

God, please give me the grace to _____. You are in all the details of my life, Jesus. I give you praise/ask your help for _____.

I trust you, Lord. Help me to glorify you in this and in every emotion I experience today, turning to you often.

In the name of the Father, and of the Son, and of the Holy Spirit. Amen.

TIP: NOTICE, TELL, INVITE THROUGHOUT THE DAY

Try to take notice of your emotions throughout your day. Stop at least once to briefly tell God how you feel and invite him into that emotion or into the situation giving rise to it. This simple pattern can become a tiny habit by which you stay more connected to Jesus (and yourself) through the ups and downs of your day.

Day 5. Give Thanks

In all circumstances give thanks, for this is the will of God
for you in Christ Jesus.
– 1 Thessalonians 5:18

Gratitude is a great place to start when setting out to grow in prayer. While it may seem easy at first glance, cultivating gratitude takes courage. The world is full of things to complain about, and our brains are wired to worry. Giving our frustrations and worries to God and thanking him for specific blessings is a powerful way to reorient our minds and hearts to goodness all around us. Thanksgiving doesn't take our struggles and sufferings away,

but it does help us know "the peace of God that surpasses all understanding" (Philippians 4:7).

Expressing our gratitude to God is a step that's easy to skip! It's one thing to enjoy a moment or a gift, it's another to give thanks for it.

> As [Jesus] continued his journey to Jerusalem, he traveled through Samaria and Galilee. As he was entering a village, ten lepers met [him]. They stood at a distance from him and raised their voice, saying, "Jesus, Master! Have pity on us!" And when he saw them, he said, "Go show yourselves to the priests." As they were going they were cleansed. And one of them, realizing he had been healed, returned, glorifying God in a loud voice; and he fell at the feet of Jesus and thanked him. He was a Samaritan. Jesus said in reply, "Ten were cleansed, were they not? Where are the other nine? Has none but this foreigner returned to give thanks to God?" Then he said to him, "Stand up and go; your faith has saved you." (Luke 17:11-19)

All ten had received the gift. Their bodies were healed. But only one returned to give thanks to God, to acknowledge the giver. Jesus calls this "faith." Gratitude gives the Samaritan far more than physical healing, it puts him in right relationship with God.

May it be so too with us. Let us not forget to thank the Lord; for "every perfect gift is from above, coming down from the Father of lights" (James 1:17).

OPEN TO GOD

In the name of the Father, and of the Son, and of the Holy Spirit. Amen.

Take a few deep breaths as you open yourself to God. Invite God's presence and help.

Jesus, I believe you are here with me. Thank you for this time together. Please help me recognize your goodness and gifts, especially in the last day or two. Help me to have a grateful heart.

PRAY FROM THE HEART

Philippians 4:8, NRSV-CE
Whatever is true, whatever is honorable, whatever is just, whatever is pure, whatever is pleasing, whatever is commendable, if there is any excellence and if there is anything worthy of praise, think about these things.

Psalm 9:1, NRSV-CE
I will give thanks to the Lord with my whole heart.

Look back over the last twenty-four hours, reviewing hour-by-hour. Pay attention to blessings you notice—big or small.

Note or write down three to five things you're grateful for. Be as specific as possible and try to choose something very small for at least one of your gratitudes, perhaps something no one else could have noticed but you.

1. _____

2. _____

3. _____

4. _____

5. _____

Linger for a few moments with each of these specific blessings. Savor each one as you would a delicious bite from a spectacular meal. For example, for each gratitude you listed, do two things:

1. Thank God for it.
2. Tell him why it delights you. Be specific and include some details.

CLOSE

End your time of prayer with one to two minutes of silence turning your grateful heart to God in silent praise.

Heavenly Father, thank you for showing me _____.

Please give me the grace to notice the many blessings you send me, and to acknowledge and thank you as the source of all that is good.

In the name of the Father, and of the Son, and of the Holy Spirit. Amen.

TIP: EVENING GRATITUDE

Each night before bed, thank God for one or two specific blessings from your day—big or small. When you repeat this practice over and over (at any time of the day), it trains your brain to look for and relish the small, simple pleasures in life, along with the bigger more obvious blessings. It's a powerful habit for cultivating joy.

Day 6. Ask, Seek, Knock

Ask and it will be given to you; seek and you will find; knock and the door will be opened to you. For everyone who asks, receives; and the one who seeks, finds; and to the one who knocks, the door will be opened.
— Matthew 7:7-8

"Father, please bless Aunt Susan with health and healing." "Jesus, help me to do my best on my math test today." "I do believe, help my unbelief!" (Mark 9:24).

Asking or petitioning God is one of the first and most basic ways we learn to pray. Though there is much more to prayer than asking, Scripture encourages and instructs us, time and again, to turn to God with our requests, both big and small. Jesus seems intent on reminding us that the Father is not bothered by our requests. He loves answering our prayers and delights when we turn our hearts to him in childlike ways.

Which one of you would hand his son a stone when he asks for a loaf of bread, or a snake when he asks for a fish? If you then, who are wicked, know how to give good gifts to your children, how much more will your heavenly Father give good things to those who ask him. (Matthew 7:9-11)

It's true that we don't always receive everything we ask for, but even then we are not left empty-handed. Luke records a time when Jesus made the same point as above, but a little differently: "If you then, who are wicked, know how to give good gifts to your children, how much more will the Father in heaven give *the holy Spirit* to those who ask him?" (Luke 11:13, emphasis added).

Sometimes we see the answers to our prayers, sometimes we don't, but we're strengthened by the Holy Spirit in the very asking. Either way, "ask and it *will* be given to you; seek and you *will* find; knock and the door *will* be opened to you." (Matthew 7:7, emphasis added). What an amazing promise from a loving Father who wants his children to run to him with the deepest desires of their hearts.

OPEN TO GOD

In the name of the Father, and of the Son, and of the Holy Spirit. Amen.

Take a few deep breaths as you open yourself to God.

Jesus, you tell me to ask you for what I need. I come to you today with my own needs and those of the people in my life. Help me trust you to provide for us and give us good gifts.

PRAY FROM THE HEART

John 16:23-24, NRSV-CE

Very truly, I tell you, if you ask anything of the Father in my name, he will give it to you. Until now you have not asked for anything in my name. Ask and you will receive, so that your joy may be complete."

- What people or situations are on your mind today?
- What will help you, or those who come to mind, experience more joy, freedom, love, generosity, kindness, healing, wholeness, closeness to God, etc.?

Bring these people and situations to our loving Father by asking for your own needs or interceding for (asking on behalf of) others. Use the prompt below to get you started. Be specific in asking God for whatever you or they need.

Good Father, in the name of Jesus I ask you to please_____.

(Repeat for any additional petitions.)

CLOSE

End your time of prayer with one to two minutes of silence. Open your hands in your lap and gently release all your petitions into God's care.

Let these words by St. Teresa of Avila, draw you into a deeper trust in God to supply for all of your needs.

Let nothing trouble you,

Let nothing scare you,

All is fleeting,

God alone is unchanging.

Patience

Everything obtains.

Who possesses God

Nothing wants.

God alone suffices.[10]

Amen.

Day 7. Meeting God in Silence

*The Father spoke one Word, which was his Son, and this
Word he speaks always in eternal silence, and in silence must it be
heard by the soul.*[11]
– St. John of the Cross

While God is closer to us than *anyone*, spending time with him in prayer is different than talking with a friend over coffee.

God doesn't (usually) speak to his people with an audible voice, but he *does* speak to us. When we pray from the heart, we not only let our words rise up to God but we also open our hearts and allow him to speak to us.

Worn out from rejection and failure, the prophet Elijah fled persecution and found himself on Mount Horeb, where God had revealed himself to Moses. A messenger of God appeared telling him, "Go out and stand on the mountain before the Lord; the Lord will pass by" (1 Kings 19:11). Elijah went.

> There was a strong and violent wind rending the mountains and crushing rocks before the Lord—but the Lord was not in the wind; after the wind, an earthquake—but the Lord was not in the earthquake; after the earthquake, fire—but the Lord was not in the fire; after the fire, a light silent sound. (1 Kings 19:11-12)

At the "light silent sound" Elijah covered his face because he knew he was in God's presence. It's a contradiction of terms, a "light silent sound," "a still small voice," "the sound of sheer silence" as three translations[12] of this verse struggle to describe it. We all have our versions of wind, earthquakes, and fire—the places we expect to find God. But the Holy Spirit most often speaks in this "language" of silence.

Many of us struggle with silence. Perhaps because in the silence we have nothing to distract us from those thoughts we were trying to avoid. Or maybe our overworked, over-scheduled bodies experience a still, silent moment as permission to fall asleep. Either way, silence takes some getting used to, and that's okay. With practice, we can learn to slow ourselves down and invite God to speak to our hearts.

> Today, get more comfortable with silence by pressing into an extended time (five minutes) of silent contemplation. Listen for the light silent sound deep within you as you dwell in God's presence

that goes deeper than words. Sit in a comfortable position, perhaps on the floor against a wall or in an upright chair with your feet flat on the floor. Rest your hands comfortably in your lap. Try not to get frustrated with your thoughts, just acknowledge them and return your focus to God. You can use a name of God to refocus you, like "Jesus" or "Father." Simply concentrate on the knowledge that you are in God's presence and let any other thoughts come and go.

Prepare a timer for 5 minutes.

OPEN TO GOD

In the name of the Father, and of the Son, and of the Holy Spirit. Amen.

Take a few deep breaths as you open yourself to God. Invite God's presence and help.

PRAY FROM THE HEART

Start your timer.

(5 minutes of contemplative silence.)

After your timer goes off, talk to God about any thoughts or emotions that surfaced during the silence. You may wish to use the Notice, Tell, Invite method from page 34 or revisit the gratitude exercise on page 23.

CLOSE

Jesus, thank you for this time together. Please continue to help me find you in silence, solitude, and stillness. In the name of the Father, and of the Son, and of the Holy Spirit. Amen.

TIP: EMBRACE SILENCE

Choose one way to build a little silence into your day outside of your prayer time. Some ideas:

- Turn off the music on your commute.
- Vacuum or do the dishes without listening to anything.
- Take a morning or evening walk in a quiet park or nature trail.

MAKE IT A HABIT
Pray from the Heart

Prayer is a practice we continue to grow in throughout our lives. See the wisdom and suggested readings below for establishing praying from the heart as a daily habit.

CONSISTENCY IS KEY

Choose a consistent time and place to pray every day. Pray in the morning if you can. A morning prayer routine puts God first in your day (literally), centers you on what is most important, and helps you take on the day's work with thoughtfulness and intentionality. It also allows you a chance to make up your prayer time later in the day if urgent or unforeseen duties prevent you from praying on a given morning. Still, morning doesn't work for everyone, and the absolute best time to pray is whenever you can actually do it! If a morning prayer routine doesn't work for you, try to tie your daily mental prayer time to another regular event in your day (e.g. immediately after lunch). Whenever you pray, do your best to decide in advance, schedule it, and show up.

DISTRACTIONS ARE NORMAL

If you get distracted during prayer, welcome to the club! St. Teresa of Avila, a doctor of the Church and a wise teacher of the practice of prayer, described the mind as a "grinding mill"[13] and "like wild horses no one can stop."[14] What do you do when your mind wants to roam wild? First, make sure to eliminate external distractions and silence your phone. Second, expect mental distraction. If you respond to your distractions by getting angry or frustrated at yourself, you've taken yourself even further away from prayer. Instead, approach your distractions with peace and a lack of surprise. Get into a habit of acknowledging the distraction and then returning your attention to prayer. If a distraction is something you're anxious not to forget, write it down or set a reminder to attend to it later. Finally, sometimes the thing you're distracted by is the very thing you need to talk to God about. In that case, bring your distractions to God and talk to him about whatever is on your mind.

MORNING OFFERING

Memorized vocal prayers can help us punctuate our days with little glances to Heaven. Many find it especially important to start their day with a vocal prayer—giving God their first thought, first glance, first words of the day. This practice disciplines our hearts into the truth that, before all else, God is. He is always there, loving and sustaining us, surer than the rising of the sun. There are various morning offering prayers in the Catholic Tradition,* but an Our Father, a Hail Mary, a Glory Be, a self-composed phrase, or even a simple "good morning, Lord" can all serve as fitting vocal prayers to accompany our first waking moments. If you don't already have a habit of praying a morning vocal prayer, consider trying it out.

THE NAME OF JESUS AS "PRAYING ALWAYS"

Reverently speaking the name of Jesus anytime, anywhere, is a great way to follow St. Paul's instruction to "pray without ceasing" (1 Thessalonians 5:17). As the *Catechism* says,

> The invocation of the holy name of Jesus is the simplest way of praying always. When the holy name is repeated often by a humbly attentive heart, the prayer is not lost by heaping up empty phrases, but holds fast to the word and 'brings forth fruit with patience.' This prayer is possible 'at all times' because it is not one occupation among others but the only occupation: that of loving God, which animates and transfigures every action in Christ Jesus. (2668)

When you feel the stress of the day building up, pause for a few deep breaths and speak the name of Jesus, aloud or interiorly. Let the name of Jesus be among the first and last words of your day. Speak the name of Jesus over your sleeping children, tracing the Sign of the Cross on their foreheads in silent blessing. "The name 'Jesus' contains all" (*Catechism*, 2666).

MIX IT UP

If you ever find yourself in a rut with your prayer routine, or avoiding it altogether out of boredom or lack of inspiration, try mixing up part of your routine to re-engage yourself. Used to praying at home? Try praying at church or outside. Usually intercede or pray a Rosary? Try meditating on Scripture or using a devotional book. Try walking, kneeling, sitting on the floor, or another posture for

---

*   Visit the Pope's Worldwide Prayer Network website from the Apostleship of Prayer for a variety of pre-written morning offerings to choose from. Available at popesprayerusa.net/daily-offering-prayers.

prayer than the one you typically choose. Try reading a book on prayer every once in a while for new inspiration and ideas.

AM I DOING THIS RIGHT?

Prayer really isn't about getting it "right" as much as showing up to spend time with God. Sometimes we experience flashes of insight, surges of love, zealous intercession, and clarity in discernment. Most of the time, however, prayer just feels . . . normal, perhaps boring, nothing amazing or life-changing. It can feel like wasting time to industrious minds because we don't always see the "result" or "return on investment." In the end, however, prayer is not about what *we do* or what *we get*, but about what *God does* in and with us, whether we perceive it or not. Our job is to show up, open our hearts and minds as best we can, and let God do the heavy lifting. So, don't evaluate yourself or your prayer times too critically. Persevere in making yourself available to God, try different methods of personal prayer to find the ones that work best for you in the various seasons of your life, and let your heavenly Father love you.

ADDITIONAL RESOURCES

For further reading on growing in mental prayer, we recommend the following works.

- *Catechism of the Catholic Church*, Part 4, "Christian Prayer," paragraphs 2558 - 2865
- *Prayer for Beginners*, Peter Kreeft
- *Time for God*, Jacques Philippe
- *Opening to God*, Thomas H. Green, S.J.

DISCIPLESHIP PRACTICES
Pray from the Heart

The 10:10 Challenge includes various discipleship practices for prayer and action that you can use (and share with others) long after taking the challenge. At the end of each chapter find the relevant discipleship practices for the week's topic. See Appendix C for an index of all twenty-six practices contained in this book.

Pray Every Day

When you pray, go to your inner room, close the door,
and pray to your Father in secret. And your Father who
sees in secret will repay you.
— Matthew 6:6

OPEN TO GOD
Settle yourself and turn your attention to God.
- Make the Sign of the Cross.
- Breathe deeply in a minute or two of silence and stillness. You may wish to repeat the name of Jesus or pray "Come, Holy Spirit" a few times.
- Invite the Lord to guide your prayer time.

PRAY FROM THE HEART
Talk to and listen to God however you wish. Some options:
- Simply talk to God about anything on your heart
- ACTS prayer (p. 33)
- Lord's Prayer as an outline, adding your own words (p. 17)
- Notice, Tell, Invite (p. 34)
- *Lectio divina* (p. 64) or Ignatian contemplation with Scripture (p. 65)
- Pray with a Psalm (p. 66)
- Examen prayer (p. 225)
- Extended contemplative silence (p. 27)
- Write in a prayer journal, especially any resolutions or convictions that came in prayer

CLOSE

Gather your prayers and resolutions. Offer them to God in trust.
- Ask for the grace you need going forward.
- Entrust your petitions and resolutions to Mary or another saint and ask for their prayers.
- Rest in God's presence for one to two minutes of silence
- Make the Sign of the Cross.

ACTS Prayer

Not sure what to say in prayer? Try spending a few minutes (or more) on each of these four topics.

ADORATION

Praise God for who he is. Consider the characteristics of God: good, faithful, loving, powerful, forgiving, etc. (See page 130 on praise.)

Try praying: "Heavenly Father, you are _____."

CONTRITION

Acknowledge your weakness and ask for the Lord's forgiveness. (See page 97 for an examination of conscience.)

Try praying: "Lord, I'm sorry for _____."

THANKSGIVING

Give thanks for the blessings in your life, big and small. (See page 22 on the power of gratitude.)

Try praying: "Thank you God for _____."

SUPPLICATION

"Make your requests known to God" (Philippians 4:6).

Try praying: "Lord Jesus, help me_____." or "Father, I lift up _____ to you; please help him/her with _____."

Notice, Tell, Invite

Emotional and spiritual health require cultivating an awareness of your emotions, developing a robust emotional vocabulary, and inviting Jesus into whatever you are feeling. Notice, Tell, Invite is one of the easiest ways to get real with God (and yourself) and develop a closer connection to Christ in prayer.

Notice one or a few emotions you're feeling. Use the lists below to help you identify and name your emotions, thinking beyond simple categories like "good" and "bad." What does the emotion feel like in your mind/heart? In your body? Is it pleasant? Unpleasant?

• *Grateful*	• *Jealous*	• *Creative*
• *Frustrated*	• *Confident*	• *Playful*
• *Bold*	• *Hopeful*	• *Ashamed*
• *Bored*	• *Angry*	• *Understood*
• *Annoyed*	• *Worthless*	• *Accepted*
• *Satisfied*	• *Loving*	• *Embarrassed*
• *Lonely*	• *Joyful*	• *Refreshed*
• *Stressed*	• *Depressed*	• *Patient*
• *Comforted*	• *Excited*	• *Hopeless*
• *Disappointed*	• *Peaceful*	• *Guilty*
• *Tired*	• *Overwhelmed*	• *Relieved*

Tell Jesus about the emotion and what it's like. Open up to him about any situations surrounding the emotion. Share freely about whatever comes to mind: the good and the bad. He already knows, but it's good to take note of your inner world and to express yourself to God.

Jesus, I feel _____ about _____.

Invite Jesus into this part of your inner life, being honest about your experience and open to his companionship and guidance.

Jesus, I invite you into my feelings of _____.
What do you want to show me here?

Linger a bit and listen. Pay attention to any shifts or changes within, such as new thoughts, clarifications, or additional emotions that surface.

ENDNOTES

1. See Genesis 3:8.

2. See Philippians 2:7-8.

3. St. John Damascene, *De fide orth.* 3.24 quoted in *Catechism*, 2559.

4. St. Teresa of Avila, *The Book of Her Life*, ch. 8.4 in *The Collected Works of St. Teresa of Avila*, vol. 1, trans. Kieran Kavanaugh, O.C.D. and Otilio Rodriguez, O.C.D. (Washington, D.C.: ICS Publications, 1987).

5. St. Augustine, *De diversis quaestionibus octoginta tribus* 64, 4: PL 40, 56, Cf. in Catechism, 2560.

6. St. Teresa of Calcutta, *In My Own Words*, comp. José Luis González-Balado (Liguori: Liguori Publications, 1996), 9.

7. See *Catechism*, 2700-2724.

8. Ibid., 2705.

9. St. John of the Cross, *Maxims and Counsels*, 53 quoted in *Catechism*, 2717.

10. St. Teresa of Avila, "Efficacy of Patience," trans. by Adrian J. Cooney, O.C.D. in *The Collected Works of Teresa of Avila*, vol. 3, trans. Kieran Kavanaugh, O.C.D. and Otilio Rodriguez, O.C.D. (Washington D.C.: ICS Publications, 1985).

11. St. John of the Cross, *The Sayings of Light and Love*, no. 100 in *The Collected Works of St. John of the Cross*, trans. Kieran Kavanaugh, O.C.D. and Otilio Rodrigues, O.C.D. (Washington D.C.: ICS Publications, 1991).

12. NABRE, RSVCE, NRSVCE translations respectively.

13. St. Teresa of Avila, *The Book of Her Life*, ch. 15.6.

14. St. Teresa of Avila, *The Way of Perfection*, ch. 19.2 in *The Collected Works of St. Teresa of Avila*, vol. 2, trans. Kieran Kavanaugh, O.C.D. and Otilio Rodriguez, O.C.D. (Washington, D.C.: ICS Publications, 1980).

WEEK 2
DWELL IN GOD'S WORD

Let the word of Christ dwell in you richly.
– Colossians 3:16

CONVERSATION TWO
Dwell in God's Word

OPENING PRAYER (3 MIN)
Select one person to open in prayer. Use the following prayer or your own words.

Come, Holy Spirit. Join us during this time. Please help us connect with you and with each other through this experience. Thank you for all you have done in our lives this week. We pray all this through Christ our Lord, Amen.

CATCH UP (5 MIN)

Share highs and lows: one positive thing (a simple joy, gratitude, or blessing) and one challenge in your life since you last met. Feel free to keep this light and not too deep.

REVIEW PRAY FROM THE HEART (15 MIN)
Read aloud.

Since you last met, you worked through the daily prayer guides for Week 1: Pray from the Heart. If one or more of you did not get to this yet, spend another week completing them before using the following discussion guide. In that case, spend today's time troubleshooting any obstacles you faced and making a concrete plan to pray daily.

Discuss a few of the following questions.

- Day 1 introduced prayer as "availability" to God. How available did you make yourself to God in prayer this week?
- Which of the following prayer practices did you find most helpful or memorable? Most challenging?
  - Extended prayer with the Our Father
  - Notice, Tell, Invite
  - Give Thanks
  - Silence
  - Ask, Seek, Knock
  - Extended silence
- What do you make of the distinction between vocal, meditative, and contemplative prayer?
- What questions came up for you this week?

ABOUT DWELL IN GOD'S WORD (15 MIN)

Read aloud.

Wouldn't it be great to hear from God more clearly and more often?

With practice, we can. God speaks to us in many ways, and one of the privileged places we can tune into his voice is in the words of Sacred Scripture. By prayerfully reading and meditating upon Scripture, we learn to recognize not only how God spoke to people of the past, but how his Spirit is stirring in each of us here and now.

We believe God is "living and effective" in the divinely inspired texts of the Scriptures (Hebrews 4:12). Praying with Scripture creates an environment where we can encounter God. This chapter challenges you to go beyond merely reading the words of Scripture to slow down and *dwell* in God's Word. To do this, you'll learn a few different methods for praying with Scripture. First is *lectio divina* (divine reading). This is an ancient practice of praying with God's Word, listening in particular for what God is saying to you in the text. You'll also use the Psalms as a springboard for conversation with God. Finally, you'll use prayerful imagination to interact with the people and places of Scripture in new ways.

No matter how familiar (or unfamiliar) you are with Scripture, the Lord can and will meet you in his Word. As St. Gregory the Great has described it, "Scripture is like a river…, shallow enough here for the lamb to go wading, but deep enough there for the elephant to swim."[1] We learn to swim in its depths more fully over time, but all the while, "in the sacred books, the Father who is in heaven meets His children with great love and speaks with them."[2]

YOUR CHALLENGE THIS WEEK:

- ☐ Dwell in God's Word by completing the readings and exercises in the daily prayer guide.
- ☐ Memorize the following Bible passage. See page 67 for info on how to do this.

> **Philippians 4:6-7, NRSV-CE**
>
> Do not worry about anything, but in everything by prayer and supplication with thanksgiving let your requests be made known to God. And the peace of God, which surpasses all understanding, will guard your hearts and your minds in Christ Jesus.

Discuss some or all of the following.

- What has been your experience praying with Scripture? (Feel free to share the good, the bad, the ugly!)
- What parts of the Bible do you find particularly moving or meaningful?
- What role do you want Scripture to play in your life?

DWELL IN GOD'S WORD TOGETHER (20 MIN)
Read aloud.

Lectio divina, or "divine reading," is an ancient practice for praying with Scripture. The four steps of *lectio divina* are to read, reflect, respond, and rest. The method helps us meditate on the passage and gives God space to speak to us through the words of Scripture. The practice calls us to listen attentively for a specific word or phrase that stands out, even slightly. Because the Holy Spirit aids our reading of the Scripture he inspired, we can have faith that this word or phrase is given by God as a personal word for us to meditate on and pray about. You can pray *lectio divina* individually or with a group. Today, pray it together using the prompts below.

Step 1: Read
One person reads the Scripture passage aloud slowly. As they read, everyone makes mental note of any word, phrase, or image that catches their attention.

Matthew 11:25-30, NRSV-CE

[25] At that time Jesus said, "I thank you, Father, Lord of heaven and earth, because you have hidden these things from the wise and the intelligent and have revealed them to infants; [26] yes, Father, for such was your gracious will. [27] All things have been handed over to me by my Father; and no one knows the Son except the Father, and no one knows the

Father except the Son and anyone to whom the Son chooses to reveal him.

[28] "Come to me, all you that are weary and are carrying heavy burdens, and I will give you rest. [29] Take my yoke upon you, and learn from me; for I am gentle and humble in heart, and you will find rest for your souls. [30] For my yoke is easy, and my burden is light."

After a minute of quiet reflection, briefly share the word, phrase, or image that stood out to each of you. Don't elaborate. Share *only* the word or phrase without commentary.

Step 2: Reflect
Choose a different person to read the passage a second time. After you read the passage, take another minute or so to reflect silently, pondering the word or phrase that caught your attention. Then, discuss your answers to the following questions:

- What do you think God is saying to you about the word, phrase, or image that stood out to you?
- Did anything in this passage attract you or sound desirable? Did anything challenge or stretch you? How so?
- What other questions arise as you ponder?

Step 3: Respond
Read the passage aloud a third time and consider how you would respond to what you heard from God in this passage. After a period of quiet reflection, take turns offering prayers in your own words.

Talk to God aloud about whatever moved you as you meditated on God's Word during this time of *lectio divina*. Here are a few examples to give you an idea:

- "Jesus, thank you for helping me understand what's going on with my parents right now and giving me insight into their concerns."
- "God, please give me the grace to give you my worries and concerns rather than trying to carry them myself."

Use your own words to respond in prayer to whatever God drew your attention to through this passage.

Step 4: Rest
Pause for a brief time of silent prayer in God's presence.

Choose one person to close using the following prayer or pray spontaneously.

Jesus, thank you for bringing us here today and dwelling with us in your Word. We are grateful for all the ways you are showing us more about who you are through prayer and Scripture. Help us to stay firm in our commitment to praying from the heart and teach us to dwell in your Word in the coming days.

We ask this through Christ our Lord, Amen.

NEXT MEETING (2 MIN)

Make sure you have your next discussion on the calendar.

PRAYER GUIDE
Dwell in God's Word

Day 1. Encounter the Living Word

Indeed, the word of God is living and effective, sharper than any two-edged sword, penetrating even between soul and spirit, joints and marrow, and able to discern reflections and thoughts of the heart.
– Hebrews 4:12

If you've read the Bible, you may have noticed it's not like other books. In fact, it's a collection of books, written over the course of hundreds of years. But it's also more than just a text—it's a living word we believe is God-breathed from the very same Spirit of God that created the world and breathed life into it.

This doesn't mean it fell from heaven. With God's help and inspiration, human authors wrote from various perspectives and in various styles. The result is not an instruction manual answering every question we could ever have. Rather, when read and interpreted correctly, the Scriptures reveal what God most wanted us to know about himself and about how to live fully and freely.

When we pray with Scripture, the Holy Spirit moves within us, penetrating the recesses of our hearts and minds to say something personal and timely to us through these ancient pages. God's living and active Spirit is why we can read a familiar passage again and again and gain new inspiration from it. The Holy Spirit can highlight new reflections, new instructions, new convictions for today that are different from other times we prayed with that passage in the past.

In order to sense the movements of the Spirit as we read the Bible, we need to slow down and follow St. Paul's counsel, "Let the word of Christ dwell in you richly" (Colossians 3:16). Dwelling calls us to stay with God's Word longer than a mere skimming or even a typical reading pace allows. We need to "chew" on God's Word, taking the time to extract the nourishment it has to offer us by reflecting on the meaning of the words, asking questions of the text, and letting God draw us into dialogue with himself.

OPEN TO GOD

Take a few deep breaths as you open yourself to God.

In the name of the Father, and of the Son, and of the Holy Spirit. Amen.

Come, Holy Spirit. Please speak to me today through the Scriptures. Help me notice the way you're moving within me and inspiring my thoughts and reflections. Amen.

PRAY FROM THE HEART

Give thanks to God for one or two blessings from the past twenty-four hours. What is good and delightful that you are grateful for?

Thank you God for _____.

Read the following Scripture passage slowly and attentively. Notice any word or phrase that grabs your attention. Consider reading it a second time before moving on to the reflection questions below.

Read

Matthew 13:1-9, 18-23, NRSV-CE
That same day Jesus went out of the house and sat beside the sea. Such great crowds gathered around him that he got into a boat and sat there, while the whole crowd stood on the beach. And he told them many things in parables, saying: "Listen! A sower went out to sow. And as he sowed, some seeds fell on the path, and the birds came and ate them up. Other seeds fell on rocky ground, where they did not have much soil, and they sprang up quickly, since they had no depth of soil. But when the sun rose, they were scorched; and since they had no root, they withered away. Other seeds fell among thorns, and the thorns

grew up and choked them. Other seeds fell on good soil and brought forth grain, some a hundredfold, some sixty, some thirty. Let anyone with ears listen!" . . .

"Hear then the parable of the sower. When anyone hears the word of the kingdom and does not understand it, the evil one comes and snatches away what is sown in the heart; this is what was sown on the path. As for what was sown on rocky ground, this is the one who hears the word and immediately receives it with joy; yet such a person has no root, but endures only for a while, and when trouble or persecution arises on account of the word, that person immediately falls away. As for what was sown among thorns, this is the one who hears the word, but the cares of the world and the lure of wealth choke the word, and it yields nothing. But as for what was sown on good soil, this is the one who hears the word and understands it, who indeed bears fruit and yields, in one case a hundredfold, in another sixty, and in another thirty."

Reflect

- Can you recall a time when you received God's love, guidance, or instruction to great effect? If so, what was that like?
- What are some rocks and weeds that tend to prevent you from receiving Jesus or his words more fruitfully?
- What type of soil most reflects your own heart lately?

Respond

- Talk to God about your answers to the previous questions and anything else on your heart.

CLOSE

Spend a few minutes in restful silence. "Be still and know that I am God" (Psalm 46:11).

Lord, thank you for your Word. Help me to keep my eyes, ears, and heart open to you and your Word, as rich soil. As I go through the rest of my day, help me remember _____.

In the name of the Father, and of the Son, and of the Holy Spirit. Amen.

TIP: GET A BIBLE

Get a physical copy of the Bible in a trusted translation that is also readable, such as the New American Bible, Revised Edition

(NABRE), the New Revised Standard Version, Catholic Edition (NRSV-CE), the Revised Standard Version, 2nd Catholic Edition (RSV-2CE), or any other Catholic edition.* The New American Bible (NAB) translation is used in the readings at Mass in the United States. If you already have a formal family Bible, consider getting an additional one in which you'd feel comfortable underlining verses, highlighting, or making notes.

Day 2. Revelation

No one has ever seen God. It is God the only Son, who is close to the Father's heart, who has made him known.
– John 1:18, NRSV-CE

Jesus reveals who God is. He is the "image of the invisible God" (Colossians 1:15). He revealed himself to his disciples during his time on earth, particularly to the Twelve who spent time with him day in and day out on the road to Jerusalem.

After Jesus' Death and Resurrection, through the power of the Holy Spirit at Pentecost, his disciples "went from place to place, proclaiming the word" (Acts 8:4, NRSV-CE). They passed on what they had learned from Jesus to the people, baptized them into his life through the Holy Spirit, and gathered for prayer, fellowship, and the breaking of bread. Some of Jesus' earliest followers committed to writing what he did and said so that the community could continue to meditate on his words and actions. In the age of the Church, the one complete revelation of God in Christ continues to spread by the power of the Holy Spirit in two ways: in the living Word of God (the Scriptures) and in the living Tradition of the Church (the community of disciples who discern the will of the Spirit and apply Jesus' teaching in each new age).

These two sources of revelation—Scripture and Tradition—work together to reveal God to us today.

> "For both of them, flowing out from the same divine wellspring, come together in some fashion to form one thing, and move towards the same goal." Each of them makes present and fruitful in the Church the mystery of Christ, who promised to remain with his own "always, to the close of the age."[3]

---

*   For more guidance on translations, visit the U.S. Catholic Conference of Bishops' website: *www.usccb.org/offices/new-american-bible/approved-translations-bible.*

What a one-two punch! Reading and meditating on Scripture, particularly the Gospels, allows us to encounter and come to know the living Jesus. The Sacraments and teachings of the Church bring us into contact with God and guide us in how to follow Jesus today.

OPEN TO GOD

Quiet yourself by taking a few deep breaths. Turn your attention to God.

In the name of the Father, and of the Son, and of the Holy Spirit. Amen.

God, I praise you today. Jesus, thank you for coming to us as a person who I can get to know. I love that you are _____.

As I come to you today, I bring you my concern for _____ _____. I entrust this matter to you, Lord. I believe you see it and will carry me/us through.

What else do you wish to say to the Lord today as you open yourself to him?

PRAY FROM THE HEART

Read

Read the passage twice, slowly and attentively. Read aloud if possible. Note any word, phrase, or image that catches your attention. Possibly underline or highlight any words or phrases that stand out to you.

John 1:1-5, 9-14, 16-18, NRSV-CE

In the beginning was the Word, and the Word was with God, and the Word was God. He was in the beginning with God. All things came into being through him, and without him not one thing came into being. What has come into being in him was life, and the life was the light of all people. The light shines in the darkness, and the darkness did not overcome it. . . .

The true light, which enlightens everyone, was coming into the world.

He was in the world, and the world came into being through him; yet the world did not know him. He came to what was his own, and his own people did not accept him. But to all who received him, who believed in his name, he gave power to become children of God, who were born, not of blood or of the will of the

flesh or of the will of man, but of God.

And the Word became flesh and lived among us, and we have seen his glory, the glory as of a father's only son, full of grace and truth. . . . From his fullness we have all received, grace upon grace. The law indeed was given through Moses; grace and truth came through Jesus Christ. No one has ever seen God. It is God the only Son, who is close to the Father's heart, who has made him known.

Reflect

- What words or phrases stood out to you? Notice how they affect you.
- Reflect on the meaning of this passage for you, or of the word/phrase that caught your attention. What is God high-lighting for you?

For help reflecting:

- What does the Word bring to the world?
- From the text, what are some of the reasons the Word (God) became flesh?
- In your experience, how is Jesus light that overcomes dark-ness?
- Into what darkness do you currently need heavenly light to shine?

Respond

- Talk to God about your answers to the previous questions and anything else on your heart.

CLOSE

Spend a few minutes in restful silence. "Be still, and know that I am God!" (Psalm 46:10, NRSV-CE).

Jesus, you are the Word of life, spoken to all of creation. Draw me deeper into fellowship with you through the Holy Spirit. Come, Lord Jesus, come into my life and be my light today.

In the name of the Father, and of the Son, and of the Holy Spirit. Amen.

TIP: STUDY TOOLS IN YOUR BIBLE

Most Catholic study Bibles include introductions to each book that provide a framework for how to read and pray with each section of the bible. Some parts, like those of eyewitness accounts such as the Gospels, convey truth about certain events and how they affected the people who lived them. Other parts can be more allegorical, like the two creation stories in Genesis 1 and 2, which use stories of people and events to convey deeper truths about God and the human condition rather than historical facts.

The notes and cross references in your Bible often offer clues to the context of a particular passage. Most Bibles use superscript letters and symbols to connect a particular verse to notes in the margins or elsewhere. If you see that the passage you're reading has notes associated with it, take a look to see if anything there sheds light on the context or meaning of the passage. When other Scripture passages are referenced, it often indicates that they include a different telling of the same story or connect with the passage thematically. Reading different accounts of the same story at times can also deepen your prayerful understanding of the events or help you make new connections.

Day 3. Abide in Me

Abide in me as I abide in you. . . . As the Father has loved me,
so I have loved you; abide in my love.
– John 15:4, 9, NRSV-CE

Jesus describes the relationship he wants with his followers using deeply intimate language. He calls his disciples to be more than students, more than even friends. He calls us to *union* with him. In the passage quoted above, he encourages his disciples to *abide* in him, to be as connected to him as a branch is to a vine. In other places he prays that we would be one with him in the same way that he is one with the Father—fully united. Still elsewhere, Jesus tells his disciples to eat his flesh and drink his blood, taking his life within us to be sustained and transformed. It's no wonder that St. Paul uses the imagery of marriage to try to describe Jesus' relationship with his Church.[4] It's that level of intimacy—and even closer than any human relationship—that Jesus invites us to have with him.

Recall the four steps of *lectio divina*: read, reflect, respond, rest. As you use this method to pray with Scripture, take note of the last step in the prayer process: rest. After chewing on the Word of God through your reflections and savoring its goodness in your prayerful responses, this last step is the moment when you figuratively push your chair back from the table and bask in the enjoyment of the meal. Here, you stop for a minute or two of silence to rest and abide in the mystery of God that goes far deeper than words. *Dwell, abide, linger* a bit in his presence. The Lord is at work.

OPEN TO GOD

Settle and center yourself with a few deep breaths.

Invite the Holy Spirit to guide your prayer time. Use your own words or the prayer below.

In the name of the Father, and of the Son, and of the Holy Spirit. Amen.

Come, Holy Spirit. Open my eyes to see and my ears to hear your Word. Help me be open to whatever you want to speak to me today.

PRAY FROM THE HEART

Read

Read the Scripture selection twice, slowly and attentively. Read aloud if possible. As you read, listen "with the ear of your heart."[5] Note any word, phrase, or image that catches your attention. Possibly underline or highlight any words or phrases that stand out to you.

John 15:1-11, NRSV-CE

"I am the true vine, and my Father is the vinegrower. He removes every branch in me that bears no fruit. Every branch that bears fruit he prunes to make it bear more fruit. You have already been cleansed by the word that I have spoken to you. Abide in me as I abide in you. Just as the branch cannot bear fruit by itself unless it abides in the vine, neither can you unless you abide in me. I am the vine, you are the branches. Those who abide in me and I in them bear much fruit, because apart from me you can do nothing. Whoever does not abide in me is thrown away like a branch and withers; such branches are gathered, thrown into the fire, and burned. If you abide in me, and my words abide in you, ask for whatever you wish, and it will be done for you. My Father is glorified by this, that you bear much fruit and become my disciples. As the Father has loved me, so I have loved you; abide in my love. If you keep my commandments, you will abide in my love, just as I have kept my Father's commandments and abide in his love. I have said these things to you so that my joy may be in you, and that your joy may be complete."

Reflect

- What words or phrases stood out to you? Notice how they affect you.
- Reflect on the meaning of this passage for you, or of the word/phrase that caught your attention. What is God highlighting for you?

For help reflecting:

- How do you understand Jesus' metaphor of the vine and the branches? How does the vine interact with the branches? What is pruning? What is the fruit?
- Jesus uses the word "abide" ten times in this passage (some translations use "remain"). What do you think he means when he says "abide in me?"
- What promises do you find in this passage?
- Why is Jesus telling his disciples these things? What does he want for them/us?

Respond

- Talk to God about your answers to the previous questions and anything else on your heart.

CLOSE

Close by resting silently for a few minutes in the love God has for you and that you have for God.

To begin this, tell Jesus you love him by slowly repeating a few times: *Jesus, I love you. I love you, Lord.*

Move into your minute or two of silence. If you get distracted simply repeat, *I love you, Jesus,* and continue to rest in his presence.

Lord, thank you for abiding in me and with me. Thank you that you are not a God who is far off, but one who dwells, who abides, with us. Increase my faith in your abiding presence.

In the name of the Father, and of the Son, and of the Holy Spirit. Amen.

Day 4. Pray with the Psalms

Let all who take refuge in you rejoice;
let them ever sing for joy.
Spread your protection over them,
so that those who love your name may exult in you.
— Psalm 5:12, NRSV-CE

The Bible is a collection of all different kinds of writing: historical records, eyewitness accounts, wisdom proverbs and instructions for living, letters, allegories, prayers, and songs. Just as we approach a news article with different expectations than a textbook or a novel, knowing the genre of a particular Scripture passage helps us know where to look for the truth the author is conveying.

The Psalms are the songbook of the Bible. Many even begin with instructions for singing the words accompanied by a particular instrument. Music has a way of opening up something deeper within the human heart. These biblical songs are no different. They are songs of joy, praise, sorrow, anger, despair, hope, and longing that deeply express the human condition. As such, the Psalms are the Bible's school of prayer. Many of them are written in the first person, making it easy for us to put ourselves in the Psalmist's shoes and take up the words as our own. In doing so, we learn a new vocabulary for prayer. Using the Psalms as a starting point, we can gain freedom and ease in using our own words to express our hearts to God.

Pray with Psalm 18. The words in italics show how to use the psalm as a starting place for spontaneous prayer. Use them to start your conversation with God, adding and substituting your own words.

OPEN TO GOD

Quiet yourself by taking a few deep breaths. Welcome God into your midst.

In the name of the Father, and of the Son, and of the Holy Spirit. Amen.

Come, Lord Jesus. Teach me to pray. Help me to find the words to speak to you. Fill my heart and mind with your Spirit, and open my lips to proclaim your praise.

PRAY FROM THE HEART

Use the words of the Psalm and the prompts below to spark prayer in your own words.

Psalm 18:1-3, NRSV-CE
I love you, O Lord, my strength.

God, you are my strength. You give me gifts of _____ that sustain me and help me to follow you. I love you, Lord. You are good. I love you, O Lord, my strength. (Add your own words.)

The Lord is my rock, my fortress, and my deliverer,
   my God, my rock in whom I take refuge,
   my shield, and the horn of my salvation, my stronghold.

Yes, Jesus, you are my rock, my sure foundation. You are solid and trustworthy. I can count on you. I take refuge in you. You come to my aid and protect me.

I call upon the Lord, who is worthy to be praised,
   so I shall be saved from my enemies.

God, you are worthy of praise. I praise you because you are _____. Father, defend me from my enemies, from anything inside or outside of me that would tempt me away from you, especially_____. I call upon you today, Lord, for help with _____. Please also help (anyone who you feel called to pray for) _____.

As I go forth from this time of prayer, please let these words of the Psalm sink deeper into my heart and guide me. Thank you, Jesus, for being my rock, my fortress, and my deliverer. I love you, Lord.

What else do you want to say to God right now?

CLOSE

Spend a few minutes in restful silence, letting God be your refuge.

God, thank you for this prayer time together. Thank you for being my strength, my rock, my fortress, my deliverer. Go before me in all I may encounter today.

In the name of the Father, and of the Son, and of the Holy Spirit. Amen.

Day 5. Jesus, Our Teacher

Remain faithful to what you have learned and believed, because you know from whom you learned it, and that from infancy you have known [the] sacred scriptures, which are capable of giving you wisdom for salvation through faith in Christ Jesus. All scripture is inspired by God and is useful for teaching, for refutation, for correction, and for training in righteousness, so that one who belongs to God may be competent, equipped for every good work.
– 2 Timothy 3:14-17

The word used for "disciple" in the Gospels is the same Greek word used for "student," and we can see how the first disciples of Jesus studied him and sought to pass on what they learned.

The most important way for disciples to act as students is to sit at Jesus' feet and learn from him. We do this by praying with Scripture. In the letter above, we hear St. Paul encourage his student St. Timothy to continue to turn back to the inspired Word of God as a sure teacher that would show Timothy the way to salvation.

Many people, when they're getting started with the Bible, feel overwhelmed or confused because they don't "know enough." That's understandable. The Bible was written over hundreds of years, thousands of years ago, in lands and cultures foreign to the modern Westerner. But you don't need a degree in biblical studies to pray with the Bible. You can choose simpler parts and passages to get started. Over time, through a habit of prayerful reading, with help from biblical notes and commentaries, and by learning from others in your community, you'll gain a deeper understanding. You will grow to think and live with "the mind of Christ" (1 Corinthians 2:16).

Two general questions can always guide your Scripture reflection: "What does this passage teach me about God/Jesus?" and "What does this passage teach me about my life?" Let the inspired words of Scripture teach, correct, and train you for righteousness as God equips you to be his disciple.

OPEN TO GOD

Start as usual, taking some deep breaths and turning your attention to God, becoming aware of his presence.

In the name of the Father, and of the Son, and of the Holy Spirit. Amen.

Jesus, you are the great teacher of humankind. Thank you for calling me to be your disciple and to share in your life. Please guide me during this time of prayer.

PRAY FROM THE HEART

Dwell in God's Word today by praying with Matthew 7:24-29.

Read

Read the passage two or three times, slowly and attentively, aloud if possible. Note any word, phrase, or image that catches your attention. Possibly underline or highlight any words or phrases that stand out to you.

Matthew 7:24-29

"Everyone then who hears these words of mine and acts on them will be like a wise man who built his house on rock. The rain fell, the floods came, and the winds blew and beat on that house, but it did not fall, because it had been founded on rock. And everyone who hears these words of mine and does not act on them will be like a foolish man who built his house on sand. The rain fell, and the floods came, and the winds blew and beat against that house, and it fell—and great was its fall!"

Now when Jesus had finished saying these things, the crowds were astounded at his teaching, for he taught them as one having authority, and not as their scribes.

Reflect

- What words or phrases stood out to you? Notice how they affect you.
- Reflect on the meaning of this passage for you, or of the word/phrase that caught your attention. What is God highlighting for you?

For help reflecting:

- What do you think Jesus means by the rain, the floods, and the winds? What might those represent?
- What is a good intention that has been on your mind or that this passage stirs up in you? What would it take for you to act on that intention?
- Ponder Jesus' authority. Why do you think it is different from the scribes'?

Respond

- Talk to God about your answers to the previous questions and anything else on your heart.

- Ask God for whatever you need (courage, creativity, resources, guidance, restraint, etc.) to act on his words.

CLOSE

Rest silently for a few minutes at the feet of the great Teacher.

Lord, I choose to build my life on the rock that is you and your Church. To whom else would I go? "You have the words of eternal life" (John 6:68). Help me always to put into practice the goodness and truth you point me to.

In the name of the Father, and of the Son, and of the Holy Spirit. Amen.

TIP: SPIRITUAL BOUQUETS

One of the best ways to extend the graces of your prayer time into the rest of your day is to write down a resolution or insight before moving on with your day. This might be your answer to the questions: What did I learn about myself from this time of prayer? What did I learn about God? Or anything else you want to make note of. St. Francis de Sales calls this gathering a "spiritual bouquet." Simply write down a sentence or two in your journal or on a notecard that you can "sniff" later to remind yourself of the fragrance of your prayer time.

Day 6. Use Your Imagination

It is profitable to use the imagination and to apply the five senses . . .
I will smell the fragrance and taste the infinite sweetness and charm
of the Divinity, of the soul, of its virtues, and of everything there . . . I
will, so to speak, embrace and kiss the places where the persons walk.[6]
– St. Ignatius of Loyola

Do you ever wonder what it would have been like to follow along at Jesus' side, to hear his voice, and to see what he did first-hand?

Reflecting on Scripture exercises our minds. We use our intellects to understand the passage and ponder the meaning it conveys. But our minds are not only analytical. They also possess great powers to imagine and empathize.

St. Ignatius of Loyola encourages us to use our imaginations to enter into the events of Christ's life. We can put all five of our senses at the disposal of the Holy Spirit to make the event more real to us.

The point of imagining is not to recreate a fully accurate picture of the scene in our mind's eye. Instead, entering the scene allows God to open up new insights and inspirations in our minds and hearts. Consider: what would it have felt like to be pushed around in a tightly packed crowd fighting to touch the hem of Jesus' cloak, like the woman in Mark, chapter 5? Would the hot sand have scorched your nostrils as you lowered yourself at his feet? What would stir in your heart as he told you your faith had made you well?

Our imaginations bring the stories to life and allow the Holy Spirit to place us in Jesus' presence in prayer. The words he speaks become words spoken to us. The decisions people face become decisions we grapple with. Their stories become part of our story, because we are all part of God's story.

OPEN TO GOD

Settle into prayer with a few deep breaths.

In the name of the Father, and of the Son, and of the Holy Spirit. Amen.

Father, Jesus, Holy Spirit: enlighten my mind. Give me new eyes to see, new ears to hear, new senses to experience this Scripture passage according to whatever you want to reveal to me. Give me the grace to pray.

PRAY FROM THE HEART

Read

Mark 5:24-34, NRSV-CE

A large crowd followed him and pressed in on him. Now there was a woman who had been suffering from hemorrhages for twelve years. She had endured much under many physicians, and had spent all that she had; and she was no better, but rather grew worse. She had heard about Jesus, and came up behind him in the crowd and touched his cloak, for she said, "If I but touch his clothes, I will be made well." Immediately her hemorrhage stopped; and she felt in her body that she was healed of her disease. Immediately aware that power had gone forth from him, Jesus turned about in the crowd and said, "Who touched my clothes?" And his disciples said to him, "You see the crowd pressing in on you; how can you say, 'Who touched me?'" He looked all around to see who had done it. But the woman, knowing what had happened to her, came in fear and trembling, fell down before him, and told him the whole truth. He said to her, "Daughter, your faith has made you well; go in peace, and be healed of your disease."

Reflect

Use your imagination to picture the scene.

- Start with any details mentioned in the passage: Where does the event take place? Does the passage mention any details about the setting? What other details do you picture?
- Use your imagination to continue painting the picture: Is it dry and dusty? Humid? Cold? What is the weather like? Who are the different people present for this event?
- Place yourself in the scene. Choose one of the people in the narrative and see the scene through their eyes. Are you the woman suffering from hemorrhages? A member of the crowd? Jesus? One of Jesus' disciples?
- Then use your imagination to extrapolate. What do you see, smell, feel, taste, hear? How close or far are you from Jesus? What emotions stir within you? What do you want to do or say? What do you see Jesus do? Hear him say? How do other people in the story interact with you? What do you see them do or hear them say?
- How do these imaginings affect you? What do they show you about yourself, Jesus, or someone else?

Respond

Talk to God about whatever emerged in your prayerful imagining.

CLOSE

Rest for a minute or two at Jesus' feet, receiving his peace.

Let this blessing of St. Paul seal your time of prayer as you close:

I pray that, according to the riches of [God's] glory, he may grant that you may be strengthened in your inner being with power through his Spirit, and that Christ may dwell in your hearts through faith, as you are being rooted and grounded in love. I pray that you may have the power to comprehend, with all the saints, what is the breadth and length and height and depth, and to know the love of Christ that surpasses knowledge, so that you may be filled with all the fullness of God. (Ephesians 3:16-19, NRSV-CE)

In the name of the Father, and of the Son, and of the Holy Spirit. Amen.

Day 7. Praying the Promises

God's promises always come true. God is Truth itself, whose words cannot deceive.
— Catechism of the Catholic Church, 215

When God makes a promise, he doesn't break it. As St. Paul reminds us, "for in [Jesus Christ] every one of God's promises is a 'Yes'" (2 Corinthians 1:20, NRSV-CE). Scripture, as God's inspired Word, is filled with "precious and very great promises" (2 Peter 1:4). Have you ever tried to find some of the promises in Scripture? Have you ever sat in prayerful meditation with the ones you have found? Doing so can be a powerful practice for bolstering faith, calming fears, and growing in courage.

This practice also clarifies for us what God has and has not promised. God never promised an easy life, protection from all suffering and temptation, or enough money to live in luxury. He did not promise to rid the world of injustice this side of heaven. What he *has* promised, however, we can rely on absolutely. He has promised to show us the way to everlasting life, that he is with us always, and that he works all things together for our good—even through trials. We can claim and stand on the promises of God's Word.

Each promise in Scripture was given in a certain context, and we may not understand the full meaning of the words at a glance. Nonetheless, they carry a sure and lasting relevance for believers in any context. The promises of Scripture reveal the heart of God and his loving will for us. God's Word continues to speak to those who seek him and follow him in every age.

OPEN TO GOD

Become aware of yourself and your surroundings. Slow yourself down and prepare for prayer.

In the name of the Father, and of the Son, and of the Holy Spirit. Amen.

Jesus, you are the fulfillment of all God's promises. Please be with me during my prayer today and help me to receive the gifts you have in store for me.

PRAY FROM THE HEART

What are you bringing with you to prayer today? Use the Notice, Tell, Invite method (page 34) to become more aware of your emotional state and invite God to be with you.

Given how you are today, which of the following Scriptural promises stands out to you? Read through all of them once, then continue to pray *lectio divina* with the one that speaks to you.

Read

Isaiah 41:10
Do not fear: I am with you;
    do not be anxious: I am your God.
I will strengthen you, I will help you,
    I will uphold you with my victorious right hand.

Jeremiah 29:11, NRSV-CE
For surely I know the plans I have for you, says the Lord, plans for your welfare and not for harm, to give you a future with hope.

Romans 8:28
We know that all things work for good for those who love God, who are called according to his purpose.

James 1:5, NRSV-CE
If any of you is lacking in wisdom, ask God, who gives to all generously and ungrudgingly, and it will be given you.

Matthew 28:20
I am with you always.

Psalm 34:19
The Lord is close to the brokenhearted,
    saves those whose spirit is crushed.

1 Corinthians 10:13
No trial has come to you but what is human. God is faithful and will not let you be tried beyond your strength; but with the trial he will also provide a way out, so that you may be able to bear it."

2 Corinthians 12:9
My grace is sufficient for you, for power is made perfect in weakness.

Isaiah 54:10
Though the mountains fall away
    and the hills be shaken,
My love shall never fall away from you
    nor my covenant of peace be shaken,
    says the Lord, who has mercy on you.

Psalm 103:12
As far as the east is from the west,
so far has he removed our sins from us.

Reflect

- What words or phrases stood out to you? Notice how they affect you.
- Reflect on the meaning of this passage for you, or of the word/phrase that caught your attention. What is God highlighting for you?

Respond

- Talk to God about your answers to the previous questions and anything else on your heart.
- Ask God for whatever you need to claim this promise in your life.

CLOSE

Rest silently for a few minutes, trusting in God's goodness.

Lord, thank you for your promises. Thank you for being my source and sustenance. I choose you today. Fill me anew with your life and your love, that I may walk in your ways and radiate your goodness to the world around me.

As I go from here, help me to _____.

In the name of the Father, and of the Son, and of the Holy Spirit. Amen.

MAKE IT A HABIT
Dwell in God's Word

We continue to grow in praying with Scripture throughout our lives. Below, find tips and suggested readings for making the practice of dwelling in God's Word a firmly established habit in your life.

GETTING STARTED WITH READING THE BIBLE

Many people who are new to reading Scripture make the understandable assumption that the best way to start is at the beginning, with the Book of Genesis. And why not? Isn't that how books work? You start at page one and continue to the end?

But the Bible isn't like most books. It's more like a little pocket library—a collection of writings by different people, in different styles and genres, written over the course of many hundreds of years.

If you're new to the Bible and looking to read more, the best place to begin is with the Gospels: Matthew, Mark, Luke, and John. These contain stories of Jesus and his disciples that will help you get to know Jesus better and familiarize you with his teachings and way of life. They contain helpful stories and teachings that are generally understandable at face value without the need for extensive study (although, of course, study can inform and deepen your understanding).

After the Gospels, the Acts of the Apostles and the New Testament letters (Romans, 1 and 2 Corinthians, and so on) introduce the activity of the early Church and how Jesus' disciples learned to live as children of God.

The Psalms, as we introduced in this chapter, are the songbook of the Bible and are another good source of passages to pray with, even for beginners with the Bible.

Once you get used to reading and praying with Scripture, you will be able to enter into the narratives, histories, wisdom literature, and prophetic texts of the Old Testament with more confidence and context.

MEMORIZE GOD'S WORD

There are some words we'll never forget: the last thing a loved one said before they died, words of pride and approval from a parent, the first time a significant person said, "I love you." But many words come and go, and we don't remember the vast majority of what we hear, read, or even say. The Bible records a long history of God's people striving to remember what God has said and done. Like us, they find it easy to forget. Moses thus instructed the Israelites about the first and greatest commandment, "You shall love the Lord, your God, with your whole heart, and with your whole being, and with your whole strength":

> Take to heart these words . . . Keep repeating them to your
> children. Recite them when you are at home and when you

are away, when you lie down and when you get up. Bind them on your arm as a sign and let them be as a pendant on your forehead. Write them on the doorposts of your houses and on your gates." (Deuteronomy 6:5-9)

Intentional memorization is something of a lost art these days; we rely on our phones to retrieve information that prior generations would have committed to memory. But memorizing Scripture still has immense value. The Holy Spirit seems to delight in recalling our memorized verses into our thoughts just when we need to hear them or share them with a friend. Having even small chunks of God's Word stored away in our minds helps us helps us meditate on it day and night[7] that we might say with the psalmist, "I treasure your word in my heart, so that I may not sin against you" (Psalm 119:11, NRSV-CE). See page 67 for tips.

PRAY WITH THE LECTIONARY

Mass is celebrated every day in the Catholic Church (except Good Friday) and every Mass includes the Liturgy of the Word where Scriptures from the Old and New Testaments and Gospels are proclaimed. The schedule of Scripture readings covers a large percentage of the Bible over the course of its three-year cycle for Sundays and two-year rotation of daily readings. This schedule of readings (called the lectionary) serves up a daily selection of Scripture readings to pray with. It may be too much to pray *lectio divina* with all of the readings each day. Instead, choose just one, such as the Gospel passage, as the focus of your prayer. You can find the readings of the day at the United States Council of Catholic Bishops website (*bible.usccb.org*). Many devotional subscription services such as *Magnificat, The Word Among Us*, or *Give Us This Day* provide the day's readings with reflections and other prayer material; and a variety of apps such as iBreviary, Magnificat, Hallow, Laudate, and Pray-as-You-Go include content centered on the lectionary.

LITURGY OF THE HOURS

The monastic tradition of the Catholic Church gave birth to a practice of praying at five fixed times (or "hours") of the day. These times of personal and communal prayer came to include meditation on various passages of Scripture, including singing or reciting all 150 psalms over the course of a four-week rotation. Today, this rotation of prayers, Scripture passages, and psalms are known as the Liturgy of the Hours. Catholic clergy and religious make a promise to pray the Liturgy of the Hours daily, but many lay people also find the Liturgy of the Hours a fruitful way to join in the prayer of the Church and meditate on Scripture. People commonly begin by choosing one or two "hours" to join in, such as Morning Prayer, Evening Prayer, or Night Prayer. These prayers do not take an hour to pray, but rather are said at specific times of the day. It typically takes twenty to thirty minutes to pray one of the "hours." You can find print versions of Liturgy of the Hours such as *Christian Prayer: The Liturgy of the Hours* or *Shorter Christian Prayer* (which contains only Morning and Evening Prayer) or access all of the daily prayers and readings for free on the iBreviary app.

JOIN A SMALL GROUP

One of the best ways to grow in your understanding of Scripture and to encounter Christ in the Word is to join a group that discusses and prays with the Bible. Often called "small groups," these groups read and discuss Scripture passages together for greater understanding and application to their lives. They usually have somewhere between four to ten people in them and might be for a specific population of people (like men's groups or moms' groups) or be a mixture of ages, genders, and life stages. Investigate if someone at your parish leads a small group you can join or start one of your own.

ADDITIONAL RESOURCES

- *Catechism of the Catholic Church*, Part I, Chapter 2 "God Comes to Meet Man," paragraphs 50-141
- *You Can Understand the Bible*, Peter Kreeft
- *An Ignatian Introduction to Prayer: Scriptural Reflections According to the Spiritual Exercises*, Timothy M. Gallagher, OMV
- *Walking with God: A Journey through the Bible*, Tim Gray and Jeff Cavins
- *Sacred Reading: The Ancient Art of Lectio Divina*, Michael Casey
- Great Adventure Bible Timeline and resources (*ascensionpress.com*)
- *The Bible in a Year* Podcast, Fr. Mike Schmitz
- *The Catechism in a Year* Podcast, Fr. Mike Schmitz
- Free video library at the Bible Project (*bibleproject.com*)

DISCIPLESHIP PRACTICES
Dwell in God's Word

Lectio Divina: The Ancient Art of Praying with Scripture

Speak, for your servant is listening. —1 Samuel 3:10

Lectio divina, or "divine reading," is a traditional way of listening to the word of God in Scripture in order to cultivate friendship with Christ through Spirit-prompted dialogue. Four movements make up the method.

READ
Lectio
- Read a Scripture passage two to three times, slowly and attentively.
- Note any word, phrase, or image that catches your attention.

REFLECT
Meditatio
- Ponder the meaning of what caught your attention.
- Imagine yourself in the scene.
- What is the Lord saying to you through this text?

RESPOND
Oratio
- Talk to God about the passage or anything else on your heart.
- Note any changes or actions you are drawn to live out.

REST
Contemplatio
- Spend a few minutes in restful silence.
- "Be still and know that I am God" (Psalm 46:11).

SUGGESTED PASSAGES FOR GETTING STARTED

Philippians 4:4-9	Romans 8:12-27	Titus 3:4-8	Luke 10:38-42
Psalm 1	John 15:1-5	John 10:7-18	Luke 18:9-14
Matthew 11:28-30	Psalm 139:1-16	Psalm 25:1-6	Psalm 19

Ignatian Contemplation: Imaginative Prayer with Scripture

It is profitable to use the imagination and to apply the five senses . . .
I will smell the fragrance and taste the infinite sweetness and charm
of the Divinity, of the soul, of its virtues, and of everything there . . . I
will, so to speak, embrace and kiss the places where the persons walk.
– St. Ignatius of Loyola

PREPARE & READ

Prepare for prayer as usual. Invite the Holy Spirit to guide you. Choose a passage to read. A narrative passage works best for this.

PICTURE THE SCENE

Prayerfully imagine the scene and any details noted in the passage.
- Where does the event take place?
- Does the passage mention any details about the setting?
- What other details do you picture?
- How is the weather? Is it dry? Dusty? Humid? Cold?
- Who are the different people present for this event?

Place yourself in the scene.
- Choose one of the people in the narrative and see the scene through their eyes.
- Are you someone interacting with Jesus? A member of the crowd? Jesus? One of his disciples?
- How close or far are you from Jesus?

Use your imagination to extrapolate.
- What do you see, smell, feel, taste, hear?
- What emotions stir with you?
- What do you want to do or say?
- What do you see Jesus do? Hear him say?
- How do other people in the story interact with you?
- What do you see them do or hear them say?
- How do these imaginings affect you? What do they show you about yourself or Jesus or someone else?

RESPOND

Talk to God about whatever emerged in your prayerful imagining.

---

*   St. Ignatius, *Spiritual Exercises*, 121, 124, 125.

Pray the Psalms

The Psalms are at once the Bible's song book and school of prayer.

- Choose any psalm (or a portion of one) to guide a prayer time.
- Read a verse or two at a time.
- Let the words of the psalm inspire your own words to God.

For example:

PSALM 19:2, 8, 13

² The heavens declare the glory of God; the firmament proclaims the works of his hands.

> *God, you created the heavens: the sun and the moon and the clouds. Creation is so beautiful, Jesus. It makes me wonder how beautiful you must be in all of your glory. I long to see your face, Lord.*

⁸ The law of the Lord is perfect, refreshing the soul. The decree of the Lord is trustworthy, giving wisdom to the simple.

> *God, I desire to follow you faithfully. Teach me wisdom. Help me to understand your teachings and to trust you above all else.*

¹³ Who can detect trespasses? Cleanse me from my inadvertent sins.

> *Jesus, please help me know my own heart. I don't want to sin. Help me become more aware of my faults so I can give them to you. Please give me the grace to love you more perfectly, Lord.*

SUGGESTED PSALMS

○ 3	○ 19	○ 34	○ 63	○ 100	○ 127
○ 4	○ 23	○ 42	○ 70	○ 103	○ 130
○ 8	○ 27	○ 51	○ 84	○ 104	○ 139
○ 13	○ 33	○ 62	○ 91	○ 121	○ 143

Memorize God's Word

I treasure your word in my heart.
– Psalm 119:11

Discover the power of keeping small portions of God's Word tucked in your heart.

PICK

Choose a Scripture passage you would like to memorize. Consider memorizing one verse for each of the ten topics in this book, such as the verse listed on the title page for each chapter. But the possibilities are endless.

PRAY

Read the passage in context in your Bible and pray *lectio divina* with it. Read, Reflect, Respond, Rest (see page 64).

PRACTICE

Practice reciting it daily until it's easy to do (word for word). Here are some helpful tips:

- Write the passage on a notecard and carry it with you.
- Practice one phrase at a time without looking. Once a phrase is locked in your memory, add the next phrase.
- Say the Bible reference ("Matthew 11:28-30") both before and after reciting the passage.
- Audio record yourself reading the passage, including the reference. Listen to the recording repeatedly while in the car, on a walk, etc. Speak along with the recording until you can recite the verse as easily as you can say the Our Father.
- Write it out from scratch to identify where your gaps are. Practice the trouble areas.
- Have a friend test you.
- Engage in friendly competition with a friend. Who can memorize it first?

REPEAT AND REVIEW

Add verses to your repertoire, reviewing all your memorized verses weekly. Watch how the Lord brings this inspired wisdom to mind when you need it most!

ENDNOTES

1. St. Gregory the Great, "Moralia, Commentary on the Book of Blessed Job," accessed November 6, 2023, https://faculty.georgetown.edu/jod/texts/moralia1.html.

2. Second Vatican Council, *Dei verbum*, sec. 21.

3. *Catechism*, 80.

4. See Ephesians 5:21-32.

5. St. Benedict, "Prologue," sec. 1 in *RB 1980: The Rule of St. Benedict in English*, ed. Timothy Fry, O.S.B. (Collegeville, MN: Liturgical Press, 1982).

6. St. Ignatius of Loyola, *The Spiritual Exercises*, sec. 121, 124, 125 in *Ignatius of Loyola: Spiritual Exercises and Selected Works*, The Classics of Western Spirituality, trans. George E. Ganss (New York: Paulist Press, 1991).

7. See Psalm 1:2.

WEEK 3
GROW IN FREEDOM

For freedom Christ set us free; so stand firm and do not submit again to the yoke of slavery.

– Galatians 5:1

CONVERSATION THREE
Grow in Freedom

OPENING PRAYER (3 MIN)

Select one person to open in prayer. Use the following prayer or your own words.

In the name of the Father, and of the Son, and of the Holy Spirit. Amen.

Heavenly Father, thank you for the ways you have met us, loved us, and led us this week. Thank you for your word in Scripture, in Tradition, and in our hearts. Come, Holy Spirit; join us as we gather here. Guide our conversation and fill us with your life, as we learn from you and one another what it means to be your disciple.

We ask these things in the name of Jesus. Amen.

CATCH UP (5 MIN)

Share highs and lows: one positive thing (a simple joy, gratitude, or blessing) and one challenge in your life since you last met.

REVIEW DWELL IN GOD'S WORD (15 MIN)

Discuss a few of the following questions.

- How did go memorizing Philippians 4:6-7? Can you recite it now?
- Did you draw any encouragement or spiritual benefit from having this verse hidden within you? Or how could you imagine this verse encouraging you in the future? (Note: It may take time for you to experience these benefits!)
- On day 1 you prayed with the parable of the sower and the seeds. Which type of ground do you think most reflects your own heart lately (the path, rocky ground, among thorns, or fertile soil)?
- Which of the following prayer practices did you find most helpful or memorable? Most challenging?
  - *Lectio divina*
  - Praying with a psalm
  - Ignatian imaginative prayer
- What promise from Scripture on Day 7 spoke to you most?

ABOUT GROW IN FREEDOM (15 MIN)

Read aloud.

We all want *freedom*. It's the rallying cry of politicians, preachers, songwriters, and teenagers alike. What is meant by the *Christian freedom* the New Testament proclaims? The answer is both freedom *from* sin and freedom *for* love.

Broadly understood, sin means to fall short of loving. Sin has inherent consequences: every unloving act injures someone, including the person committing the wrong. Too often, though, self-interest, temptation, and poor judgment lead us to choose the harm of sin over the freedom and blessing of love.

Through accepting Jesus in faith and receiving the sacraments, we are set free from slavery to sin,[1] but it still clings to us. We are like prisoners with unlocked shackles who must choose to let go of the familiar chains and walk into unfamiliar freedom.

The content this week requires courage, humility, and commitment. We'll take a hard look at the realities of sin, evil, and darkness, both in ourselves and in our world, so that we can cling more robustly to our Savior Jesus Christ, and grow in the abundant freedom he offers.

YOUR CHALLENGE THIS WEEK:

☐ Grow in freedom—*from* sin and *for* love—by praying with the daily prayer guide.

☐ Receive the Sacrament of Reconciliation (if you are Catholic). The prayer guide will walk you through preparing for the sacrament.

Discuss the following questions.

- What is your experience of the Sacrament of Reconciliation (also known as "confession")?
- What are the options and times for confession near you? If you don't know, how can you find out?*

---

* The website and app *masstimes.org* can help you locate Catholic parishes, Mass times, and confession times. Always check with the actual parish web-

- Are there any roadblocks (in your schedule or your mind / heart) that would prevent you from receiving this sacrament* in the next few weeks?

READ AND DISCUSS (15 MIN)

Read aloud.

Galatians 5:1, 13-25 (NRSV-CE)†

[1] For freedom Christ has set us free. Stand firm, therefore, and do not submit again to a yoke of slavery.

[13] For you were called to freedom, brothers and sisters; only do not use your freedom as an opportunity for self-indulgence, but through love become slaves to one another. [14] For the whole law is summed up in a single commandment, "You shall love your neighbor as yourself." [15] If, however, you bite and devour one another, take care that you are not consumed by one another.

[16] Live by the Spirit, I say, and do not gratify the desires of the flesh. [17] For what the flesh desires is opposed to the Spirit, and what the Spirit desires is opposed to the flesh; for these are opposed to each other, to prevent you from doing what you want. [18] But if you are led by the Spirit, you are not subject to the law. [19] Now the works of the flesh are obvious: fornication, impurity, licentiousness, [20] idolatry, sorcery, enmities, strife, jealousy, anger, quarrels, dissensions,

---

site or call the parish to verify the information you find on secondary websites. If times are not listed or are too sporadic, call the parish and request an appointment for confession. Don't ever worry about being an inconvenience; it's the priest's very vocation to make himself available to you for this sacrament of healing!

* If you are not Catholic, you may certainly still schedule time with a priest for conversation, encouragement, and spiritual guidance. If you're interested in exploring more about the sacraments or becoming Catholic, reach out to any local Catholic parish or friends to help you inquire further and get the support you need.

† When reading St. Paul, it's important to know that his use of the word "flesh" does not simply mean "body." "The flesh" means the whole of a person (body and soul) without reference to God and God's grace. Living by the flesh, then, means relying on one's own powers apart from God's guidance and help. Embracing Christ, by contrast, is the pathway to living not according to "the flesh" but according to the Spirit by faith.

factions, [21] envy, drunkenness, carousing, and things like these. I am warning you, as I warned you before: those who do such things will not inherit the kingdom of God.

[22] By contrast, the fruit of the Spirit is love, joy, peace, patience, kindness, generosity, faithfulness, [23] gentleness, and self-control. There is no law against such things. [24] And those who belong to Christ Jesus have crucified the flesh with its passions and desires. [25] If we live by the Spirit, let us also be guided by the Spirit.

Discuss the following questions.

- What do you think Paul means by "slavery?" How does he describe the freedom God offers?
- Have you ever experienced a season of growth in freedom away from any of these "works of the flesh" and / or towards any of these "fruits of the spirit?" How so?
- What is one "work of the flesh" or "fruit of the Spirit" that you want to pray about in your life right now?

NEXT MEETING (2 MIN)

Make sure you have your next discussion on the calendar.

CLOSING PRAYER (5 MIN)

Choose someone to lead the closing prayer time. Use the prompts below and add your own words. Invite the other(s) to add their prayers when you prompt them.

In the name of the Father, and of the Son, and of the Holy Spirit. Amen.

Jesus, thank you for your promise to keep doing a good work in us. It is the desire of our hearts to know you and to walk freely in your ways of love. Help us to trust always in your mercy and run to you for strength, forgiveness, healing and guidance.

Lord, we lift up our thanksgiving and our petitions to you. In particular:

_____ , _____ , _____ , _____ .

(Add some of your own and invite the other(s) to add theirs as well.)

Thank you for always hearing our prayers and leading us into your will.

Mother Mary, we ask you to pray for us and our loved ones, as we say together:

Hail Mary, full of grace, the Lord is with thee; blessed art thou among women, and blessed is the fruit of thy womb, Jesus. Holy Mary, Mother of God, pray for us sinners, now and at the hour of our death, Amen.

PRAYER GUIDE
Grow in Freedom

Day 1. Weeds and Wheat

Man is split within himself. As a result, all of human life, whether individual or collective, shows itself to be a dramatic struggle between good and evil, between light and darkness.
– Gaudium et spes, 13

Our world is a profound mix of grace and sin, goodness and evil, light and darkness. In the parable of the weeds and the wheat,[2] Jesus told us it would be this way until the end of time.

If we're honest and even a little self-aware, we'll acknowledge that we all have some weeds and wheat in us. We all contribute not only to what is right and good in this world, but also to what is broken. Indeed, "the line dividing good and evil cuts through the heart of every human being."[3] For even as we are "wonderfully made" (Psalm 139:14) and created in God's very "image and likeness" (Genesis 1:26), still we "all have sinned and fall short of the glory of God" (Romans 3:23, NRSV-CE).

Let's face it: it's much easier to complain about the sins and flaws of others than to see, admit, and deal with our own. As Tolstoy put it, "Everybody thinks of changing humanity, and nobody thinks of changing himself."[4]

Jesus was intent on teaching the importance of staying aware of our own need for mercy and continual conversion instead of fixating on the flaws of others. "Why do you notice the splinter in your brother's eye, but do not perceive the wooden beam in your own eye?" (Matthew 7:3). One of the signs of human and spiritual maturity lies precisely here: can we look squarely at those less desirable qualities in ourselves, those failures to love, those specific sins as well as our sinful tendencies, and respond, not with blame or excuses or self-loathing, but with genuine repentance?

Today, you begin to face some of the tensions in your own heart. Because of God's great love for us, and what he has done for us in

Christ Jesus, we can face our less admirable qualities and our sins with the blessed assurance that we are not disqualified or cast out. We are invited, instead, to experience the tender mercy that God longs to give us, especially where we need it most.

OPEN TO GOD

Open yourself to God in your usual way.

In the name of the Father, and of the Son, and of the Holy Spirit. Amen.

Come, Holy Spirit. Move me today to consider how much I need your merciful love, your gentle corrections.

PRAY FROM THE HEART

Begin by casting your cares on the one who loves you. What are you carrying today that you can entrust into God's care? *Lord, I give you* _____.

Use the steps of *lectio divina* (read, reflect, respond, rest) to pray with the following passage.

> Luke 18:9-14, NRSV-CE
> He also told this parable to some who trusted in themselves that they were righteous and regarded others with contempt: "Two men went up to the temple to pray, one a Pharisee and the other a tax collector. The Pharisee, standing by himself, was praying thus, 'God, I thank you that I am not like other people: thieves, rogues, adulterers, or even like this tax collector. I fast twice a week; I give a tenth of all my income.' But the tax collector, standing far off, would not even look up to heaven, but was beating his breast and saying, 'God, be merciful to me, a sinner!' I tell you, this man went down to his home justified rather than the other; for all who exalt themselves will be humbled, but all who humble themselves will be exalted."

For help reflecting:

- What word or phrase stands out to you as you read this passage a few times? What meaning does God have for you in this word or phrase today?
- To whom did Jesus address this parable?
- What do you think it means to go home justified?
- It's easy to write off the Pharisee as a self-righteous, arrogant man. Is there any way, perhaps more subtly, that you sometimes think, feel, or act like him?

- Repeat the tax collector's prayer several times, slowly. Talk to God about whatever comes into your consciousness as you do this.

CLOSE

Rest in quiet prayer for a minute or two. Allow God's loving mercy and help to surround you.

Jesus, forgive me for the ways I've trusted in myself rather than in you. Increase my faith in you, Lord. Please give me the grace to be humble before you and trust in your goodness rather than my own.

In the name of the Father, and of the Son, and of the Holy Spirit. Amen.

Day 2. What Is Sin?

*Sin is an offense against reason, truth, and right conscience;
it is failure in genuine love for God and neighbor caused by a perverse
attachment to certain goods. It wounds the nature of man and
injures human solidarity.*
— Catechism of the Catholic Church, 1849

Sin is not just anything we feel badly about, but a genuine offense against God, self, or others. Sometimes we feel badly about things and situations in which we have not sinned, and we sometimes commit genuine sins without feeling any accompanying guilt. The more our conscience is formed through the guidance of the Holy Spirit, the wisdom of the Church, and our ongoing practice in recognizing and confessing our sin, the more we will respond to sin with proper contrition (sorrow).

The Church gives words to a dynamic we're all familiar with: some sins are worse than others. 1 John 5:17 states: "All wrongdoing is sin, but there is sin that is not deadly."

A sin is "mortal" (deadly) if it is a grave (serious) matter, and if it is freely chosen with full knowledge of its seriousness.[5] "Mortal sin destroys charity in the heart of man by a grave violation of God's law; it turns man away from God, who is his ultimate end and his beatitude, by preferring an inferior good to him."[6] Venial sin (sin that is not "mortal") "allows charity to subsist, even though it offends and wounds it."[7] While venial sins slow us down and injure us on the road of charity and grace (and should be taken very seriously), through mortal sin we effectively jump off "the road that leads to life" and choose instead "the road . . . that leads to destruction" (Matthew 7:14, 13).

Remember, the Lord longs to forgive you and to keep leading you in victory. And all along the way—through both victories and failures—his love for you never falters. Jesus has provided a sure route out of the darkness and death of sin and into the joy of love. In Jesus, who brings life from death, "we have redemption by his blood, the forgiveness of transgressions, in accord with the riches of his grace that he lavished upon us" (Ephesians 1:7-8).

OPEN TO GOD

Open yourself to God in your usual way.

In the name of the Father, and of the Son, and of the Holy Spirit. Amen.

Jesus, you have the words of eternal life. You are eternal and abundant life itself. I trust in your love for me. Continue giving me courage to reflect on my need for your tender mercy and loving guidance. Speak, Lord, your servant is listening.

PRAY FROM THE HEART

Begin by celebrating growth and giving thanks.

- What area of your life feels more firmly set on the narrow path of goodness and right than in the past?
- Reflect on your experience of this change. To what extent has it increased your freedom or joy?
- Say a prayer of thanks to God for the good work he has done in you.

Use the steps of *lectio divina* (read, reflect, respond, rest) to pray with the following passage.

1 John 1:5-2:2, NRSV-CE

This is the message we have heard from him and proclaim to you, that God is light and in him there is no darkness at all. If we say that we have fellowship with him while we are walking in darkness, we lie and do not do what is true; but if we walk in the light as he himself is in the light, we have fellowship with one another, and the blood of Jesus his Son cleanses us from all sin. If we say that we have no sin, we deceive ourselves, and the truth is not in us. If we confess our sins, he who is faithful and just will forgive us our sins and cleanse us from all unrighteousness. If we say that we have not sinned, we make him a liar, and his word is not in us.

My little children, I am writing these things to you so that you may not sin. But if anyone does sin, we have an advocate with the Father, Jesus Christ the righteous; and he is the atoning sacrifice for our sins, and not for ours only but also for the sins of the whole world.

For help reflecting:

- What does John mean by walking "in the light"? Is he simply saying "don't sin"? Or is there more to it than that?
- How would you put his message into your own words?
- What phrases do you find most encouraging? Most challenging?

CLOSE

Rest for a few minutes in the light of God, in whom there is no darkness.

Jesus, you are the light of the world, and in you there is no darkness. This week and always, keep me from hiding and isolation when I sin. Help me bring my shortcomings into your radiant light. Thank you for your promise to forgive and to cleanse me from all unrighteousness.

In the name of the Father, and of the Son, and of the Holy Spirit. Amen.

Day 3. Sin and Wounds

He himself bore our sins in his body upon the cross, so that, free from sin, we might live for righteousness. By his wounds you have been healed. For you had gone astray like sheep, but you have now returned to the shepherd and guardian of your souls.
– 1 Peter 2:24-25

All sins inflict wounds. Sin wounds both the one who commits sin and the one(s) wronged. But while sin leads to wounds, wounds can also lead to sins. When we are hurting from wounds like abandonment, fear, confusion, rejection, or shame,[8] we often turn to sin, rather than God, as a (false) form of comfort. We may eat too much, drink too much, watch too much TV, overuse social media, escape into an erotic or emotional fantasy, or strive desperately to prove our worth through various praise-winning projects. We may lash out verbally at family members, become impatient with friends, or gossip about coworkers.

False comforts can distract us from our pain or bring quick

relief—for a time. But they never heal our wounds. And unhealed wounds, no matter how small at first, are prone to infection. They grow and spread. When this happens, we consume larger doses of our false comforts, and a vicious cycle develops. Our pain leads us to sin's doorstep, and sin only causes more pain in the long run.

We've all been wounded by the brokenness and sins of others. We've all been wounded by our own attempts to numb our pain through false comforts. It takes humility and grace to understand and admit that we are not exempt from this vicious cycle. But this is precisely the cycle that our savior Jesus interrupts and works to overturn in us. "Those who are well do not need a physician, but the sick do. I did not come to call the righteous but sinners" (Mark 2:17).

OPEN TO GOD

Take a few deep breaths and prepare for prayer.

In the name of the Father, and of the Son, and of the Holy Spirit. Amen.

Holy Spirit, guide my prayer today. Give me courage to face the patterns of pain and brokenness in my life. Help me to see how I tend to turn to people and things to fill in me what only you can fill. As St. Augustine prayed, so do I: "You have made us for yourself, and our heart is restless until it rests in you."[9]

PRAY FROM THE HEART

Consider the patterns of sin and grace described above. Ask God to show you where this "vicious cycle" has had an effect in your own life.

- What pains, hardships, or insecurities tend to cause you restlessness?
- What people or things do you tend to turn to for comfort, health, or healing that ultimately cannot give these to you?

Bring these prayerful reflections with you as you pray with the following passage using *lectio divina.*

Mark 2:1-12, NRSV-CE

When he returned to Capernaum after some days, it was reported that he was at home. So many gathered around that there was no longer room for them, not even in front of the door; and he was speaking the word to them. Then some people came, bringing to him a paralyzed man, carried by four of them. And when they could not bring him to Jesus because of the crowd, they removed the roof above him; and after having dug through it, they let down the mat on which the paralytic lay. When Jesus saw their faith, he said to the paralytic, "Son, your sins are forgiven." Now some of the scribes were sitting there, questioning in their hearts, "Why does this fellow speak in this way? It is blasphemy! Who can forgive sins but God alone?" At once Jesus perceived in his spirit that they were discussing these questions among themselves; and he said to them, "Why do you raise such questions in your hearts? Which is easier, to say to the paralytic, 'Your sins are forgiven,' or to say, 'Stand up and take your mat and walk'? But so that you may know that the Son of Man has authority on earth to forgive sins"—he said to the paralytic—"I say to you, stand up, take your mat and go to your home." And he stood up, and immediately took the mat and went out before all of them; so that they were all amazed and glorified God, saying, "We have never seen anything like this!"

Ultimately, only Jesus can heal us of our wounds and our sins. Turn to him now with sorrow for your sins and faith in his saving help.

I give you the wounds I bear and those I have inflicted on others, Lord. I'm sorry for the times I've failed to love you, others, and myself, and for being slow to turn to you for the love and guidance I so desperately need. In particular, I'm sorry for _____.

Please heal me from my sins and the wounds they cause, Lord. Give me your divine healing, especially in _____.

CLOSE

Rest in the silent embrace of your Maker, who loves you and desires to make you fully well.

Jesus, my heart is indeed restless until it rests in you. Continue your saving, healing, restoring work in me. Thank you for coming as the Divine Physician into this world and into my life.

In the name of the Father, and of the Son, and of the Holy Spirit. Amen.

TIP: KNOW THYSELF

Growing in freedom is a process of continual conversion. This includes a greater awareness of both our strengths and weaknesses, seen under the light of God's love for us. Various personality profiling tools and strengths or gifts inventories can help in this quest to know ourselves, provided we don't expect any of these tests or systems to provide comprehensive insight or to replace the role of prayer and the Holy Spirit in our self-examination. Listening to the input of people in our lives is also crucial; we all have blind spots and need feedback from others who know us.

Day 4. Repentance and Reconciliation

For we do not have a high priest who is unable to sympathize with our weaknesses, but one who has similarly been tested in every way, yet without sin. So let us confidently approach the throne of grace to receive mercy and to find grace for timely help.
– Hebrews 4:15-16

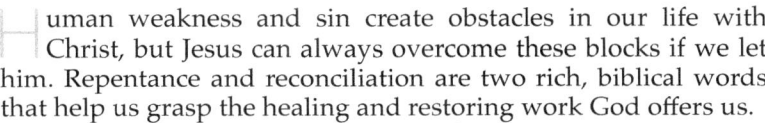

Human weakness and sin create obstacles in our life with Christ, but Jesus can always overcome these blocks if we let him. Repentance and reconciliation are two rich, biblical words that help us grasp the healing and restoring work God offers us.

"This is the time of fulfillment. The kingdom of God is at hand. Repent, and believe in the gospel" (Mark 1:15). These are Jesus' first words in the Gospel of Mark. "Repentance" (*metanoia*) implies a radical turning around. It is a change of one's perspective and entire direction away from sin and evil, towards goodness and God. It includes genuine sorrow for doing wrong, desire and resolve to change, and trust in God's mercy and help.

"Reconciliation" means to remove the tension between two parties, to restore a previously fractured bond, to make whole again. Jesus accomplished reconciliation between the world and God once and for all by his Death and Resurrection (Colossians 1:20), but each person must allow this reconciling love to reach their own heart.

We see this reconciling love reach Peter's heart on the beach on that first Easter morning. Peter must have felt awful on Holy Saturday. He fell asleep in Gethsemane, denied Jesus three times, and now his friend and Savior was dead. But this was not the end. For each of Peter's denials, the risen Jesus gently led him through a process of repentance, reconciliation, and recommitment (see John 21:15-19).

God gave the Church a visible means of experiencing this same reconciling love of Jesus. In the Sacrament of Reconciliation, we see, hear, touch, feel, and know, with a blessed assurance, that we are embraced, forgiven, healed, strengthened, and sent by the Lord *himself.*

Today, prepare for the Sacrament of Reconciliation by prayerfully examining your conscience. Doing so will prepare you to repent and receive reconciliation by naming the sins you are sorry for.

OPEN TO GOD

Prepare for prayer in your usual way.

In the name of the Father, and of the Son, and of the Holy Spirit. Amen.

Jesus, I love you. I don't want anything to come between us. Please help me examine my conscience, repent of my sins, and seek reconciliation with you.

PRAY FROM THE HEART

Use the prompts below to review your actions, thoughts, and attitudes. Make note of sins and omissions to confess, either mentally or written on a piece of paper, to bring with you to confession.

Let your conscience speak to you:

- When have you neglected to do what you knew was good?
- When have you chosen to do what you knew was evil, wrong, or against God's will?
- When have you thought or acted in a way that was unloving to yourself or others?
- When have you neglected to love God?

For further help examining your conscience in light of the Ten Commandments, see page 97.

Talk to God about the things that examining your conscience stirred up in you. Express your sorrow and contrition to God and resolve to repent and participate in the Sacrament of Reconciliation as soon as possible.

CLOSE

Remember, the Lord loves to forgive you and to keep leading you in victory. All along the way—through both victories and failures—his love for you never falters. Rest in his love now in one to two minutes of silence.

My God, I am sorry for my sins with all my heart. In choosing to do wrong and failing to do good, I have sinned against you whom I should love above all things. I firmly intend, with your help, to do penance, to sin no more, and to avoid whatever leads me to sin.

In the name of the Father, and of the Son, and of the Holy Spirit. Amen.

TIP: TELL SOMEONE

Sin and temptation prefer the darkness of secrecy and isolation. The first thing Adam and Eve did after they ate the forbidden fruit was hide. We do the same thing. We're embarrassed. We're ashamed. Or perhaps we're rather content with our sin and don't want to be reminded that we're called to a higher standard of love.

When we hide our sin and try to "get it under control" by ourselves or with just "Jesus and me," we are sure to grow more enslaved to its pull. Simply put, Jesus didn't choose to free us from sin all by himself. He chose to make our path to freedom a profoundly communal one. He gave us the Church and the sacraments as our ordinary means of receiving his grace; he calls us to speak our confession aloud to a priest, forcing us to courageously confront our sins and open our hearts wide to his healing mercy. In addition to confessing to a priest, telling a mature Christian friend or mentor about our struggles with a particular temptation brings additional levels of accountability and support we cannot give ourselves.

"For all of you are children of the light and children of the day. We are not of the night or of darkness" (1 Thessalonians 5:5). Talking about our sins and temptations brings them out of the darkness of hiding, and into the light of Christ.

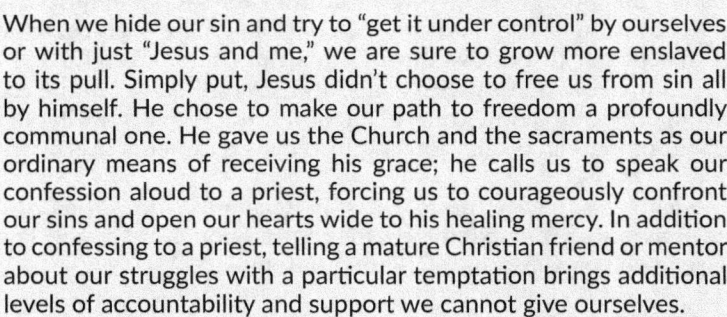

Day 5. Amazing (Sacramental) Grace

Through the sacraments of Christian initiation, man receives the new life of Christ... This new life as a child of God can be weakened and even lost by sin. The Lord Jesus Christ, physician of our souls and bodies...has willed that his Church continue, in the power of the Holy Spirit, his work of healing and salvation, even among her own members. This is the purpose of the two sacraments of healing: the sacrament of Penance and the sacrament of Anointing of the Sick.
—Catechism of the Catholic Church, 1420-1421

Confessing our sins forces us to be vulnerable—naming our brokenness and inadequacy. But the beautiful promise of the Sacrament of Reconciliation is that God longs to forgive and strengthen us. There is no need for fear. God entered our human condition, experienced all the suffering our sin causes, so that he could free us from sin's tyranny. In the words of St. Paul, "We implore you on behalf of Christ, be reconciled to God. For our sake he made him to be sin who did not know sin, so that we might become the righteousness of God in him" (2 Corinthians 5:20-21). God promises freedom, wholeness, life, righteousness. Like the father of the prodigal son, God runs to us, longing to forgive us when we return to him.

By virtue of Holy Orders, the priest acts *in persona Christi*—"in the person of Christ," pronouncing the words of absolution.[10] This means that the priest's ability to administer sacramental power flows not from himself, but from God's all-sufficient grace, which he has chosen to bestow through his ministers. Therefore, it is Christ himself who forgives, heals, and strengthens us in the confessional. The amazing grace of encountering Jesus is available to us, without fail, in confession and in every sacrament. This is truly good news!

So let us frequently run to Christ in Reconciliation. "The Lord's acts of mercy are not exhausted, his compassion is not spent; They are renewed each morning" (Lamentations 3:22-23).

OPEN TO GOD

Prepare for prayer in your usual way.

In the name of the Father, and of the Son, and of the Holy Spirit. Amen.

Come, Holy Spirit. I give you this time and I thank you for it. Open my mind and heart to listen to the words you want me to hear today. Come, Holy Spirit.

PRAY FROM THE HEART

Today, pray with this famous story of a father and his two sons. Jesus tells this story in response to the Pharisees and scribes who were grumbling (see Luke 15:2) about Jesus spending time with sinners. This is one of three stories Jesus tells them about the joy in heaven over even one person who repents of their sins.

If this is a familiar passage for you, you may need to exercise extra diligence in order to be open to the "living and effective" word of God (Hebrews 4:12) speaking a new word to you today. Trace each line with your finger as you read or read it aloud to yourself to deepen your attentiveness.

Use the steps of *lectio divina* (read, reflect, respond, rest) to pray with the following passage.

Luke 15:11-32, NRSV-CE

Then Jesus said, "There was a man who had two sons. The younger of them said to his father, 'Father, give me the share of the property that will belong to me.' So he divided his property between them. A few days later the younger son gathered all he had and traveled to a distant country, and there he squandered his property in dissolute living. When he had spent everything, a severe famine took place throughout that country, and he began to be in need. So he went and hired himself out to one of the citizens of that country, who sent him to his fields to feed the pigs. He would gladly have filled himself with the pods that the pigs were eating; and no one gave him anything. But when he came to himself he said, 'How many of my father's hired hands have bread enough and to spare, but here I am dying of hunger! I will get up and go to my father, and I will say to him, 'Father, I have sinned against heaven and before you; I am no longer worthy to be called your son; treat me like one of your hired hands.' So he set off and went to his father. But while he was still far off, his father saw him and was filled with compassion; he ran and put his arms around him and kissed him. Then the son said to him, 'Father, I have sinned against heaven and before you; I am no longer worthy to be called your son.' But the father said to his slaves, 'Quickly, bring out a robe—the best one—and put it on him; put a ring on his finger and sandals on his feet. And get the fatted calf and kill it, and let us eat and celebrate; for this son of mine was dead and is alive again; he was lost and is found!' And they began to celebrate."

"Now his elder son was in the field; and when he came and approached the house, he heard music and dancing. He called one of the slaves and asked what was going on. He replied, 'Your brother has come, and your father has killed the fatted calf, because he has got him back safe and sound.' Then he became angry and refused to go in. His father came out and began to plead with him. But he answered his father, 'Listen! For all these years I have been working like a slave for you, and I have never disobeyed your command; yet you have never given me even a young goat so that I might celebrate with my friends. But when this son of yours came back, who has devoured your property with prostitutes, you killed the fatted calf for him!' Then the father said to him, 'Son, you are always with me, and all that is mine is yours. But we had to celebrate and rejoice, because this brother of yours was dead and has come to life; he was lost and has been found.'"

For help reflecting:

- What does the son envision will happen when he gets home? What actually happens?
- Take a closer look at the actions of the father in the story. What does he show you about our heavenly Father?
- Imagine the celebration that takes place at the return of the prodigal son. Put yourself in his place.
- What type of conversion is the older son in need of?
- Which of the two sons do you see more of in yourself lately?
- How does this story affect your understanding of how God views you when you approach the Sacrament of Reconciliation?

CLOSE

Imagine yourself being held in the Father's loving, forgiving embrace. Stay there in a moment or two of silent prayer.

Let the words of absolution, which the priest pronounces in the Sacrament of Reconciliation, draw you into a greater longing to run frequently to this wellspring of grace.

God, the Father of mercies through the death and resurrection of his Son has reconciled the world to himself and poured out the Holy Spirit for the forgiveness of sins; through the ministry of the Church may God grant you pardon and peace, and I absolve you from your sins in the name of the Father, and of the Son, and of the Holy Spirit.[11]

Amen.

TIP: DON'T LOSE HEART!

We must not let our weakness and failures discourage us. The spiritual masters of the Catholic tradition insist that one of the first lessons we must learn is to always return to God even in our shortcomings; by this we come to trust his mercy and develop the habit of clinging to him. Thus, St. Francis de Sales instructs us:

Be patient with everyone, but above all with yourself; I mean, don't be disturbed about your imperfections, and always have the courage to pick yourself up after a fall...There is no better way of growing...in the spiritual life than to be always starting over again and never thinking that we have done enough.

But most important, don't lose heart... I have no doubt that God is holding you by the hand; if he allows you to stumble, it is only to let you know that if he were not holding your hand, you would fall. This is how he gets you to take tighter hold of his hand.[12]

Day 6. We Have an Enemy

A thief comes only to steal and slaughter and destroy; I came so that they might have life and have it more abundantly.
—John 10:10

We humans are not the only characters on the stage with God in the real-life drama we live in. There are angels, helping us along, as well as evil spirits actively seeking to draw us away from the love of God, self, and neighbor.

The existence of evil spirits might be an uncomfortable truth to consider, but we must not ignore it. Jesus referred to Satan as the "father of lies" (John 8:44), fended off his temptations in the desert, and frequently cast out demons. St. Paul reminds us that "our struggle is not with flesh and blood but with the principalities, with the powers, with the world rulers of this present darkness, with the evil spirits in the heavens" (Ephesians 6:12). St. Peter exhorts, "Be sober and vigilant. Your opponent the devil is prowling around like a roaring lion looking for [someone] to devour. Resist him, steadfast in faith, knowing that your fellow believers throughout the world undergo the same sufferings" (1 Peter 5:8-9).

The point is not to scare us but to alert us to reality and to teach us to cling to our Savior and his ample resources as we learn to fight the good fight of faith. To ignore or deny the existence of active, personal evil only gives it more power to wreak havoc in our world.

The great news is that Satan has no actual power over Christ, whose victory was sealed in the Cross and Resurrection. We can call on Jesus' name in faith and cling to the sacraments to abide in his victory and protection. We can learn the powerful practice of claiming God's truth for ourselves over and against the enemy's lies. We can call upon the saints and our guardian angels, who intercede and fight for us.

OPEN TO GOD

Pause to center yourself and your attention on God.

In the name of the Father, and of the Son, and of the Holy Spirit. Amen.

Lord, "even though I walk through the valley of the shadow of death, I will fear no evil, for you are with me" (Psalm 23:4). Good Shepherd, be with me and guide me in this time of prayer and protect me from all evil.

PRAY FROM THE HEART

Sit with St. Paul's description of the armor of God given to every believer in Jesus Christ. It's not because of our own resources or strength that we have hope in the face of our spiritual battle with evil. "Our help is in the name of the Lord, who made heaven and earth" (Psalm 124:8, NRSV-CE).

Use the steps of *lectio divina* (read, reflect, respond, rest) to pray with the following passage.

Ephesians 6:13-18, NRSV-CE

Therefore take up the whole armor of God, so that you may be able to withstand on that evil day, and having done every-thing, to stand firm. Stand therefore, and fasten the belt of truth around your waist, and put on the breastplate of righteousness. As shoes for your feet put on whatever will make you ready to proclaim the gospel of peace. With all of these, take the shield of faith, with which you will be able to quench all the flaming ar-rows of the evil one. Take the helmet of salvation, and the sword of the Spirit, which is the word of God.

Pray in the Spirit at all times in every prayer and supplication. To that end keep alert and always persevere in supplication for all the saints.

For help reflecting:

- What are all the distinct pieces of armor St. Paul's lists here? For each one, is it primarily defensive in nature (protecting you from attacks) or offensive (used for launching proactive attacks)?
- Which piece of armor are you in most need of at this time?
- What are some practical ways for you to "keep alert"?
- What might it look like for you to "always persevere in sup-plication for all the saints"? (recall that "saints" here means other believers)

"Pray in the Spirit at all times in every prayer and supplication" (v. 18). Ask the Holy Spirit what or who to pray for today. Pray briefly for whatever comes to mind.

CLOSE

"Do not fear! Stand your ground and see the victory the Lord will win for you today . . . The Lord will fight for you; you have only to keep still" (Exodus 14:13-14).

Keep still now, for a few minutes of restful trust in God, who fights for you.

St. Michael the Archangel,
defend us in battle.
Be our defense against the wickedness
and snares of the Devil.
May God rebuke him, we humbly pray,
and do thou, O Prince of the heavenly hosts,
by the power of God,
thrust into hell Satan,
and all the evil spirits,
who prowl about the world
seeking the ruin of souls.

In the name of the Father, and of the Son, and of the Holy Spirit. Amen.

TIP: TURN TO MARY

On the cross, Jesus gave his mother to John, and in turn, to all who would believe in and follow Jesus. She is not only our spiritual mother, but through her prayers, a warrior who commands legions of angels on our behalf! In the words of St. Bonaventure, "Men do not fear a powerful hostile army as the powers of hell fear the name and protection of Mary."[13] If you are ever feeling overwhelmed by the darkness or confusion of sin or by a particularly concerning or complicated problem, remember to turn to Mary in your prayers. Even one simple Hail Mary prayer, uttered in faith, is a more powerful weapon for good than we can even imagine.

Day 7. Live in Freedom

For freedom Christ set us free; so stand firm and do not submit again to the yoke of slavery.
— Galatians 5:1

Baptism is the sacrament that initiates us into the abundant life promised us in Christ. We become children of God, heirs of an imperishable inheritance. And yet, as we've been reflecting on in this chapter, sin still clings to us. We feel a gravitational pull to its deceptive comfort and power.

Perhaps that is why so many of the letters to the early Church found in the New Testament include encouragement for the newly baptized to live into their identity as "children of the light" (1 Thessalonians 5:5). Jesus invites us to be born anew, "of water and Spirit" (John 3:5). And St. Paul writes, "So whoever is in Christ is a new creation: the old things have passed away; behold, new things have come" (2 Corinthians 5:17). Baptism re-makes us into these new creations, but we have to choose every day to reject sin and live the new life Jesus has given us.

The readers of the New Testament letters were already baptized, and yet, like us, they still struggled with sin. "My children, I am writing this to you so that you may not commit sin. But if anyone does sin, we have an Advocate with the Father, Jesus Christ the righteous one" (1 John 2:1).

Growing in holiness means never tiring of rejecting sin and accepting the glorious freedom Christ offers us. When we live for God, we can put aside selfishness, fear, control, greed, and our own comforts, knowing our identity is secure in him. Grace empowers us to do courageous and noble things out of love for God and others, even when they are difficult or cost us. And when we fail or fall short of who we are in Christ, he is ready to forgive us and strengthen us to get back up. Like Japanese pottery that's broken and then fused back together with gold in the cracks, we're even more radiant and resilient because of what the Lord's mercy has done for us.

OPEN TO GOD

Open yourself to God in your usual way.

In the name of the Father, and of the Son, and of the Holy Spirit. Amen.

Father, Son, and Holy Spirit, you have made me a new creation in Baptism. Draw me deeper into your abundant life and empower me to live within the glorious freedom that you give me. As I begin this prayer time, I cast my cares upon you today. I give you my concerns about _____. Thank you for receiving me today. Open my heart to receive your Word.

PRAY FROM THE HEART

Use the steps of *lectio divina* (read, reflect, respond, rest) to pray with the following passage.

Romans 6:3-11, NRSV-CE

Do you not know that all of us who have been baptized into Christ Jesus were baptized into his death? Therefore we have been buried with him by baptism into death, so that, just as Christ was raised from the dead by the glory of the Father, so we too might walk in newness of life.

For if we have been united with him in a death like his, we will certainly be united with him in a resurrection like his. We know that our old self was crucified with him so that the body of sin might be destroyed, and we might no longer be enslaved to sin. For whoever has died is freed from sin. But if we have died with Christ, we believe that we will also live with him. We know that Christ, being raised from the dead, will never die again; death no longer has dominion over him. The death he died, he died to sin, once for all; but the life he lives, he lives to God. So you also must consider yourselves dead to sin and alive to God in Christ Jesus.

For help reflecting:

- What role does Christ play in our freedom, according to this passage?
- What does it mean for you to walk in newness of life?
- Are there things you would do differently if "death no longer [had] dominion" over you? How so?
- Many people have willingly died rather than submit to sin. How do you understand their actions in light of this passage?
- What part of the "old self" are you knowingly holding on to? Talk to Jesus about this, asking for mercy and the courage and grace to let it go.

Spend a few moments thanking God for the ways you have experienced "newness of life" in him or the ways in which he has given you freedom from sin.

CLOSE

You were created and recreated by God out of love. Let your Creator love you for a few minutes, sitting silently in his presence, just as you are.

Jesus, I trust in the words of Scripture, that you have freed us from the power of sin and death. Thank you, Lord, for all that you have done in my life, heart, and soul. I give you permission to continue leading me into the newness of life with you.

In the name of the Father, and of the Son, and of the Holy Spirit. Amen.

TIP: USE YOUR SWORD

Jesus used Scripture to fend off the devil's temptations in the desert. We, too, can adopt this powerful defense against the enemy of our souls. In fact, it's more than defense: St. Paul calls the Word of God the "sword of the spirit" (Ephesians 6:17) which is the only offensive weapon in his list of spiritual armor (Ephesians 6:10-17). Choose a verse that helps you resist a particular temptation or one that reminds you of your identity in Christ. If you're not sure which verse to choose, try this one from Philippians: "I have the strength for everything through him who empowers me" (4:13). Memorizing a verse makes it readily available to us (and our guardian angels) to call to mind whenever a temptation arises. For more on memorizing Scripture, see page 67.

MAKE IT A HABIT
Grow in Freedom

As its name implies, growing in the freedom of Christ is an ongoing process we continually embrace, as we become fit for the Kingdom we inherit by grace. Below, find additional information, tips, and suggested readings to make Grow in Freedom a life-giving habit going forward.

NURTURE HEALTH

The proper care of our bodies—rest, healthy food, and exercise—remains essential not only for physical well-being but also for our mental and spiritual health. Are you typically getting enough sleep? How is your physical health (or at least what you can control of it)? Is there a simple goal about diet, exercise, or sleep that you want to bring into this season of discipleship growth?

THE JESUS PRAYER

St. Paul encourages us to "pray without ceasing" (1 Thessalonians 5:17). One way to do that is to repeat a simple prayer in your mind throughout the day. The Eastern Orthodox and Catholic Churches practice a form of continuous prayer called the "Jesus Prayer." Pray the Jesus Prayer by repeating this short phrase again and again throughout your day: "Jesus Christ, Son of God, have mercy on me, a sinner." Repeating this often makes it part of the fabric of your mind and heart, almost like continuous background music to your thoughts. Many people adopt variations of the classic prayer to turn to God in the midst of daily life. Try repeating, "Lord Jesus Christ, have mercy on me," or simply "Jesus" to make the tax collector's prayer your own throughout the day.

REGULAR CONFESSION

The Church urges us not to wait until we're conscious of mortal sin to receive the Sacrament of Reconciliation but to go to confession regularly in order to grow in freedom over venial sins and to become more merciful like our Heavenly Father:

> Without being strictly necessary, confession of everyday faults (venial sins) is nevertheless strongly recommended by the Church. Indeed the regular confession of our venial sins helps us form our conscience, fight against evil tendencies, let ourselves be healed by Christ and progress in the life of the Spirit. By receiving more frequently through this sacrament the gift of the Father's mercy, we are spurred to be merciful as he is merciful.[14]

Just as restarting a computer regularly allows it to function at its best, so we receive a full spiritual "reset" when we examine our conscience and bring all the brokenness we can see to Jesus in Confession. We therefore highly recommend going to confession monthly, in addition to any times you are conscious of committing a grave sin. If monthly is too difficult at first, start with the seasons of Lent and Advent, and work up from there.

GROW IN VIRTUE WITH A PARTICULAR EXAMINATION

In the battle to overcome certain sins and grow in the freedom of virtue, it can be very helpful to focus on proactively living out a specific virtue rather than merely trying to avoid a vice. The virtue that opposes pride, for example, is humility. Admiration directly contradicts envy. Forgiveness counteracts anger. Zeal for good causes works against sloth. Generosity opposes greed. Asceticism and temperance oppose gluttony, and chastity is the opposite of lust.

The practice of a daily "particular examination," as distinct from a "general examination of conscience," zeros in on one chosen area of growth you want to focus on for a time. Choose one sin or vice you are working to avoid, or one virtue you want to cultivate in a tangible way. For example, perhaps you want to be more present to your spouse in the evenings and on weekends. Ask God for the help you need for this at the beginning of the day. At the end of the day, look back and make note of the times you did well along with the times you could have done better. Thank God and ask for mercy and grace as needed. Try choosing a different virtue or practice every few weeks as the subject of your ongoing particular examination, helping you build healthy habits of loving God, others, and yourself well. See page 98.

SEEKING PROFESSIONAL HELP

This chapter touches on many topics that require fuller explanation and, in some cases, the help of trained professionals. Spiritual warfare, mental health, and addictions, for example, are topics not to explore in isolation. Seek the help of a mental health professional and your pastor or other trusted local experts in these fields for personalized support.

ADDITIONAL RESOURCES

- *Catechism of the Catholic Church*, "The Sacrament of Penance and Reconciliation," paragraphs 1422-1498
- *The Return of the Prodigal Son*, Henri Nouwen
- *Loved as I Am: An Invitation to Conversion, Healing, and Freedom through Jesus*, Miriam James Heidland, S.O.L.T.
- *Be Healed: A Guide to Encountering the Powerful Love of Jesus in Your Life*, Bob Schuchts
- *Be Transformed: The Healing Power of the Sacraments*, Bob Schuchts
- *Back to Virtue: Traditional Moral Wisdom for Modern Moral Confusion*, Peter Kreeft
- "Making a Good Confession," Fr. Mike Schmitz on YouTube

- "Going to Confession for the First Time in a Long Time," Fr. Mike Schmitz on YouTube
- "A Guided Examination of Conscience," Fr. Mark-Mary on YouTube
- "Why You Need Jesus AND a Counselor," Mari Pablo on YouTube
- "Seven Deadly Sins, Seven Lively Virtues," Word on Fire video series
- *Healing the Whole Person* retreats and resources from John Paul II Healing Center

DISCIPLESHIP PRACTICES
Grow in Freedom

A Guide to Confession

Blessed is the one whose fault is removed, whose sin is forgiven.
— Psalm 32:1

PREPARE

Prayerfully reflect on your life since your last confession. Use an examination of conscience such as the one found on page 97 and take some notes.

GREETING

The priest will welcome you, and together, you will make the Sign of the Cross. You may begin by saying: "Bless me, Father, for I have sinned. It has been [give weeks, months, or years] since my last confession."

CONFESSION

Confess all your sins to the priest. Be as specific and straightforward as you can. When you are finished, conclude with these or similar words: "I am sorry for these and all my sins."

PENANCE

The priest will propose an act of penance. He might counsel you on how you can grow in the Christian life.

ACT OF CONTRITION

After the priest has given your penance, pray an Act of Contrition, such as:

My God, I am sorry for my sins with all my heart. In choosing to do wrong, and failing to do good, I have sinned against you whom I should love above all things. I firmly intend, with your help, to do penance, to sin no more, and to avoid whatever leads me to sin. Our Savior Jesus Christ suffered and died for us. In his name, my God, have mercy.

ABSOLUTION

The priest will extend his hands over your head and say the words of absolution. You respond, "Amen."

Examination of Conscience with the Ten Commandments

The examination below uses the Ten Commandments to prompt deeper reflection on your thoughts, actions, and motivations.

1. I am the Lord your God: you shall not have strange gods before me.
- Have you put people, things, or events ahead of God?

2. You shall not take the name of the Lord your God in vain.
- Have you used your words to defame God, others, or the Church?

3. Remember to keep holy the Lord's Day.
- Have you attended Mass on Sundays and other Holy Days?
- Do you put God ahead of your work and other responsibilities, setting aside intentional time to be with God?

4. Honor your father and your mother.
- Have you shown your parents love and respect?
- Have you made efforts to communicate with and visit your parents where possible?
- Are you holding any grudges over your parents' shortcomings?

5. You shall not kill.
- Have you physically or emotionally harmed anyone?
- Have you damaged others' reputations through gossip or slander?
- Have you been mean or unjustly angry to others?

6. You shall not commit adultery.
- Have you respected the sexual dignity due yourself and others?
- Have you lusted after someone physically or emotionally?
- Have you engaged in illicit romantic fantasies, used pornography, or masturbated?

7. You shall not steal.
- Have you taken physical or intellectual property that does not belong to you?
- Have you hoarded, wasted, or otherwise improperly used money or resources?

8. You shall not bear false witness against your neighbor.
- Have you lied to, misled, or manipulated others?

- Have you stayed quiet when you ought to have defended another?

9. You shall not covet your neighbor's spouse.
- Have you been inappropriately intimate (physically or emotionally) with someone who is not your spouse?
- Have you sought the romantic attention of others through inappropriate flirtation or immodesty?

10. You shall not covet your neighbor's goods.
- Do you seek to outstrip others for the sake of status or power?
- Do you compare yourself to others unnecessarily?
- Do you rely on the Lord for your needs?
- Have you harbored envy or jealousy?

The Particular Examination: A Tool for Growing in Virtue

Identifying one specific virtue to focus on can help you grow through concentrated effort and attentiveness. Perhaps you want to be more fully present to your family in the evenings and less distracted by media and household tasks; or to grow in purity of the eyes, generosity with your finances, listening to others, or patience with someone who gets under your skin.

SELECT ONE VIRTUE

Pray about and identify one virtue you want to grow in.

7 DEADLY SINS & OPPOSITE VIRTUES	
Pride	Humility
Envy	Admiration
Anger	Forgiveness
Sloth	Zeal
Avarice	Generosity
Gluttony	Asceticism
Lust	Chastity

OTHER SUGGESTED VIRTUES

Patience	Cheerfulness	Honesty	Courage
Orderliness	Excellence	Self-control	Temperance
Responsibility	Gratitude	Affability	Prudence

ENVISION LIVING THIS VIRTUE

Think about how, practically, you can live this virtue well.

- In what concrete ways will you act to live out this virtue?
- In what situations do you typically fail to live it?
- What is the opposite vice, and what does it look like when you fall into it?

PRAY FOR THE VIRTUE DAILY

- In the morning, ask God for help to live this virtue well.
- In the evening, review your day in light of this virtue.
  - How/when did you live it well?
  - How/when could you have done better?
- Thank God and ask for mercy and grace as you see fit.

ASSESS PROGRESS

After a few weeks, decide if you want to continue with this same examination, or choose a new one.

Taking Thoughts Captive to Christ

For, although we are in the flesh, we do not battle according to the flesh, for the weapons of our battle are not of flesh but are enormously power-ful, capable of destroying fortresses. We destroy arguments and every pretension raising itself against the knowledge of God, and take every thought captive in obedience to Christ.
– 2 Corinthians 10:3-5

Counteract the lies of the enemy with the truth of God's revelation. Begin by noticing when your thoughts do not align with God's truth about himself or your identity in him. Use the formula, "I renounce the lie that _____, and I announce the truth that _____" to articulate your own prayers of spiritual combat in the name of Jesus.

Below are powerful examples from Dr. Bob Schuchts addressing what he calls the "Seven Deadly Wounds."

REJECTION

In the name of Jesus Christ, I renounce the lie that I am unloved and unlovable.

In Jesus' name, I announce the truth that by virtue of my Baptism, I am a beloved son or daughter of the Father. I announce the truth that I am loved and valued, wanted and desired, and that I am precious in the Father's eyes.

ABANDONMENT

In the name of Jesus Christ, I renounce the lie that I am alone, unprotected, and that God has abandoned me.

In Jesus' name, I announce the truth that Jesus lives and dwells in me by virtue of my receiving him in Holy Communion. I am connected, understood, and cared for. Jesus and the Communion of Saints are always with me.

POWERLESSNESS

In the name of Jesus Christ, I renounce the lie that I am powerless, weak, not capable, stuck, trapped, or helpless. I renounce the lie that I am a victim and can't change.

In Jesus' name, I announce the truth that I have been anointed . . . with the power of the Holy Spirit to share in Christ's mission, therefore, "I have the strength for everything through him who empowers me" (Phil 4:13).

CONFUSION

In the name of Jesus Christ, I renounce the lie that everything is chaotic and confusing and that it is up to me to figure things out on my own.

In Jesus' name, I announce the truth that Jesus has shown me the path to the Father. I reclaim his divine order through the Church . . . and trust this authority to reveal the truth and guide my path.

FEAR

In the name of Jesus Christ, I renounce the lie that if I trust I will be hurt, disappointed, or die. I renounce all fear, anxiety, mistrust, and distrust.

In Jesus' name, I announce the truth that in Christ perfect love casts out all fear. I announce the truth that I am secure in Jesus' faithful love.

SHAME

In the name of Jesus Christ, I renounce the lie that I am bad, dirty, ugly, stupid, worthless, perverted, and (fill in any area of struggle).

In Jesus' name, I announce the truth that Jesus died for my sins and wounds and that I am forgiven, washed, cleansed, justified, and accepted (see 1 Cor 6). I announce the truth that through the sacrament of Reconciliation, Jesus washes me clean and forgives my sin; therefore, in Jesus I am pure and undefiled.

HOPELESSNESS

In the name of Jesus Christ, I renounce the lie that nothing ever changes and I will never have what I want. I renounce the lie that my life is meaningless and that I have nothing to live for.

In Jesus' name, I announce the truth...that my hope is steadfast in Christ, and that I have been raised to life in him.

My final hope is in the resurrection from the dead and eternal life with the Trinity and the Communion of Saints (see Jn 21:5).

I pray all of this in the powerful name of the Father, the Son, and the Holy Spirit. Amen.*

---

*   Excerpted from *Be Transformed: The Healing Power of the Sacraments*. Pages 162-163. Copyright © 2017 by Bob Schuchts. Used with permission of the publisher, Ave Maria Press®, Inc., P.O. Box 428, Notre Dame, IN 46556. *www.avemariapress.com*. For more on the Seven Deadly Wounds see also *Be Healed: A Guide to Encountering the Powerful Love of Jesus in Your Life* (Notre Dame: Ave Maria Press, 2014), 107-123.

ENDNOTES

1. See Romans 6.

2. Matthew 13:24-30.

3. Aleksandr Solzhenitsyn and Daniel J. Mahoney, *The Ascent from Ideology* (New York: Rowman & Littlefield Publishers, Inc., 2001), 50.

4. Leo Tolstoy, "Some Social Remedies," In *Pamphlets. Translated from the Russian* (Christchurch, Hants: Free Age Press: 1900), 29.

5. See *Catechism*, 1857.

6. Ibid., 1855.

7. Ibid., 1855.

8. Bob Schuchts, "Seven Deadly Wounds" in *Be Transformed: The Healing Power of the Sacraments* (Notre Dame: Ave Maria Press, 2017), 30.

9. St. Augustine, *Confessions*, trans. Henry Chadwick (New York: Oxford University Press, 2008), sec. 1.1.1.

10. See *Catechism*, 1548, and John 20:21-22.

11. United States Conference of Catholic Bishops, "Newsletter, Committee on Divine Worship," last modified April, 2022, https://www.usccb.org/resources/newsletter-2022-04.pdf.

12. St. Francis de Sales, *Golden Counsels of Saint Francis de Sales*, ed. Mary Paul McCarthy, VHM, and Mary Grace McCormack, VHM, trans. Peronne Marie Thibert, VHM (St. Louis: Monastery of the Visitation, 2018), 9.

13. Quoted in St. Aphonsus Ligori, *The Glories of Mary*, 2nd Edition (New York: P. O'Shea Publisher, 1868), 124.

14. *Catechism*, 1458.

WEEK 4
WORSHIP THE LORD

Jesus said to him in reply, "It is written: 'You shall worship the Lord, your God, and him alone shall you serve.'"

– Luke 4:8

CONVERSATION FOUR
Worship the Lord

OPENING PRAYER (2 MIN)
Select one person to open in prayer. Use the following prayer or your own words.

In the name of the Father, and of the Son, and of the Holy Spirit. Amen.

Heavenly Father, thank you for the ways you have met us, loved us, and led us this week. Thank you for not turning your back on us or anyone because of sin, and for running to our aid. Help us to grow in awareness of who you are and what you have done for us in Christ. May our conversation today encourage us to draw ever closer to you.

We ask these things in the name of Jesus. Amen.

CATCH UP (5 MIN)
Share highs and lows: one positive thing (a simple joy, gratitude, or blessing) and one challenge in your life since you last met.

REVIEW GROW IN FREEDOM (15 MIN)
Discuss a few of the following questions.

- What was your overall experience of Week 3: Grow in Freedom?
- Were you able to receive the Sacrament of Reconciliation yet?
- What prayer session was particularly helpful or meaningful, and why?
- What questions came up for you this week?

ABOUT WORSHIP THE LORD (15 MIN)
Read aloud.

Having reflected on God's amazing love and graciousness in the face of human waywardness, we now challenge ourselves to respond to the Lord's goodness with our sincerest worship. Throughout Scripture, God and his prophets exhort the people to worship God and God *alone*. The biblical word for worship means to lay prostrate, to bow low, to reverence, to give homage. Far more than a physical gesture, worship is expressing to God (and therefore reminding ourselves) that he alone is the "one God and

Father of all, who is over all and through all and in all" (Ephesians 4:6).

Communal liturgies, songs of praise, silent adoration, and striving to cling more to God (and less to something other than God) are just a few forms that worship can take. In the Catholic understanding of Christian faith, the Holy Mass is the highest, most perfect form of worship. In Mass, we communally worship and glorify God in the way he called us to do, around the table of the Eucharist and through the ministry of the Church. The Mass both sums up and leads to all other forms of worship, prayer, and service.

YOUR CHALLENGE THIS WEEK:

☐ Worship the Lord with all your heart. The daily prayer guide will lead you in several ways to do this.

☐ Go to daily Mass at least one time (in addition to Sunday Mass).*

Discuss a few of the following questions.

- How do you understand the concept of worship? Why do you think it's such an important and repeated exhortation in Scripture?
- What would you say is the opposite of worship?
- What is your favorite part of the Mass?
- How would you answer someone who asks, "Why go to Mass, when I can pray and worship anywhere?"

READ AND DISCUSS (10 MIN)

Read aloud.

The book of Revelation contains several glimpses into the glorious, unending worship of the saints and angels in heaven, such as in chapter 7 below.

---

* See local parish websites and *www.masstimes.org* to locate various daily Masses near you. Always verify times you find on third-party sites with the parish website itself.

Revelation 7:9-17, NRSV-CE

[9] After this I looked, and there was a great multitude that no one could count, from every nation, from all tribes and peoples and languages, standing before the throne and before the Lamb, robed in white, with palm branches in their hands. [10] They cried out in a loud voice, saying,

> "Salvation belongs to our God who is seated on the throne, and to the Lamb!"

[11] And all the angels stood around the throne and around the elders and the four living creatures, and they fell on their faces before the throne and worshiped God, [12] singing,

> "Amen! Blessing and glory and wisdom
> and thanksgiving and honor
> and power and might
> be to our God forever and ever! Amen."

[13] Then one of the elders addressed me, saying, "Who are these, robed in white, and where have they come from?" [14] I said to him, "Sir, you are the one that knows." Then he said to me, "These are they who have come out of the great ordeal; they have washed their robes and made them white in the blood of the Lamb.

> [15] For this reason they are before the throne of God,
> and worship him day and night within his temple,
> and the one who is seated on the throne will shelter them.
> [16] They will hunger no more, and thirst no more;
> the sun will not strike them,
> nor any scorching heat;
> [17] for the Lamb at the center of the throne will be their shepherd,
> and he will guide them to springs of the water of life,
> and God will wipe away every tear from their eyes."

- Pause for a minute or two of silence as you ponder this vision of heavenly worship.
- Share any brief reflections or thoughts about what spoke to you.

WORSHIP THE LORD TOGETHER (10 MIN)

In this week's first prayer time, you'll reflect on the role of praise as a unique expression of our worship of God. In praise, we declare the Lord's goodness. Praising God is closely related to thanking God, but different in an important way. We might thank someone for a gift, but to tell them they are a generous person expresses something even deeper. God's praises fill the mouths and hearts of the saints and angels in heaven, and of his followers here on earth. The Bible frequently exhorts us to "praise the Lord!" (the literal meaning of the word "hallelujah") in every type of circumstance.

Pray together now in a way that incorporates praise as well as three other types of prayer you have practiced in the 10:10 Challenge so far. Use the ACTS acronym to guide you according to the prompts below. Speak directly to God, using your own words. Spend a few minutes on each of the four topics for prayer, allowing each person to pray aloud. It's okay if there are some brief pauses for silence while further prayers emerge. Everyone should feel free to pray more than once within each category. Build on each other's prayers as you lift your minds and hearts to God in adoration (praise), contrition, thanksgiving, and supplication.

In the name of the Father, and of the Son, and of the Holy Spirit. Amen.

Adoration
Praise God for who he is. Consider the characteristics of God: good, faithful, loving, all-powerful, forgiving, etc.

Try praying: *"Heavenly Father, you are _____."*

Contrition
Acknowledge your weakness and ask for forgiveness.

Try praying: *"Lord, I'm sorry for _____."*

Thanksgiving
Give thanks for the blessings from the past day or week.

Try praying: *"Thank you for _____."*

Supplication
"Make your requests known to God" (Philippians 4:6).

Try praying: *"Lord Jesus, help me _____."* Or *"Father, I lift up _____ to you; please help them with _____."*

CLOSING PRAYER (1 MIN)

Choose someone to close the prayer. Use the prompts below or your own words.

Jesus, you are the Lamb of God who takes away the sins of the world. We worship you, and we give you thanks for our time together today. Please help us stay faithful to our prayer times this week, and lead us to a deeper understanding and experience of worship. Increase our appreciation for the gift of Holy Mass.

Thank you for always hearing our prayers and leading us into your will.

Together let us pray: Glory be to the Father, and to the Son, and to the Holy Spirit, as it was in the beginning, is now, and ever shall be, world without end. Amen.

NEXT MEETING (2 MIN)

Make sure you have your next discussion on the calendar.

PRAYER GUIDE
Worship the Lord

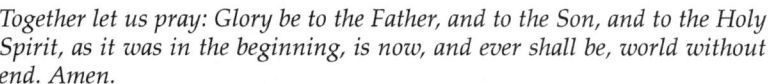
Day 1. Praise the Lord!

Praise the Lord, all you nations! Extol him, all you peoples! His mercy for us is strong; the faithfulness of the Lord is forever. Hallelujah!
– Psalm 117:1-2

One core expression of worship, found in nearly every chapter of the Bible, is to declare the praises of God. The Psalms, especially, are the storehouse and songbook of Israel's praises to God. The oft-repeated cry of "Hallelujah!" literally means "praise the Lord!"

What is praise? Praise is closely related to thanksgiving but is also distinct from it in an important way. When we thank God, we express gratitude for the good things he has given or done for us. When we praise God, we relish *who he is* and *what he is like* (God's character). It's the difference between saying to a friend, "thank you for this generous gift" and "you are such a generous person." Both are good, and each gets at something a little different. Praise can be more unfamiliar for us than thanksgiving at first, but it also can draw us into a deep intimacy with God.

Praise is first and foremost an act of justice. "You are indeed Holy, O Lord, and all you have created *rightly* gives you praise."[1] It's the resounding keynote of all creation, the very song of heaven. As an orchestra tunes its instruments to the keynote before a concert, we too are invited to bring our voices (and lives) into harmony with this eternal song. As an old hymn puts it, "tune my heart to sing Thy grace."[2]

In heaven, we won't be able to help but praise the Lord. It will be the most natural thing imaginable and the great joy of our hearts. Here on earth, where "we see in a mirror, dimly" (1 Corinthians 13:12), we may not always feel like praising God, but we can choose a regular rhythm of it all the same. As an evergreen tree stays green throughout the year, we also grow to praise the Lord in every season of our lives. It is right and just. Hallelujah!

OPEN TO GOD

Take a few deep breaths as you open yourself to God.

In the name of the Father, and of the Son, and of the Holy Spirit. Amen.

Come, Holy Spirit. Live in me today. Help me as I grow in the language of praise. You are good and full of love and mercy. "Lord, open my lips, and my mouth will proclaim your praise" (Psalm 51:15, Grail Psalter).

PRAY FROM THE HEART

Read the following passage. When you get to the last line, picture yourself in the boat with the disciples. Join them in worshiping Jesus. Use the prompts following the passage to help guide you.

Matthew 14:22-33

Immediately he made the disciples get into the boat and go on ahead to the other side, while he dismissed the crowds. And after he had dismissed the crowds, he went up the mountain by himself to pray. When evening came, he was there alone, but by this time the boat, battered by the waves, was far from the land, for the wind was against them. And early in the morning he came walking toward them on the sea. But when the disciples saw him walking on the sea, they were terrified, saying, "It is a ghost!" And they cried out in fear. But immediately Jesus spoke to them and said, "Take heart, it is I; do not be afraid."

Peter answered him, "Lord, if it is you, command me to come to you on the water." He said, "Come." So Peter got out of the boat, started walking on the water, and came toward Jesus. But when he noticed the strong wind, he became frightened, and beginning to sink, he cried out, "Lord, save me!" Jesus immediately reached out his hand and caught him, saying to him, "You of little faith, why did you doubt?" When they got into the boat, the wind ceased. And those in the boat worshiped him, saying, "Truly you are the Son of God."

"Truly, you are..." is a helpful formula for practicing the language of worship and praise. Spend a few minutes speaking similar sentences to God, filling in a different word or phrase each time. What are five to ten names, titles, or descriptors you can say to Jesus in worship today? (See the lists below for help from Scripture, but choose what *you* most want to say.)

Jesus, truly, you are _____.

Truly, you are _____.

Truly, you are _____.

Truly, you are _____.

Truly, you are _____.

Relationship

- *my hope*
- *my joy*
- *my refuge*
- *my rock*
- *my shepherd*
- *my song*
- *my strength*
- *my Lord and my God*
- *my portion and cup*

- *my hiding place*
- *my deliverer*
- *my healer*
- *my treasure*
- *my provider*
- *my all in all*
- *my Father*
- *my salvation*
- *my righteousness*

Attributes

- *holy*
- *merciful*
- *steadfast*

- *glorious*
- *beautiful*
- *faithful*

- *just*
- *awesome*
- *loving*

- *mighty*
- *good*
- *forgiving*

Titles

- *The Anointed One*
- *The One True God*
- *The Bread of Life*
- *True God and True Man*
- *The Lion of Judah*
- *The Word Made Flesh*
- *The Great I AM*
- *The Lord of Hosts*
- *The Lamb of God*
- *The Living Water*
- *The Good Shepherd*
- *The Most High*

- *The King of the Universe*
- *The Prince of Peace*
- *Emmanuel*
- *The Holy One*
- *The Light of the world*
- *The King of Kings*
- *The Lord of Lords*
- *The Alpha and the Omega*
- *The Wonderful Counselor*
- *The True Vine*
- *The Eternal Word*
- *The King of Glory*

CLOSE

Spend a minute in silence. Rest in the presence of our great God, who inhabits the praises of his people (cf. Psalm 22:3).

As long as I live, I will praise you, my God. And even after my time on earth is over, I look forward to joining the heavenly choirs of angels in praise of you. Help my actions today align with the praises of my lips, giving glory and honor to you in word and in deed.

In the name of the Father, and of the Son, and of the Holy Spirit. Amen.

Day 2. Mighty and Merciful

When Simon Peter saw this, he fell at the knees of Jesus and said, "Depart from me, Lord, for I am a sinful man." For astonishment at the catch of fish they had made seized him and all those with him. . . . Jesus said to Simon, "Do not be afraid."
— Luke 5:8-9, 10

Many people assume that the Old Testament presents a mighty and fearful picture of God, while in the New Testament Jesus reveals, once and for all, the loving, merciful, tender view of God. In reality, both views of God, the mighty and the merciful, run throughout both Testaments and must be held together. God is mighty, awesome, and powerful, not to be trifled with; and no one who beholds his glory can help but fall down in a holy fear and awe. At the very same time, God is caring—intimate even—full of love, mercy, gentleness, patience, and peace.

If the Lord were only mighty but not merciful, we'd rather run than worship. Yet, if mercy, meekness, and gentleness were his only qualities, we would soon find him weak and voiceless in the face of the world's grave injustices. We might also find God conveniently approving of just about everything we did. Rather than worship this "god" (who appears more like Santa than the great I AM), we'd likely forget about him entirely.

It's all too easy to create God or Jesus in our own image or fit him into our preconceived molds. In the long run, though, this only deepens our pain and keeps us trapped in patterns of self-indulgence and small-mindedness. Scripture keeps us grounded in the truth: the one true God, who came into this world as Jesus Christ, is both awesome and compassionate, both mighty and loving beyond our comprehension. In fact, it's just this combination that makes him so amazingly good. Before him, we rightly fall down like Peter because of our unworthiness. And when we do, he says to us, as to Peter, "Do not be afraid."

OPEN TO GOD

Take a few deep breaths as you open yourself to God.

In the name of the Father, and of the Son, and of the Holy Spirit. Amen.

Heavenly Father, you are awesome—in the truest sense of the word. "Mountains melt like wax before [you,] Lord" (Psalm 97:5); for no one and nothing is more powerful than you.

Yet, no one outshines you in mercy either, Lord. You look with compassion on your children. Thank you, God, for your strength and your merciful love. Fill me today with renewed awe and gratitude in your presence.

PRAY FROM THE HEART

For prayer today, consider how people in the stories of Scripture often bow down, kneel, or even fall down or lie prostrate upon first entering the Lord's presence. Read the following excerpts and reflect on the questions that follow.

Psalm 95:6
Enter, let us bow down in worship; let us kneel before the Lord who made us.

Genesis 17:3-4
Abram fell face down and God said to him: For my part, here is my covenant with you: you are to become the father of a multitude of nations.

Exodus 34:6, 8, NRSV-CE
The Lord passed before him . . . and Moses quickly bowed his head toward the earth, and worshiped.

Matthew 2:11, NRSV-CE
On entering the house, they saw the child with Mary his mother; and they knelt down and paid him homage.

Matthew 15:25, NRSV-CE
But she came and knelt before him, saying, "Lord, help me."

Luke 17:15-16
And one of them, realizing he had been healed, returned, glorifying God in a loud voice; and he fell at the feet of Jesus and thanked him.

Philippians 2:10
At the name of Jesus every knee should bend.

Revelation 7:11, NRSV-CE
And all the angels stood around the throne and around the elders and the four living creatures, and they fell on their faces before the throne and worshiped God.

- Have you ever felt like bowing, kneeling, or bending low in some way before the Lord?
- When you enter a Catholic church, how attentive are you to where the tabernacle is?
- Do you have any preferred ways of gesturing towards the Eucharistic presence when you enter a church or a pew or pass by the tabernacle (genuflect, bow, make the Sign of the Cross, etc.)?
- Other than postures and gestures, what are some ways to show reverence to Jesus when you are at Mass (e.g. listening attentively to the proclaimed Word, acknowledging your neighbors and saying a kind word before or after Mass, taking notes during the homily, following along with a missalette, etc.)?

- Inspired by Jesus' words in Matthew 25, St. Teresa of Calcutta said the poor are Jesus in his "most distressing disguise."[3] How does this phrase challenge your understanding of what showing Jesus reverence ought to look like or entail?

Talk to Jesus about whatever is weighing on your mind today.

CLOSE

Spend a few minutes in reverent, restful silence, as you sit in the presence of the One who is mighty and merciful.

I love you, Jesus. You are my God, my Savior, my friend. Together with all the saints and angels who know and love you, I bow before you in awe, in worship, and in dependence on you. Thank you for seeing me, knowing me better than I know myself, and loving me always.

In the name of the Father, and of the Son, and of the Holy Spirit. Amen.

Day 3. Work, Rest, and Worship

Remember the sabbath day — keep it holy.
— Exodus 20:8

From the very first book of the Bible, God makes his top priority for human life clear. God never wanted us to just keep going and going and going. He calls us to establish a holy rhythm of work, rest, and worship.

The modern human sciences affirm the importance of such a rhythm to life as well, but the biblical teaching is much more than a call for work-life balance. The sabbath carves out time not only for rest but for worship. God instructed his people to set aside a day (Saturday in Jewish tradition) to cease from all other activity, to remember, celebrate, and rely fully on God, who alone is worthy of all our hope and trust.

For Christians who believe in the world-changing event of the Resurrection of Jesus, a further revelation has dawned. The *Catechism* explains,

> Jesus rose from the dead "on the first day of the week."[4] Because it is the "first day," the day of Christ's Resurrection recalls the first creation. Because it is the "eighth day" following the sabbath,[5] it symbolizes the new creation ushered in by Christ's Resurrection. For Christians it has

become the first of all days, the first of all feasts, the Lord's Day… Sunday.

Every Sunday, then, is the holiest of days. While we can and should worship the Lord every day and in many different ways, we especially do so in the way and at the time God himself has given us through the Church: in Sunday Mass.

Words can hardly express how central and important the Mass is. Holy Mass is the universal prayer of the global Church, a joining with the choirs of angels, the definitive meeting place of heaven and earth. The Eucharist is "the source and summit of the Christian life."[6] Therefore, the people of God have a sacred responsibility to gather on the Lord's Day to worship and receive Jesus in the special, privileged way available to us in the Mass. Mass is the chief way we respond to God's gracious invitation to abide in him, as branches abide on the vine.[7]

OPEN TO GOD

Begin in your usual way, with a few deep breaths to center yourself on God.

In the name of the Father, and of the Son, and of the Holy Spirit. Amen.

"Teach me, Lord, your way that I may walk in your truth, single-hearted and revering your name" (Psalm 86:11).

PRAY FROM THE HEART

"I will give thanks to the Lord with my whole heart" (Psalm 9:1, NRSV-CE).

Look back over the last twenty-four hours. Find two or three specific blessings for which you are grateful, big or small, and spend a few minutes savoring them and expressing your gratitude to God.

Thank you God for_____.

Reflect prayerfully on your relationship with Mass and the Lord's day.

- Why do you think God, from the very beginning, communicated his desire for people to dedicate one day a week to rest and worship?
- What is your current routine surrounding rest and worship on the Lord's day?

- Where does Sunday Mass fall in your current priorities?
- What's your "why" for going to Sunday Mass? What draws you again and again? What about the Mass do you find most important, meaningful, or helpful?

The phrase "the sacrifice of the Mass" rightly reminds us of Jesus' sacrifice on the Cross, which is re-presented to us at every Mass. But going to Mass often involves our own sacrifice of time and effort to get there.

- What are you sacrificing when you go to Mass? A more relaxed Sunday morning, or an event-free Saturday evening? More time for leisure, work, and other activities? The stress of getting kids ready or enduring their meltdowns? A desire for better music or homilies than you find at your parish?
- How can making this sacrifice of time and effort be an act of worship?
- If you must work on Sundays due to the nature of your job or career, where else in your week or weekend can you set aside time for holy rest, extra prayer, and God-honoring leisure?

Talk to God about any desires or struggles you have about keeping the Lord's day holy.

CLOSE

Spend a minute with God in silence.

Good Father, thank you for instructing your people, since the creation of the world, to bring glory to your name not only through their hard work, but also through their rest, their holy leisure, and their communal worship. Help me to live by the holy rhythms and priorities you prescribed for us in your Word and through your Church. When it is difficult to arrange my schedule on a weekend to get to Mass, help me do it as an offering of my sacrifice of praise to you, remembering that you are never outdone in generosity.

In the name of the Father, and of the Son, and of the Holy Spirit. Amen.

TIP: REFLECT ON THE READINGS BEFORE MASS

Take some time to read and reflect on the upcoming Sunday readings (or just the Gospel reading). You can do this as a private prayer practice, as a family, or with a small group.

Day 4. An Offering to God

The lives of the faithful, their praise, sufferings, prayer, and work, are united with those of Christ and with his total offering, and so acquire a new value. Christ's sacrifice present on the altar makes it possible for all generations of Christians to be united with his offering.
– Catechism of the Catholic Church, 1368

Jesus' whole life was an offering of love to God the Father. Free to do anything with his life, Jesus only wanted to do God's saving work: "From the first moment of his Incarnation the Son embraces the Father's plan of divine salvation . . . The sacrifice of Jesus 'for the sins of the whole world' (1 John 2:2) expresses his loving communion with the Father."[8] Jesus' friendships, his intellect, his love and respect of Mary and Joseph, his persistent trajectory toward Jerusalem—all of it was an offering of love to God, culminating in the Cross.

He gave his Body and Blood for us and sustains us with them every time we celebrate the Eucharist. We, too, are called to offer ourselves to God in union with Jesus. Through Baptism we can say with St. Paul: "I have been crucified with Christ; yet I live, no longer I, but Christ lives in me" (Galatians 2:19-20).

In Jesus, the smallest action or decision made for love of God or neighbor can become a gift we offer to the Father. We can offer our lives to God in our work, our play, our sufferings, our joys, our time with family and friends. When we come to Mass, we bring all of that with us and place our lives on the altar beside the bread and wine. United with the perfect offering of Jesus' Body and Blood, our offerings "acquire a new value."[9] God knows the details of our lives, and he is pleased when we bring them to him in worship.

Today, you'll take stock of your life in a number of different areas. Not all of the scenarios listed below may apply to you; focus on those that do.

OPEN TO GOD

Quiet your body and mind for prayer.

In the name of the Father, and of the Son, and of the Holy Spirit. Amen.

Jesus, dear Savior, draw me deeper into union with you. I love you, Lord. Help me to offer myself to you as an act of love. Give me greater faith, greater trust, Jesus.

PRAY FROM THE HEART

Hebrews 4:14-16, NRSV-CE

Since, then, we have a great high priest who has passed through the heavens, Jesus, the Son of God, let us hold fast to our confession. For we do not have a high priest who is unable to sympathize with our weaknesses, but we have one who in every respect has been tested as we are, yet without sin. Let us therefore approach the throne of grace with boldness, so that we may receive mercy and find grace to help in time of need.

Jesus, you are the great high priest who knows me inside and out. Please help me make an offering of my life to God during this time of prayer.

Identify one or more people or situations that stand out as you review these potential areas of life:

- Situations with family members
- Projects or interpersonal dynamics at work
- Areas of personal/professional growth
- Virtues you are striving after
- Sins you are struggling with
- Financial concerns or decision making
- Questions of vocation or discernment
- Hopes and desires for your life or family members' lives
- Physical, emotional, or spiritual suffering
- Wounds from and grievances with others
- People who have asked for your prayers

Use your imagination to picture yourself bringing these people and/or situations to Jesus.

Picture yourself approaching the altar at your local church like the people bringing the bread and wine offerings. Consciously hand over each of your offerings, placing them on the altar.

What are you hoping for from God for these people or situations? Boldly approach the throne of grace and ask God to provide what is needed in your life or the lives of those you are bringing to him in prayer today.

CLOSE

Rest silently in God's care for a moment, perhaps opening your hands in a posture of trust.

Father, I believe that you love me and the people I just mentioned more than I ever could. I know you care about _____. I give it/ them to you, Father. Please provide the _____ (grace/heal- ing/direction/etc) they/I need.

In the name of the Father, and of the Son, and of the Holy Spirit. Amen.

TIP: INTERIOR OFFERING

Make note of people and situations you offered to God during this prayer time. Next time you go to Mass, call them to mind as the gifts of bread and wine are presented to the priest. Join your prayers to the Eucharistic Prayer as the priest prepares the altar. Trust that God is giving you the grace you need as you receive Communion and head into the rest of your day.

Day 5. True Food and True Drink

This saying is hard; who can accept it?
— John 6:60

Jesus said some shocking things. When he told his followers that his body was "true food" and his blood was "true drink" (John 6:55), his disciples responded with: "This saying is hard; who can accept it?" (John 6:60). Jesus pressed them further: "Does this shock you?" (John 6:61). After many people left him, Jesus turned to the Twelve, saying, "Do you also want to leave?" (John 6:67).

Believing that the Eucharist is Jesus' real presence—Body, Blood, Soul, and Divinity—takes as much faith today as it did then. But since the earliest times, the Church has proclaimed that Jesus "was made known to them in the breaking of the bread" (Luke 24:35). We encounter Christ in the Eucharist.

Jesus told his followers that he was true food and drink, not to shock them or to drive them away, but to assure them that he alone was the source of their life. He offered them a closeness they could hardly conceive of. "Whoever eats my flesh and drinks my blood remains in me and I in him. Just as the living Father sent me and I have life because of the Father, so also the one who feeds on me will have life because of me" (John 6:56-57). His Body and Blood sustain us, giving us the true food we need to nourish our life in God.

When the Eucharistic minister lifts the host before you at Mass and declares, "The Body of Christ," they are not only announcing the true substance of what they offer you; they are declaring the true substance of each of us who receives the Eucharist! Bread is transformed, and so is Christ's Church. We are the body of Christ.

Draw near to Christ. He offers you true food, true drink, and true life. Let him dwell within you. His very presence will transform you.

OPEN TO GOD

Open yourself to God, quieting your mind and body in your usual way.

In the name of the Father, and of the Son, and of the Holy Spirit. Amen.

Invite God to be with you during this time of prayer using your own words or the prayer below:

Come, Holy Spirit, fill the hearts of your faithful and kindle in them the fire of your love. Send forth your Spirit and they shall be created, and you shall renew the face of the earth.

I cast my cares upon you, Lord. I entrust to you my concern about _____. Grant me your peace which surpasses understanding.

PRAY FROM THE HEART

Pray *lectio divina* with the passage below. Read the passage slowly and attentively. Note any word, phrase, or image that catches your attention. Possibly underline or highlight any words or phrases that stand out to you. Then reflect, respond, and rest.

John 6:35-40, 48-59, NRSV-CE

Jesus said to them, "I am the bread of life. Whoever comes to me will never be hungry, and whoever believes in me will never be thirsty. But I said to you that you have seen me and yet do not believe. Everything that the Father gives me will come to me, and anyone who comes to me I will never drive away; for I have come down from heaven, not to do my own will, but the will of him who sent me. And this is the will of him who sent me, that I should lose nothing of all that he has given me, but raise it up on the last day. This is indeed the will of my Father, that all who see the Son and believe in him may have eternal life; and I will raise them up on the last day." . . .

"I am the bread of life. Your ancestors ate the manna in the wilderness, and they died. This is the bread that comes down from heaven, so that one may eat of it and not die. I am the living bread that came down from heaven. Whoever eats of this bread will live forever; and the bread that I will give for the life of the world is my flesh."

The Jews then disputed among themselves, saying, "How can this man give us his flesh to eat?" So Jesus said to them, "Very truly, I tell you, unless you eat the flesh of the Son of Man and drink his blood, you have no life in you. Those who eat my flesh and drink my blood have eternal life, and I will raise them up on the last day; for my flesh is true food and my blood is true drink. Those who eat my flesh and drink my blood abide in me, and I in them. Just as the living Father sent me, and I live because of the Father, so whoever eats me will live because of me. This is the bread that came down from heaven, not like that which your ancestors ate, and they died. But the one who eats this bread will live forever." He said these things while he was teaching in the synagogue at Capernaum.

For help reflecting:

- How does Jesus describe himself? Does anything surprise or challenge you?
- What is the will of the Father that Jesus is carrying out?
- What promises is Jesus making to those who eat his flesh?
- Jesus says he gives his flesh "for the life of the world." What do you think he means by this?
- In what area or situation do you need more of the life that Jesus gives?

Talk to Jesus about whatever arose in your reflections, or anything else on your mind. Tell him about any doubts you carry or desires you have to grow in faith.

CLOSE

Spend a few minutes in restful silence. "Be still and know that I am God" (Psalm 46:11).

Close with the *Anima Christi* prayer from St. Ignatius of Loyola:

Soul of Christ, sanctify me;
Body of Christ, save me;
Blood of Christ, inebriate me;
Water from the side of Christ, wash me;
Passion of Christ, strengthen me;
O good Jesus hear me;

Within your wounds hide me;
Separated from you, let me never be;
From the evil one protect me;
At the hour of my death, call me;
And close to you bid me; That with your saints,
I may be praising you forever and ever. Amen.

In the name of the Father, and of the Son, and of the Holy Spirit. Amen.

TIP: PREPARE TO RECEIVE JESUS

Because Jesus is truly present in the Eucharist, we take great care to receive such an exalted gift with proper reverence and interior preparation. As early as the first century, St. Paul warned against carelessness when gathering for the Lord's Supper (see 1 Corinthians 11:27-29).

Several prayers and guidelines of the Church are based on this principle. The Mass begins, for example, with a penitential rite by which we "acknowledge our sins, and so prepare ourselves to celebrate the sacred mysteries." We also say before Communion, "Lord, I am not worthy that you should enter under my roof, but only say the word and my soul shall be healed." The Church instructs the faithful to fast at least one hour before receiving the Eucharist,* and to abstain from receiving the Eucharist if you are conscious of having committed a mortal sin that you have not yet confessed in the Sacrament of Reconciliation.[10] Embrace each of these moments and instructions as part of your deliberate preparation for receiving Jesus in the Eucharist.

Day 6. Finding the Center

No one can serve two masters; for a slave will either hate the one and love the other, or be devoted to the one and despise the other. You cannot serve God and wealth.
— Matthew 6:24, NRSV-CE

The call to worship the Lord extends far beyond going to Mass or using certain words in prayer. At its root, it's a call to place

---

*   "A person who is to receive the Most Holy Eucharist is to abstain for at least one hour before holy communion from any food and drink, except for only water and medicine." *Code of Canon Law: Latin-English Edition* (Washington, D.C.: Canon Law Society of America, 1998), can. 919.

God and God's Kingdom in the very center of our lives.

In the passage above, Jesus used wealth as the example of a rival "master" perhaps because of how common it is to put our ultimate hope or trust in money over the Lord. Of course, it might be something else that vies for that central place in our hearts—esteem from others, a desire for romance, a need to be right.

Serving the Lord above all else does not mean doing only religious things. It's a matter of prioritizing who or what is in the central place. Who or what is our ultimate concern and greatest pursuit? Who or what gives shape, direction, and strength to all the other plans and projects of our lives?

Bishop Robert Barron points to the massive rose windows of Gothic cathedrals to illustrate this point. Classically, at the center of these beautiful, stained-glass windows stands an image of Christ.

> The message of the window is clear: When one's life is centered on Christ, all the energies, aspirations, and powers of the soul fall into a beautiful and satisfying pattern. And by implication, whenever something other than Christ—money, sex, success, adulation—fills the center, the soul falls into disharmony.[11]

Our hearts were created to desire infinite love, infinite joy. And nothing other than God, who is infinite, can ultimately satisfy this longing. "Those who choose another god multiply their sorrows" (Psalm 16:4, NRSV-CE). Worshiping the Lord means learning to place all our hope and trust in God, our only sure foundation and reliable guide.

OPEN TO GOD

Open in your usual way, with a few deep breaths and calling on the name of the Lord.

In the name of the Father, and of the Son, and of the Holy Spirit. Amen.

"Teach me your way, O Lord, that I may walk in your truth; give me an undivided heart to revere your name" (Psalm 86:11, NRSV-CE).

PRAY FROM THE HEART

Consider a rose window (see the previous page) as an image of a life that is centered on Christ. Ponder the questions below in prayerful meditation and conversation with Jesus.

- What do you think it means for something to be at the center of a person's life?
- What do you think it means or looks like for you to center your life on Jesus Christ?
- Is this idea:
  - New or foreign to you?
  - Scary or intense sounding?
  - A reality you have tasted and seen, and want more of?
  - Nice sounding but confusing or difficult to put into practice?
  - An aspirational goal you feel you are moving toward?
  - Something else entirely?
- In what relationship, project, or aspect of your life is Jesus already at or near the very center?
- In this area, what are the evident fruits of putting Christ first? (Peace, clarity, confidence, a deep joy, etc?)
- In your experience, what pursuits, people, or things tend to vie for that center spot in people's lives today? Think especially within your demographic (age group, location, etc.).
- What about you, personally? What pursuits, people, or things do you find yourself tempted to assign a higher place in your heart or mind (or calendar or bank account) than is healthy or pleasing to God?

CLOSE

Spend a few minutes resting in God, who loves you and embraces the whole you—those parts that truly have him in the center and those parts that are not yet in alignment with his heart. He's not withholding his love until you get it all together. He sees, loves, and holds you now—offering you grace, peace, and rest.

"Teach me your way, O Lord, that I may walk in your truth; give me an undivided heart to revere your name" (Psalm 86:11, NRSV-CE). Thank you, Jesus, for being the Good Shepherd of my heart and the greatest news of my life. I trust in you and in your great love for me. Help me grow in conformity to your will, so that I may come to love what you love and desire what you desire in all things.

In the name of the Father, and of the Son, and of the Holy Spirit. Amen.

Day 7. Idolatry

Therefore, my beloved, avoid idolatry.
– 1 Corinthians 10:14, NRSV-CE

To study the subject of "worship" in the Bible leads very quickly to warnings against idolatry. Inspired prophets and sages repeatedly call God's people to turn from idols (false gods) and to worship the one and only true God.

At first blush, these warnings and instructions might sound a bit outdated to our modern ears. Yet, as we saw yesterday, we all experience the temptation to put ourselves, another person, or a certain good in the center of our lives—a place designed only for God. It's in this broader understanding of worship and idolatry that the biblical challenge still hits home.

Dr. Timothy Keller offers some helpful language worth pondering in prayer:

> What is an idol? It is anything more important to you than God, anything that absorbs your heart and imagination more than God, anything you seek to give you what only God can give… An idol is whatever you look at and say, in your heart of hearts, "If I have that, then I'll feel my life has meaning, then I'll know I have value, then I'll feel significant and secure." There are many ways to describe that kind of relationship to something, but perhaps the best one is worship.[12]

This challenging but clarifying definition helps us see how reputation, popularity, a certain possession, income level, relationship, or career might become an idol for us. The same could even be said for very noble pursuits, like fighting for a just cause or concern for a loved one.

It takes both courage and community to wade into this territory, because we rarely see how much weight we are giving certain fears, pursuits, and desires deep within us. Yet Jesus, "the leader and perfecter of our faith" (Hebrews 12:2), gently leads us to grow in placing his love above all else in our lives. As zealous as the prophets were for God's people to avoid sacrificing to idols, so ought we, the followers of Jesus, be watchful about turning to anything less than Christ for our deepest identity, happiness, and worth.

OPEN TO GOD

Quietly turn your attention to God, opening to this time of prayer.

In the name of the Father, and of the Son, and of the Holy Spirit. Amen.

Our hearts are restless, Lord, until they rest in you. Come and guide me today. Grant me courage to see where I'm tempted to give other people or things my worship instead of giving it to you. Help me trust in you as the only source and center of my life.

PRAY FROM THE HEART

Trusting in God's love for you, without scolding or shaming yourself, reflect courageously on the following:

- What people or things tend to absorb your heart and imagination more than God?
- For what are you sometimes tempted to think, "If I have that, then my life will have meaning" or "then I will feel significant and secure"?
- Recall the image of the rose window from yesterday's prayer time (page 124). How do the things you called to mind vie for the central place in your mind and heart?

Idolatry is also a lens through which we can understand sin better. Pride, for example, is idolatry of self; envy is idolatry of status or possessions; gluttony is idolatry of food and drink; lust idolizes sex or a relationship; anger idolizes control or justice; greed idolizes security or wealth; and sloth idolizes comfort.[13]

Are there one or two of these that especially hit home for you? Spend a little time reflecting on that.

Colossians 1:15-22

He is the image of the invisible God, the firstborn of all creation; for in him all things in heaven and on earth were created, things visible and invisible, whether thrones or dominions or rulers or powers—all things have been created through him and for him. He himself is before all things, and in him all things hold together. He is the head of the body, the church; he is the beginning, the firstborn from the dead, so that he might come to have first place in everything. For in him all the fullness of God was pleased to dwell, and through him God was pleased to reconcile to himself all things, whether on earth or in heaven, by making peace through the blood of his cross.

And you who were once estranged and hostile in mind, doing evil deeds, he has now reconciled in his fleshly body through death, so as to present you holy and blameless and irreproachable before him—provided that you continue securely established and steadfast in the faith, without shifting from the hope promised by the gospel that you heard, which has been proclaimed to every creature under heaven.

Tell Jesus that he alone is worthy of all your worship. Spend a few minutes worshiping him with your words or pondering something that stood out to you from this passage.

Talk to Jesus about anything you desire greater freedom from. How do you need his help to avoid becoming obsessed with or overly attached to something?

CLOSE

Rest for a few minutes in the love of God.

Close today's prayer time with the following prayer from the Mass:

O God, who has prepared for those who love you good things which no eye can see, fill our hearts, we pray, with the warmth of your love, so that, loving you in all things and above all things, we may attain your promises, which surpass every human desire.[14]

In the name of the Father, and of the Son, and of the Holy Spirit. Amen.

MAKE IT A HABIT
Worship the Lord

Worship is a deep well we continue to grow in throughout the course of our lives. Below, find tips and suggested readings for making worship a habit in your life.

UNWAVERING COMMITMENT TO MASS

When her children would complain about having to attend Mass on vacations, one mom's go-to reply was this: "There are two things we don't take vacations from: Mass and vegetables." Good one, Mom!

Mass attendance on Sundays and holy days* is among the highest priorities of Catholic life and discipleship. Mass on the

---

*   In addition to Sundays, there are six holy days of obligation observed in the United States. Your parish will inform you of Mass times for these celebrations when they fall outside of Sunday Mass.

Lord's day is the focal point of the week, around which everything else is built and takes its reference. There are only five "precepts of the Church"* which comprise "the indispensable minimum in the spirit of prayer and moral effort, in the growth in love of God and neighbor."[15] Make every reasonable effort, therefore, to never miss Mass on a Sunday/Saturday evening or another holy day of obligation, and confess in the Sacrament of Reconciliation any time you do miss for non-essential reasons.† See *masstimes.org* (also a mobile app) to help you find Mass options near you, especially when you travel.

PRAY IN THE PRESENCE

Praying in the presence of the Eucharist, even outside of Mass, can deepen your relationship with Jesus. Most Catholic churches keep the Eucharist reserved in a tabernacle where you can go to pray with Jesus. Many parishes also provide designated hours when the Eucharist is made visible in a gold stand called a monstrance. This is commonly called Eucharistic adoration. Stop by a church for your prayer time or a brief visit before the tabernacle. See if your church has scheduled times of Eucharistic adoration or find a perpetual Eucharistic adoration chapel where you can pray before Jesus' Eucharistic presence. Gaze upon him who loves you. Soak up the rays of the Son.

GO TO MASS MORE THAN ONCE A WEEK

Celebrating the Eucharist weekly at Sunday Mass is part of our sacred responsibility as worshipers of the Lord. But did you know the Church celebrates the Eucharist every day? You can deepen your habit of worship by carving out time on one or more additional days each week to attend a daily Mass at a local church (if

---

*   The five precepts are: (1) attend Mass on Sundays and holy days of obligation, (2) confess your sins at least once a year, (3) receive the sacrament of the Eucharist at least during the Easter Season, (4) observe the days of fasting and abstinence established by the Church, and (5) help to provide for the needs of the Church. See *Catechism,* 2041-2043.

†   "If participation in the eucharistic celebration becomes impossible because of the absence of a sacred minister or for another grave cause, it is strongly recommended that the faithful take part in a Liturgy of the Word if such a liturgy is celebrated in a parish church or other sacred place according to the prescripts of the diocesan bishop or that they devote themselves to prayer for a suitable time alone, as a family, or, as the occasion permits, in groups of families." *Code of Canon Law,* can. 1248.

it's possible for you to do so given your work and family responsibilities). Daily Masses typically have just two readings instead of three and are shorter than Sunday Masses. They are a wonderful and grace-filled way to put Christ in the center of your day and life.

REFRAIN FROM UNNECESSARY WORK ON SUNDAYS

The literal meaning of "holy" is "set-apart." To keep holy the sabbath means to set this day apart as especially dedicated to God. Even though every waking (and sleeping) hour is rightly lived in, for, and with God, the Lord saw fit to call his people to dedicate one special day a week for enhanced prayer, rest from labor, and enjoying community and family. Some people have jobs they must attend to on Sundays in today's world and so there is flexibility in discerning how to live out the sabbath rest. Pray about what might make your Sundays truly set-apart for God, not only by attending Mass, but also through rest, additional prayer and reflection, and quality time with family or community.

PRAISE WITH MUSIC

Music can powerfully shape our thoughts and minds in praise of God. Listen to a modern or traditional rendition of "Joyful, Joyful, We Adore Thee" or another song of praise to lead you in singing God's praise. Many music streaming services have "Praise and Worship" or contemporary Christian playlists, or tune into your local Christian radio station to listen and sing along with songs of praise. Don't overlook traditional hymns either. Many include beautiful words of praise and worship directed toward God. Lift up your voice both during and outside of Mass, joining the earthly and heavenly choirs in their endless songs of praise to God!

ADDITIONAL RESOURCES

- *Catechism of the Catholic Church,* Part 2, "The Lord's Day," paragraphs 2174-2196
- *God is Near Us: The Eucharist, the Heart of Life,* Joseph Cardinal Ratzinger
- *Real Presence: What Does it Mean and Why Does it Matter?* Timothy P. O'Malley
- *Bored Again Catholic: How the Mass Could Save Your Life,* Timothy P. O'Malley
- *This is My Body: A Call to Eucharistic Revival,* Bishop Robert Barron

DISCIPLESHIP PRACTICES
Worship the Lord

Praise the Lord!

I will bless the Lord at all times;
his praise shall always be in my mouth.
— Psalm 34:2

"Praise is the form of prayer which recognizes most immediately that God is God. It lauds God for his own sake and gives him glory, quite beyond what he does, but simply because HE IS" (*Catechism of the Catholic Church*, 2639).

To strengthen your vocabulary of praise, repeatedly pray "Jesus, you are _____," filling in the blank with different words each time. Consider the scriptural titles for God, his attributes, and his relationship with you in particular. Some examples follow, but the possibilities are endless.

TITLES

The Anointed One	The King of the Universe
The One True God	The Prince of Peace
The Bread of Life	Emmanuel
True God and True Man	The Holy One
The Lion of Judah	The Light of the world
The Word Made Flesh	The King of Kings
The Great I AM	The Lord of Lords
The Lord of Hosts	The Alpha and the Omega
The Lamb of God	The Wonderful Counselor
The Living Water	The True Vine
The Good Shepherd	The Eternal Word
The Most High	The King of Glory

ATTRIBUTES

holy	glorious	just	mighty
merciful	beautiful	awesome	good
steadfast	faithful	loving	forgiving

130

RELATIONSHIP

my hope	my hiding place
my joy	my deliverer
my refuge	my healer
my rock	my treasure
my shepherd	my righteousness
my song	my provider
my Lord and my God	my all in all
my strength	my Father
my portion and cup	my salvation

Get More Out of Mass

Come, let us climb the Lord's mountain, to the house of the God of Jacob, that he may instruct us in his ways, that we may walk in his paths.
— Micah 4:2

Climbing the mountain of the Lord is a fitting image for what we do at Mass. It takes some effort and sacrifice to get there, but on top of that mountain, we are transformed by gaining a far-reaching perspective on life and on the God we worship. From that vantage point, we can see more clearly in four directions:

LOOK BACKWARD at all of salvation history and at the previous week of our own lives.

LOOK INWARD at our hearts, giving thanks (*eucharistia*) for the gifts received that week, and repenting of our shortcomings ("Lord have mercy").

LOOK UPWARD to God as we praise with choirs of angels, listen to his Word, bring him our needs, and eat his heavenly food.

LOOK FORWARD as re-commissioned missionaries, sent back to the valleys and plains with good work to do and good news to share.

TIPS

- Identify one thing to place spiritually on the altar to be transformed along with the bread and the wine: a gratitude, worry, fear, request…
- Read that day's Scripture readings before coming to Mass; discuss the homily after Mass.
- Arrive early to pray and prepare yourself interiorly. Check out St. Thomas Aquinas' Prayer Before Communion
- If you are aware of having committed a serious sin, receive the Sacrament of Reconciliation before receiving Communion.
- Pray silently after receiving the Eucharist.
- Build community by saying hello to someone before you leave.
- If young children prevent you from the more meditative strategies, take heart! The Lord is honored by your sacrifice to bring your family to Mass, and his grace is powerfully at work even amidst the wiggles, squiggles, and constant distractions.

Honor the Lord's Day

How will you (and your family, if relevant) keep holy the Lord's Day? Review the following guide each week until planning your Sunday becomes second nature. The excerpts below are from the *Catechism of the Catholic Church*.

EUCHARISTIC WORSHIP

"The Eucharist is 'the source and the summit of the Christian Life'" (1324).

- When and where will you attend Mass?
- What preparations would you like to build into your routine? (See page 131 for ideas.)

REST AND LEISURE

"Just as God 'rested on the seventh day from all his work which

he had done,' human life has a rhythm of work and rest. The institution of the Lord's Day helps everyone enjoy adequate rest and
leisure to cultivate their familial, cultural, social, and religious
lives" (2184).

- What kind of rest and leisure can you take up to cultivate
  one or more of these dimensions of life?

WORKS OF MERCY

"Those Christians who have leisure should be mindful of their
brethren who have the same needs and the same rights, yet
cannot rest from work because of poverty and misery. Sunday is
traditionally consecrated by Christian piety to good works and
humble service of the sick, the infirm, and the elderly. Christians
will also sanctify Sunday by devoting time and care to their families and relatives, often difficult to do on other days of the week"
(2186).

- Who needs your care and support?
- Does Sunday (or the weekend in general) afford you more
  opportunities to tend to them?

REFLECTION

"Sunday is a time for reflection, silence, cultivation of the mind,
and meditation which furthers the growth of the Christian interi-
or life" (2186).

- How might you engage in deeper thought, prayer, and reflection over the weekend?

PRUDENCE

"Family needs or important social service can legitimately excuse
from the obligation of Sunday rest. The faithful should see to it
that legitimate excuses do not lead to habits prejudicial to reli-
gion, family life, and health" (2185).

ENDNOTES

1. "Eucharistic Prayer III," in the *Roman Missal*, 3rd ed. (Vatican City State: Libreria Editrice Vaticana, 2010). Emphasis added.

2. Robert Robinson, "Come Thou Fount of Every Blessing" (1758).

3. St. Teresa of Calcutta, *Where there is Love, There is God: Her Path to Closer Union with God and Greater Love for Others* (New York: Doubleday, 2010), 158.

4. See Matthew 28:1; Mark 16:2; Luke 24:1; John 20:1.

5. See Mark 16:1; Matthew 28:1.

6. Second Vatican Council, *Lumen gentium*, 11, quoted in *Catechism*, 1324.

7. John 15:1-5.

8. *Catechism*, 606.

9. Ibid., 1368.

10. See *Catechism*, 1395.

11. Bishop Robert Barron, "Bishop Barron on Making Christ the Center of your Life," Word on Fire, February 17, 2017, accessed December 4, 2023, https://www.wordonfire.org/articles/bishop-barron-on-making-christ-the-center-of-your-life/.

12. Timothy Keller, *Counterfeit Gods: The Empty Promises of Money, Sex, and Power, and the Only Hope that Matters* (United States: Penguin Publishing Group, 2009), xix.

13. This insight is from Bob Schuchts, *Be Healed: A Guide to Encountering the Powerful Love of Jesus in Your Life* (Notre Dame, IN: Ave Maria Press, 2014), 95.

14. "Collect Prayer for 20th Sunday in Ordinary Time," in the *Roman Missal*, 3rd ed.

15. *Catechism*, 2041.

WEEK 5
LOVE YOUR NEIGHBOR

You shall love your neighbor as yourself.
– Matthew 22:39

CONVERSATION FIVE
Love Your Neighbor

OPENING PRAYER (3 MIN)

Select one person to open in prayer. Use the following prayer or your own words.

In the name of the Father, and of the Son, and of the Holy Spirit. Amen.

Jesus, you are worthy of all our worship and all our praise. Thank you for the ways you have met us, loved us, and led us this week. We want to continually grow in placing you at the very center of our lives. For apart from you, we can do nothing, and you alone have the words of everlasting life. May our conversation today deepen our resolve to worship you above all things and to love our neighbors as you love us.

We ask this in the name of Jesus. Amen.

CATCH UP (5 MIN)

Share highs and lows: one positive thing (a simple joy, gratitude, or blessing) and one challenge in your life since you last met.

REVIEW WORSHIP THE LORD (15 MIN)

Discuss a few of the following questions.

- Did you get to a daily Mass this past week? If so, how did it feel the same or different from your experience of Sunday Mass?
- Which of the following prayer sessions did you find most helpful or memorable? Most challenging?
  ○ Praising God in your own words
  ○ Examining your reverence toward God
  ○ Reflecting on the importance of the Lord's Day
  ○ Considering your offering at Mass
  ○ Praying with John 6 about the Eucharist
  ○ The Rose Window meditation on putting Christ at the center of your life
  ○ Identifying your temptation toward idolatry
- How does the Church's understanding of Sunday differ from the prevailing cultural view today?
- What questions came up for you this week?

Read aloud.

The first four weeks have focused on prayer and the interior life. You have been guided through many forms of talking and listening to God, both individually and communally. The richness of the Catholic tradition on prayer, Scripture, and the sacraments is inexhaustible. Yet, growing disciples can face discouragement about their seeming lack of progress or depth in prayer and meditation. If you've ever experienced this, keep in mind the following perspective and encouragement from Catholic philosopher and author Dr. Peter Kreeft. "One moment of prayer, of weak worship, confused contrition, tepid thanksgiving, or pitiful petition, will bring us closer to God than all the books of theology in the world."[1]

Discuss the following questions.

- What do you think of Kreeft's point?
- Do your prayer times ever seem (to you) to be weak, confused, tepid, or even pitiful? If so, what is your reaction to Kreeft's reassurance here?

ABOUT LOVE YOUR NEIGHBOR (15 MIN)

Read aloud.

"You shall love your neighbor as yourself" (Matthew 22:39, Leviticus 19:18). "Do to others whatever you would have them do to you" (Matthew 7:12). What is commonly referred to as "the golden rule" appears not only in the Bible but also as one of the most central and important standards for living a blessed and godly life across traditions. This call to "love your neighbor" is astoundingly simple in theory, yet very challenging to live out. Christians aren't the only people to promote this rule, but we ought to be among its most enthusiastic practitioners!

Last week's theme (Worship the Lord) and this week's theme (Love Your Neighbor) point to the two greatest commandments: "'You shall love the Lord your God with all your heart, with all your soul, with all your mind, and with all your strength.' The second is this: 'You shall love your neighbor as yourself.' There is no other commandment greater than these" (Mark 12:29-31). Placing Jesus more firmly in the center of our lives through worship leads us not only to do good to others, but to see, love, and care about what Jesus himself sees, loves, and cares about.

YOUR CHALLENGE THIS WEEK:

☐ Love your neighbors (whomever you discern them to be) in concrete ways, as directed by the prayer guide.

☐ Send one person in your life a handwritten note. See the tip on page 144.

Discuss the following question.

- What is a current relationship or situation in which you find it especially difficult to "love your neighbor as yourself"?

READ AND DISCUSS (15 MIN)

Read aloud.

In Mark 12 and Matthew 22, Jesus is asked which commandment is the greatest of them all. Given that there were over six hundred laws in first-century Judaism, this is certainly a good question! In response, Jesus recites not one commandment, but two. Read and discuss Matthew's account here.

Matthew 22:34-40, NRSV-CE

[34] When the Pharisees heard that he had silenced the Sadducees, they gathered together, [35] and one of them, a lawyer, asked him a question to test him. [36] "Teacher, which commandment in the law is the greatest?" [37] He said to him, "'You shall love the Lord your God with all your heart, and with all your soul, and with all your mind.' [38] This is the greatest and first commandment. [39] And a second is like it: 'You shall love your neighbor as yourself.' [40] On these two commandments hang all the law and the prophets."

Discuss the following questions.

- What is generally harder for you: showing proper love and acceptance for others or for yourself?
- Jesus also told his disciples, "love one another *as I love you*" (John 15:12, cf. John 13:34, emphasis added). How do you think the meaning of loving *as Christ loved us* is similar to or

different from "love your neighbor as yourself"?

- How does this passage inspire you to show greater love to someone close to you? What, specifically, can you do this week to "love your neighbor as yourself"?

NEXT MEETING (2 MIN)

Make sure you have your next discussion on the calendar.

CLOSING PRAYER (5 MIN)

Choose someone to lead the closing prayer time. Use the prompts below or your own words. Invite the other(s) to add their prayers when you prompt them.

In the name of the Father, and of the Son, and of the Holy Spirit. Amen.

Jesus, thank you for your Word and for our conversation today. Help us grow in loving others and ourselves as you love us, Lord. We give you permission to challenge us in the upcoming weeks, to open our eyes and hearts even more to our neighbors, whoever and wherever they may be. Teach us who our neighbors are and how you're calling us to be good news to them, in your name.

We lift up our needs and deepest desires to you, Lord. In particular, we ask for _____; _____; _____. What else should we pray for?

Thank you for always hearing our prayers and leading us into your will.

Mother Mary, we ask you to pray for us and our loved ones, as we say together: Hail Mary, full of grace, the Lord is with thee; blessed art thou among women, and blessed is the fruit of thy womb, Jesus. Holy Mary, Mother of God, pray for us sinners, now and at the hour of our death. Amen.

PRAYER GUIDE
Love Your Neighbor

Day 1. The Fragrance of Christ

But thanks be to God, who in Christ always leads us in triumphal procession, and through us spreads in every place the fragrance that comes from knowing him.
— 2 Corinthians 2:14, NRSV-CE

Think of that moment when you walk into a house where someone is preparing your favorite meal. The tantalizing aroma fills the air. It's attractive. It's inviting. It brings a smile to your face. You immediately look forward to enjoying the food, along with the company you'll share it with.

We who follow Jesus are the very fragrance of Christ in the world. We are meant to attract and invite those around us to Jesus. What a lofty calling! St. Paul himself marveled at this vocation, just as we might: "Who is qualified for this?" (2 Corinthians 2:16). No one, apart from God, is qualified or worthy. "But thanks be to God, who in Christ always leads us in triumphal procession, and through us spreads in every place the fragrance that comes from knowing him" (v. 14). It's Christ's fragrance, not our own, that is good news to the world. And he has both willed and equipped us to spread his aroma wherever we go.

This fragrance of Christ, in a word, is love. Love is the very essence of God[2] and the reason Jesus came into the world. Love, then, is also the one-word summary of our deepest calling: "for the one who loves another has fulfilled the law" (Romans 13:8). Without love, we are but noisy gongs and clanging cymbals that amount to nothing.[3]

We often limit our modern understanding of love to the romantic kind, but the Greek word *agape,* used in the New Testament, best captures the meaning of God's love for us and our call to love others. *Agape* means selfless love that wills and acts only for the highest good of the beloved. This is no small feat. It is this word that St. Paul describes poignantly in his famous poem to the Corinthians. For today's prayer time, pray with Paul's powerful and gritty description of love.

OPEN TO GOD

Slow down, breathe deeply, and open your heart to God.

In the name of the Father, and of the Son, and of the Holy Spirit. Amen.

Jesus, you are perfect love made visible for us. I praise you with all my heart. Lord you are _____.

Come into my heart today and teach me what it means to love those you have placed in my life.

PRAY FROM THE HEART

Read the following passage prayerfully.

1 Corinthians 13:1-8
If I speak in human and angelic tongues but do not have love, I am a resounding gong or a clashing cymbal. And if I have the gift of prophecy and comprehend all mysteries and all knowledge; if I have all faith so as to move mountains but do not have love, I am nothing. If I give away everything I own, and if I hand my body over so that I may boast but do not have love, I gain nothing.

Love is patient, love is kind. It is not jealous, [love] is not pompous, it is not inflated, it is not rude, it does not seek its own interests, it is not quick-tempered, it does not brood over injury, it does not rejoice over wrongdoing but rejoices with the truth. It bears all things, believes all things, hopes all things, endures all things.

Love never fails.

For help reflecting:

- Who has been the fragrance of Christ for you, even if imperfectly? Say a brief prayer of thanks to God for this person or these people.
- Which trait of love do you find you live out fairly well, or with relative ease? After you identify it, thank God for giving you this gift.
- What negative description here (what love is *not*) is most challenging for you this week?
- What positive description here (what love *is*) is most challenging for you this week?
- Ask the Lord for forgiveness for any specific ways you're aware of in which you failed to love recently.

- Is there anyone you want to apologize to or reconcile with?
- Is there anyone you need to forgive in your heart (or to work toward this), in order to avoid brooding over injury? If so, talk to Jesus about this.
- Consider: this description is not just how you're called to love; it also describes how God loves you. Re-read St. Paul's words in the second paragraph through this lens. "God's love for me is patient. It is kind." Etc.

Talk to God about anything weighing on your mind or heart today.

CLOSE

Rest for a few minutes in the presence of God, who is love.

God, you are the author of love. You call me to love others as you love me. Thank you that this call is not just a duty, but a joyful privilege you help me to carry out. Without you, Jesus, I cannot love others as I ought. But with you, I can and I will. When others see me, I pray that they get a glimpse of you too, Jesus. Continue to spread your fragrance through me and through all who call you Lord.

In the name of the Father, and of the Son, and of the Holy Spirit. Amen.

TIP: SHOW GENUINE INTEREST

In a world full of screens, soundbites, gossip, pontificating, and polemical divisions, it is beyond refreshing to converse with someone who delights in getting to know us a little better; someone who asks questions and listens attentively to our thoughts and experiences; someone who takes joy in our joys and sorrow in our sorrows. Whether extroverted or introverted, we, as the Body of Christ, can intentionally extend this grace to others. One of the simplest and most profound starting points for loving others well is to take a genuine interest in the people around you. Put focused energy into growing in attentiveness through others-centered conversation in your daily life. Who is someone you could be more attentive to? This could be a spouse, a child, a roommate, a co-worker, or a next-door neighbor. Read the Ten Tips for Better Conversations on page 164 and look for natural opportunities to put these tips into practice.

Day 2. The Spiritual Works of Mercy

When he had washed their feet . . . he said to them, ". . . If I, therefore, the master and teacher, have washed your feet, you ought to wash one another's feet. I have given you a model to follow, so that as I have done for you, you should also do . . . If you understand this, blessed are you if you do it."
– John 13:12, 14-15, 17

The God of the universe took a towel and washed the dirty feet of the apostles. It was a lowly, stinky job that needed to be done, and it wasn't beneath him to do it. Service. Kindness. Generosity. Attentiveness to the needs of others. These ought to characterize the Body of Christ because they characterize Christ.

Growth in holiness comes with a greater care for others. Human and spiritual maturity involve becoming less ego-centric and more attuned and empathetic to the needs of friends, family, neighbors, and co-workers. We desire their true good; to serve them in some concrete way; to make someone else's day just a little better, if it's within our ability and calling to do so.

So, what does it look like to "wash the feet" of others? There is no end to the number of ways we might answer this important question. The spiritual and corporal works of mercy are a treasure of the Catholic tradition that can greatly aid our reflection on this question.* These two lists of seven actions are drawn from Scripture and Tradition, one focusing on the bodily / material / corporal needs, and the other focusing on the spiritual needs all people share.

They are not for the faint of heart. They call us to courageous love-in-action, just as Jesus has loved us. In today's prayer time, pray over the spiritual works before turning to the corporal works tomorrow. Wash the feet of someone in your life today in one of these concrete ways. "Let your light shine before others, so that they may see your good works and give glory to your Father in heaven" (Matthew 5:16, NRSV-CE).

OPEN TO GOD

Open to God in your usual way.

In the name of the Father, and of the Son, and of the Holy Spirit. Amen.

I give you praise, Heavenly Father, for you are good and worthy of

---

* For a quick reference guide, see page 165.

all honor and glory. Open my heart to whomever you wish to bless through me today or this week. I give you permission to guide me, Lord.

PRAY FROM THE HEART

As you pray over the list of the spiritual works of mercy,[4] first ask the Lord to help you remember when you have been the recipient of some of these loving acts. Gratefully ponder the ways in which others have blessed your faith and your life in these concrete ways.

- Counsel the doubtful
- Instruct the ignorant
- Admonish the sinner
- Comfort the sorrowful
- Forgive injuries
- Bear wrongs patiently
- Pray for the living and the dead

Go back over the list, this time asking the Lord to direct your thoughts to one specific way you can live out one of these works of mercy more intentionally this week, or in this season of your life. For each work, ponder prayerfully: who comes to mind? What, if anything, is God calling me to do with or for this person?

Spend a few minutes right now praying for one or a few of the people who came to mind.

CLOSE

Rest with Jesus in contemplative silence. As you do, trust that he is interceding not only for you but also for those you prayed for and thought about in this prayer time.

Come, Holy Spirit. Help me live more freely and abundantly according to your ways. Let it become second nature for me to forgive offenses willingly, to bear wrongs patiently, to comfort the sorrowful, to pray for others. With you, Lord, all things are possible.

In the name of the Father, and of the Son, and of the Holy Spirit. Amen.

TIP: SEND A HANDWRITTEN NOTE

In our fast-paced, digital world, getting a physical card or letter in the mail stands out. Sending a card shows attentiveness and care and makes someone feel remembered. Buy or make a thank you, birthday, or sympathy card, and send it with a personal note to someone in your life. Or send a note without an occasion, simply to let them know you're thinking of them and praying for them.

Day 3. The Corporal Works of Mercy

Then the righteous will answer him and say, "Lord, when did we see you hungry and feed you, or thirsty and give you drink? When did we see you a stranger and welcome you, or naked and clothe you? When did we see you ill or in prison, and visit you?" And the king will say to them in reply, "Amen, I say to you, whatever you did for one of these least brothers of mine, you did for me."
– Matthew 25:37-40

J esus communicates with a staggering and perhaps unsettling clarity what the call of discipleship looks like in a world of winners and losers, powerful and weak, haves and have-nots. The sick, the impoverished, the imprisoned, the foreigner don't only need aid from those who can help, but these "least" ones are the people with whom Jesus (the king in passage above) identifies himself. It is simply impossible to imagine a more elevated view of those who might appear to be small, powerless, and insignificant.

The implications are both comforting and challenging. We can take great comfort in knowing that when we are in a position of weakness, suffering, and vulnerability, God is close and on our side. The challenge is equally clear: we simply cannot seek the Lord and remain unmoved by the plight of those in need. "Those who shut their ears to the cry of the poor will themselves call out and not be answered" (Proverbs 21:13).

Serving others is not about solving every problem in the world or chasing utopia; it's about sharing God's heart. It's about seeing what God sees, loving what God loves, and doing what God does. It's about doing what we can to be salt, light, and leaven in a hurting, unjust world. "Whoever has two coats must share with anyone who has none; and whoever has food must do likewise" (Luke 3:11, NRSV-CE).

OPEN TO GOD

Open to God in your usual way.

In the name of the Father, and of the Son, and of the Holy Spirit. Amen.

Lord, you speak words of love and of challenge to your friends and followers. As one of your friends and followers, I open my heart and mind to your words today. Help me hear your voice and respond with courage and trust. I cast my cares on you today, Lord. In particular, I give you my concern for_____.

PRAY FROM THE HEART

Use the steps of *lectio divina* (read, reflect, respond, rest) to pray with the following passage. These are the words of Jesus to his disciples at the end of his final teaching discourse in Matthew's Gospel.

Matthew 25:31-46, NRSV-CE

When the Son of Man comes in his glory, and all the angels with him, then he will sit on the throne of his glory. All the nations will be gathered before him, and he will separate people one from another as a shepherd separates the sheep from the goats, and he will put the sheep at his right hand and the goats at the left. Then the king will say to those at his right hand, "Come, you that are blessed by my Father, inherit the kingdom prepared for you from the foundation of the world; for I was hungry and you gave me food, I was thirsty and you gave me something to drink, I was a stranger and you welcomed me, I was naked and you gave me clothing, I was sick and you took care of me, I was in prison and you visited me." Then the righteous will answer him, "Lord, when was it that we saw you hungry and gave you food, or thirsty and gave you something to drink? And when was it that we saw you a stranger and welcomed you, or naked and gave you clothing? And when was it that we saw you sick or in prison and visited you?" And the king will answer them, "Truly I tell you, just as you did it to one of the least of these who are members of my family, you did it to me." Then he will say to those at his left hand, "You that are accursed, depart from me into the eternal fire prepared for the devil and his angels; for I was hungry and you gave me no food, I was thirsty and you gave me nothing to drink, I was a stranger and you did not welcome me, naked and you did not give me clothing, sick and in prison and you did not visit me." Then they also will answer, "Lord, when was it that we saw you hungry or thirsty or a stranger or naked or sick or in prison, and did not take care of you?" Then he will answer them, "Truly I tell you, just as you did not do it to one of the least of these, you did not do it to me." And these will go away into eternal punishment, but the righteous into eternal life.

146

For help reflecting:

- What emotions arise in you as you read this parable? Notice these, tell Jesus about them, and invite him into these emotions.
- What word or phrase stands out to you? Pray with this and seek the Lord's message for you today.
- What do you make of the element of surprise among both groups of people ("Lord, when was it that we saw you...")? What does this seem to imply about the motivations of those who fed the hungry, etc? Were they doing it because they were trying to earn a reward from God, or was it something deeper than that?

Pray over the list of the corporal works of mercy,[5] asking the Lord to show you one specific way he is calling you to live one of these out in the next few weeks or months.

- Feed the hungry
- Give drink to the thirsty
- Shelter the homeless
- Visit the sick
- Visit the prisoners
- Bury the dead
- Give alms to the poor

CLOSE

Dwell in silence and solitude for a minute or two under the compassionate gaze of God.

Jesus, I feel _____ as I ponder your words about the sheep and the goats. I invite you into these feelings; Help me grow to see what you see, want what you want, and do what you do. Thank you for loving me just as I am and for nudging me toward greater love for my neighbor.

In the name of the Father, and of the Son, and of the Holy Spirit. Amen.

Day 4. Charity and Justice

Then the Lord asked Cain, Where is your brother Abel? He answered,
"I do not know. Am I my brother's keeper?"
– Genesis 4:9

The word "charity" is commonly used to describe acts of alms-giving to the poor. This is for good reason; charity (Latin: *caritas*) means love, and love is both God's nature and our highest calling. We give alms out of love. Yet, the term can take on a diminished meaning in our culture. Charity can connote doing something extra nice for others, something beyond the demands of duty. When we think of aiding the poor merely as something extra, something God or others would be impressed by because we "didn't have to do that," we greatly distort the biblical call of love. Biblical love—the *caritas* or *agape* to which we are called—is not something extra, but included within the concept of justice. It is simply our duty to aid the poor and vulnerable as we are able. Many saints and spiritual writers sought to make this point clear. For example, St. John Chrysostom and St. Gregory the Great said, respectively:

> Not to enable the poor to share in our goods is to steal from them and deprive them of life. The goods we possess are not ours, but theirs.

> When we attend to the needs of those in want, we give them what is theirs, not ours. More than performing works of mercy, we are paying a debt of justice.[6]

Words like these can challenge our deeply held convictions about fairness and justice. We are so accustomed to thinking of ourselves more as autonomous individuals than as a body of interconnected members who share responsibility for and with one another. After killing his brother Abel, Cain deflected God's question ("Where is your brother?") by retorting "I do not know. Am I my brother's keeper?" His question resounds throughout human history. Yet, St. John Paul II reminds us that it's a question with a clear answer: "Yes, every man is his 'brother's keeper', because God entrusts us to one another."[7]

OPEN TO GOD

Open to God in your usual way.

In the name of the Father, and of the Son, and of the Holy Spirit. Amen.

Holy Spirit, come and enkindle in me a fire for your righteousness, goodness, justice, and charity. I trust you, Lord. You have the words of eternal life. Open my ears and my heart to your Word today.

PRAY FROM THE HEART

Pray with the following prophetic exhortation from the book of Isaiah. For some context: as the people of Israel re-established life in Jerusalem after the upheaval of the Babylonian exile, they struggled to hear God's voice and know his comfort. At the same time, they performed religious fasts and ceremonies without amending their life or caring for the poor among them. Some of them oppressed their workers (verse 3). This exhortation seeks to correct the people's hypocrisy and serves as a timeless reminder to all God's people that right worship and right action must go hand in hand.

Isaiah 58:6-14, NRSV-CE
Is not this the fast that I choose:
    to loose the bonds of injustice,
    to undo the thongs of the yoke,
to let the oppressed go free,
    and to break every yoke?

Is it not to share your bread with the hungry,
    and bring the homeless poor into your house;
when you see the naked, to cover them,
    and not to hide yourself from your own kin?

Then your light shall break forth like the dawn,
    and your healing shall spring up quickly;
your vindicator shall go before you,
    the glory of the Lord shall be your rear guard.

Then you shall call, and the Lord will answer;
    you shall cry for help, and he will say, Here I am.

If you remove the yoke from among you,
    the pointing of the finger, the speaking of evil,

if you offer your food to the hungry
    and satisfy the needs of the afflicted,
then your light shall rise in the darkness
    and your gloom be like the noonday.

The Lord will guide you continually,
    and satisfy your needs in parched places,
    and make your bones strong;
and you shall be like a watered garden,
    like a spring of water,
    whose waters never fail.

Your ancient ruins shall be rebuilt;
    you shall raise up the foundations of many generations;
you shall be called the repairer of the breach,
    the restorer of streets to live in.

If you refrain from trampling the sabbath,
    from pursuing your own interests on my holy day;
if you call the sabbath a delight
    and the holy day of the Lord honorable;
if you honor it, not going your own ways,
    serving your own interests, or pursuing your own affairs;

then you shall take delight in the Lord,
    and I will make you ride upon the heights of the earth;
I will feed you with the heritage of your ancestor Jacob,
    for the mouth of the Lord has spoken.

For help reflecting:

- How does the prophet's message speak to you personally?
- What words or phrases stand out? What might the Lord be saying to you in this?
- What are some of God's promises mentioned? Are there any conditions on those promises?
- Have you ever thought about helping those in need as a type of "fast"? How does this connection add to your understanding of the meaning of the passage?
- How does the prophet's message help you connect the two ways of "worship the Lord" and "love your neighbor"?
- Respond to God. Bring him anyone or anything on your mind today. Pray from the heart.

CLOSE

Rest in stillness, letting the God of mercy and justice continue doing a deep work in your heart.

Father, thank you for your Word in Scripture, which constantly refines your people, including me. Help me see as you see and love as you love.

In the name of the Father, and of the Son, and of the Holy Spirit. Amen.

Day 5. Balance and Boundaries

Rising very early before dawn, he left and went off to a deserted place,
where he prayed. Simon and those who were with him pursued him and
on finding him said, "Everyone is looking for you."
– Mark 1:35-37

With all this talk of loving our neighbors, helping those in need, and caring attentively for people in our lives, it might be tempting to think we have to be "on" all the time. Developing a "savior complex," thinking everything depends on us, is a trap that's all too easy to fall into. We might even experience an unhealthy attachment to our own self-image as "that amazingly generous and helpful person." Do we have a need to be needed? Are we overly worried about letting others down? Do we have enough freedom and confidence to say "no" to good causes and requests—not out of laziness or selfishness, but so we can say a stronger "yes" to a few important things?

God's call to love our neighbor is not a call to be the answer to everyone's problems. It's not a call to deny our legitimate needs for balance, leisure, self-care, and boundaries. Jesus lived this holy rhythm of service, solitude, prayer, and time with friends. He had to let some people down—not healing everyone who called out from the crowds. He fiercely prioritized time in solitude with the Father, even while everyone was looking for him.

The spaces between musical notes are just as important as the notes themselves in making a beautiful song. We must never cease to seek the Lord in prayer and solitude and to find our rest and identity in him. He is all we have to give others, anyway: "I am the vine, you are the branches. Whoever remains in me and I in him will bear much fruit, because without me you can do nothing" (John 15:5).

If, because of our attempts to serve others, our prayer life suffers, our family life suffers, our physical or mental health suffers, then we're likely doing too much.[8] We're forgetting who is the Savior of the world.

OPEN TO GOD

Open to God in your usual way.

In the name of the Father, and of the Son, and of the Holy Spirit. Amen.

Jesus, you are the Savior of the world and of my life. Thank you for doing the heavy lifting in my life and in the renewal of all things. Come, be my light and my strength today. Teach me how to live as a contemplative in action. Show me how to work and how to rest in you.

PRAY FROM THE HEART

Begin today's prayer time by giving thanks for a few specific blessings from the past day or two.

Lord, thank you for _____.

Read the following words from Jesus and pray with the reflection questions below.

Matthew 11:28-30, NRSV-CE
Come to me, all you that are weary and are carrying heavy burdens, and I will give you rest. Take my yoke upon you, and learn from me; for I am gentle and humble in heart, and you will find rest for your souls. For my yoke is easy, and my burden is light.

Take stock of your commitments to others and your own need for balance and boundaries.

- How consistently are you carving out time daily for prayer?
- How consistent is your commitment to Sunday Mass? To regular Confession?
- What are your recurring, most demanding responsibilities and commitments to others?
- How are *you* doing as you serve these people and responsibilities? Are you generally joyful and filled up? Exhausted and depleted? Super stressed or overwhelmed? Bitter? Anxious? Do you feel like the proverbial camel whose back might break from one more straw placed on it?
- How are your friendships? Do you have one or a few friends with whom you can recharge in healthy, God-honoring ways?
- How is your health? Are you sleeping enough? Eating well? Getting any regular exercise?
- What do you love to do outside of work or school? Are you able to prioritize at least a little time and space for this?
- Is there any commitment or responsibility you feel pressure from others to carry, but which might not be God's will for you? If so, is it time to start praying about and discerning a possible change?

Notice, Tell, Invite

As you take stock of the many demands on your time and priorities in your life, what emotions emerge? Spend a few minutes using the Notice, Tell, Invite method (page 34) of prayer to identify your feelings, talk to God about them, and invite him to meet you right where you are, bringing his light and grace.

Did any resolutions or questions emerge that you want to pray into further? If so, write them down and talk briefly to God about them.

CLOSE

Rest for a few minutes in the enduring love of your Heavenly Father, who sustains and strengthens you in unseen ways. Breathe deeply, trusting he is close.

Lord God, you see me and know me better than I know myself. You see all that I am carrying, and you tell me to take your yoke upon me, which is easy and light. Teach me what this means, Lord. Help me find my rest in you always and serve with joy and energy those you call me to love.

In the name of the Father, and of the Son, and of the Holy Spirit. Amen.

Day 6. Care before Cure

And Jesus wept.
— John 11:35

A few days after their brother Lazarus died, Jesus visited Martha and Mary in Bethany. In their grief and pain, the women did not hold back their frustrations, even blaming Jesus for not arriving sooner. "Lord, if you had been here, my brother would not have died" (John 11:21, 32).

How did Jesus respond? Did he scold them for talking that way to the Messiah? Did he get on with the miracle of raising Lazarus to avoid such a tense moment? Did he defend himself, giving reasons for his timing?

No. "Jesus wept" (John 11:35).

The Bible often uses the Greek word *splanchna*—translated variously as compassion, tender mercy, and affection—to describe Jesus' reaction to people in need. It's a word that involves the innards. Jesus is physically moved—in his guts—in the face of human suffering. His stomach turns. He feels the pain of others.

The Latin roots of the word compassion, meaning "to suffer with," capture something of this *splanchna* as well. Before saving the day and raising Lazarus from the dead, Jesus feels and shares the pain of his grieving friends.

Why? Because he loves them. That's what love does. "If [one] part suffers, all the parts suffer with it" (1 Corinthians 12:26). Rejoicing with those who rejoice and weeping with those who weep[9] is what it means to be family, to be Church, to be human.

Fr. Henri Nouwen reflects on our desire to fix problems ("cure") without entering into the pain of others ("care"):

> Our tendency is to run away from the painful realities or to try to change them as soon as possible. But cure without care makes us into rulers, controllers, manipulators, and prevents a real community from taking shape. Cure without care makes us preoccupied with quick changes, impatient and unwilling to share each other's burden. And so cure can often become offending instead of liberating.[10]

Care must come before cure. Sometimes there is no "cure" we can offer, but we can always show care. And it matters. We share the *splanchna* of God, whose guts twist when his children suffer.

OPEN TO GOD

Open to God in your usual way.

In the name of the Father, and of the Son, and of the Holy Spirit. Amen.

Thank you, God, for looking with compassion on me and on the whole world. You are not a God who is callous to our joys or sorrows. Increase my faith in you, and give me a greater share in your compassion for my family, friends, neighbors, and even my enemies.

PRAY FROM THE HEART

Reflect prayerfully on the following questions.

- Have you ever been on the receiving end of someone attempting "cure without care"? If so, how did that experience leave you feeling?
- In what situations do you tend to jump into "fixing" mode or solution-finding too quickly, bypassing the person's need to be cared for and loved right where they are? Is there a time you did this recently, or might be tempted to do so in the near future?

Pray with the passage and questions below.

Romans 12:14-21, NRSV-CE

Bless those who persecute you; bless and do not curse them. Rejoice with those who rejoice, weep with those who weep. Live in harmony with one another; do not be haughty, but associate with the lowly; do not claim to be wiser than you are. Do not repay anyone evil for evil, but take thought for what is noble in the sight of all. If it is possible, so far as it depends on you, live peaceably with all. Beloved, never avenge yourselves, but leave room for the wrath of God; for it is written, "Vengeance is mine, I will repay, says the Lord." No, "if your enemies are hungry, feed them; if they are thirsty, give them something to drink; for by doing this you will heap burning coals on their heads." Do not be overcome by evil, but overcome evil with good.

- What is your reaction to St. Paul's punchy phrases and challenging advice here?
- Who in your life is rejoicing right now? What would it look like to honor God and them by rejoicing with them?
- Who in your life is weeping (suffering or struggling) right now? What would it look like to honor God and them by "weeping" with them?
- Is there a situation in your life where you have an opportunity to overcome evil with good? If so, what is it? Consider how to do this. Talk to God about it.
- Lift up anyone who came to mind during this prayer time in some brief intercessory prayer. Pray also for yourself, that you can love them well according to God's will.

CLOSE

Sit quietly for a few moments of peaceful rest, entrusting yourself to God.

Jesus, you lead the way in overcoming evil with good. Breathe your life into me, that I may walk the same path. Show me ways that I can care for people in my path this week, even those who are quite different from me. Show me where I can share in your splanchna for the world.

In the name of the Father, and of the Son, and of the Holy Spirit. Amen.

TIP: LOOK THE BEGGAR IN THE EYE

Plan ahead for how you can respond to people asking for help with kindness and humanity. Think of simple ways to alleviate their suffering even a little bit, for instance giving out hand warmers or warm socks if it's cold outside or rain ponchos in summer months. Stock your car or backpack with easy-to-share snacks like granola bars or gift cards to nearby grocery stores. When you hand someone something—or even if you don't have anything to give—look the person begging in the eye, say hello, and ask their name. While these simple acts won't eliminate the larger issues leading to homelessness and poverty, they show the person compassion and help us treat them with a small dose of the dignity deserving of all God's children.

Day 7. Intercessory Prayer

Simon's mother-in-law was afflicted with a severe fever, and they interceded with [Jesus] about her. He stood over her, rebuked the fever, and it left her.
– Luke 4:38-39

The people who walked and talked with Jesus in the Gospels often asked him to do things. Mary asks Jesus to help the couple in need on their wedding day (John 2:1-11). Peter and the disciples ask Jesus to help Peter's sick mother-in-law (Luke 4:38-39). A faithful centurion asks Jesus to heal his servant (Matthew 8:5-13; Luke 7:1-10). A group brings a paralyzed man through a roof to be healed. When Jesus saw their faith he healed the man of his sins and of his physical ailments (Mark 2:1-12).

In many places in Scripture, people act as go-betweens, bringing the needs of others to Jesus and asking him to act. The word "intercede" comes from the Latin word *inter* for "between" and *cedere* meaning "to go." One who intercedes goes between one party and another, asking for something to be done on their behalf.

Together with loving actions, praying for others is one of the most basic ways we are able to love our neighbors. It's a practice that is part and parcel of all the monotheistic religions: "Since Abraham, intercession—asking on behalf of another has been characteristic of a heart attuned to God's mercy."[11] Jesus repeatedly instructed his followers to do it, offering staggering promises we might be tempted to think were exaggerations: "Again, [amen,] I say to you, if two of you agree on earth about anything for which they are to pray, it shall be granted to them by my heavenly Father" (Matthew 18:19).

Of course, we don't always see the difference that prayer makes, but Jesus could not have made himself any clearer: our prayers matter. Intercessory prayer makes a difference—in us, in others, and in the world. Thankfully, we don't have to understand just how prayer works to take up this practice with gusto as we're called to. It's one of the primary and universal ways we are called to love our neighbor and spread the fragrance of Christ.

OPEN TO GOD

Open to God in your usual way with a few deep breaths and centering yourself on God.

In the name of the Father, and of the Son, and of the Holy Spirit. Amen.

Lord, I confess that intercessory prayer is a mystery I don't fully understand. But I trust that you love to hear and answer my prayers, even if I can't see every result. Increase my faith, and further awaken me to my role in bringing more light and life into the world through prayer. Help me see and attend to the people you have placed in my life, according to your will. Holy Spirit, in this prayer time I ask you to draw my attention to one person whom you would have me pray for and love more attentively this week.

In the name of the Father, and of the Son, and of the Holy Spirit. Amen.

PRAY FROM THE HEART

Read the following passage prayerfully.

Romans 8:26-27, NRSV-CE
Likewise the Spirit helps us in our weakness; for we do not know how to pray as we ought, but that very Spirit intercedes with sighs too deep for words. And God, who searches the heart, knows what is the mind of the Spirit, because the Spirit intercedes for the saints according to the will of God.

Spend a few minutes now asking the Holy Spirit to bring someone to mind.

God, thank you for bringing to mind _____. Please fill my heart with your love for him/her. I want to care for _____ as your heart cares, and to see them as you do.

Prayerfully consider how well you know this person, with the following prompts. It's okay if you can't answer all of these. Even if you know them well, spend some time prayerfully attending to who they are. Ask Jesus to lead you to really see them and know them even better over the next several weeks.

- What is one of this person's best qualities or strengths?
- What do you delight in most about this person?
- What makes them tick? What makes them happy? What are they interested in?
- What sorrows or struggles does this person carry?
- What do you know of this person's faith? Do they draw strength from God and the Church? Are they seemingly distant from one or both?
- What needs (physical, spiritual, psychological) do they have? What healing or encouragement do you want to ask God for on behalf of this person?

A Recipe for Intercession

Read through the following steps and examples, then pray.

1. Talk directly to God. Use one of the names of God as you address him in prayer. Begin your prayer with "Jesus," "Heavenly Father," "Lord," "Holy Spirit," or "God."
2. Be specific. Pray for the person by name and be specific in your requests.
3. Name the darkness. What is broken or in need of help? What ought not to be? Where is sin or sickness causing fear, a lack of freedom, or pain? (For instance: "Jack doubts that you love him." "Lucia was diagnosed with cancer this week.")
4. Ask for light in the name of Jesus. What graces or virtues do you want God to impart? What could help the situation this person is in? What obstacles do you want God to remove? ("In Jesus' name, set loose faith in Jack's heart today." "Please give Lucia strength and heal her in the name of Jesus.")
5. Make an act of trust or thanksgiving. In the end, we trust God: that he is good, that he is able to fight for us, and that his will is the best answer to our prayer. ("Thank you for hearing my prayer, Lord." "I know you are always there for us, Jesus, I trust in you." "Your will be done, Father.")

Putting It Together

Example: "Heavenly Father, Lucia was diagnosed with cancer this week. Please give her your strength to fight, and please heal her in the name of Jesus. I trust you, God."

Your Turn

- Talk directly to God by name: _____
- Be specific: _____
- Name the darkness: _____
- Ask for light: _____
- Make an act of trust: _____

Continue lifting this person / these people up to the Lord, using the following prayer adapted from St. Paul's words in Ephesians 1:17-19 (NRSV-CE). The pronouns have been changed so that the prayer addresses God and allows you to pray for the person or people you identified.

Heavenly Father, thank you for (name(s))_____.

I lift them up to you in prayer right now.

> *God of our Lord Jesus Christ, the Father of glory, . . . give [them] a spirit of wisdom and revelation as [they] come to know [you], so that, with the eyes of [their] hearts enlightened, [they] may know what is the hope to which [you] have called them, what are the riches of [their] glorious inheritance among the saints, and what is the immeasurable greatness of [your] power for us who believe, according to the working of [your] great power. Amen.*

What else do you want to bring to God today?

CLOSE

Rest for a few minutes in the Lord's presence, trusting that Jesus sees, cares for, and loves the people you just prayed for. He holds all of you in his loving care.

As you close today, ask the Blessed Virgin Mary for her prayers.

Mother Mary, please pray for (name) _____, that they may know the joy of the Lord and be protected from all evil. Pray also for me, that I would know how best to love (name) _____.

Hail Mary, full of grace, the Lord is with thee; blessed art thou among women, and blessed is the fruit of thy womb, Jesus. Holy Mary, Mother of God, pray for us sinners, now and at the hour of our death. Amen.

In the name of the Father, and of the Son, and of the Holy Spirit. Amen.

MAKE IT A HABIT
Love Your Neighbor

Below, find additional tips and suggested readings for continuing to grow in a lifestyle of loving your neighbor.

LOVE THE PERSON IN FRONT OF YOU

In seeking to love others and make the world a better place, it's tempting to think first and foremost about supporting big, organized efforts that can make a broad impact (a great thing) while neglecting to consider the small ways we're called to love the people around us. C.S. Lewis cleverly articulates this temptation in his insightful book of fiction, *The Screwtape Letters*. Screwtape, a senior demon, advises his apprentice and nephew Wormwood on how to lead Wormwood's "patient" (a young man) away from God and God's will. In one letter, he advises,

> The great thing is to direct the malice to his immediate neighbors whom he meets every day and to thrust his benevolence out to the remote circumference, to the people he does not know. The malice thus becomes wholly real and the benevolence largely imaginary."[12]

While it's very good to support organizations that effect far-reaching change, and we should do this wholeheartedly, the call to love others we see every day is in some ways even more challenging and transformative. Consider the perspective of St. Teresa of Calcutta, who said,

> I don't agree with the big way of doing things. To us, what matters is an individual...I believe in person to person. Every person is Christ for me, and since there is only one Jesus, there is only one person in the world for me at that moment.[13]

That kind of relational attentiveness softens hearts (including our own) and changes the world.

GIVE MONEY

"Honor the Lord with your wealth, with first fruits of all your produce" (Proverbs 3:9). Sharing a portion of our financial resources is a clear biblical call and an important discipline for our spiritual growth and freedom. Consider how you can give God your "first fruits" by intentionally choosing a percentage of your income to give to the Church and other good causes. Doing so reminds us that all we have is a gift from God, even the resources we work hard for and earn. It also protects us against unhealthy attachments to our money and helps us grow in generosity, the joy of giving, and a deeper trust in God.

The Old Testament laid out a clear call to the people of Israel to give away the first ten percent of their earnings and produce, which is where the term "tithe" comes from (meaning tenth). Today, this is not a hard and fast rule of the Church, but it remains a biblical guide for Christians to pray about and strive for (or to exceed). If you are not in the habit of giving ten percent, pray about what percentage you are able and called to give now, and continue revisiting this question in months and years to come.

ENGAGE IN DIRECT SERVICE

Find a local opportunity to serve people in need in your community either through your parish or another charitable organization such as a local food bank, a women's care center, a ministry to troubled youth or the homeless, etc. Go on your own, bring your family, or invite some friends to serve with you. Providing direct service personalizes our charity. We can gain a better understanding of what life is like for those who are suffering or in need in some way, which helps us to love, serve, and pray for them more personally.

STUDY CATHOLIC SOCIAL TEACHING

In its care for the dignity of every human being, the Church has developed teaching and guidelines for living that are collectively referred to as "Catholic social teaching." This branch of moral theology helps us apply the gospel messages of love for our neighbor and care for the least among us in very real and specific issues in our world. Start by gaining a deeper understanding of the four major guiding principles of Catholic social teaching: the dignity of the human person, subsidiarity, the common good, and solidarity. See the *Compendium of the Social Doctrine of the Church* (book) and the U.S. Conference of Catholic Bishops webpage: *www.usccb.org/offices/justice-peace-human-development/catholic-social-teaching*.

SHARE YOUR STUFF

The Catholic social teaching principle of the *universal destination of goods*[14] teaches that while we're given the right to private property (it's good and dignifying to own things), this right is also circumscribed within a larger ethical responsibility: to use our private property in ways that serve the common good. Our private property is given to us as a blessing not only to ourselves but to others. One practical and enjoyable way to live out this principle is to think about what things you have that you are willing to share with others. This could include specialized tools or yard equipment, recreational gear for certain hobbies, kids' clothes, etc. Write these down and distribute the list to neighbors and local friends, telling them they are welcome to borrow these items when you're not using them.

SUPPORT LIFE FROM WOMB TO TOMB

The Catholic teaching on the dignity of every human person created in the image of God extends from the moment of a new creation at conception to the final breath we breathe. Joining in Jesus' love and concern for people includes doing our part to advocate for societal structures, laws, and supports that protect people at all stages of life. Supporting life at all stages includes protection for unborn babies, material and emotional support for mothers, affordable childcare, living wages, quality education opportunities, community programs for at-risk teens, protection for the elderly and vulnerable, and loving and attentive end-of-life care. Research local organizations that support the protection and flourishing of people at risk in your community. Make referrals, get involved, or support some of these financially if you're able. Advocate with local or national organizations that work to create just laws and structures. No political party aligns perfectly with the teachings of Jesus or the Church. Challenge yourself to think beyond party lines to advocate for the true good of all.

LIVE SIMPLY

Cultivate disciplines that help you live more simply, including using fewer resources, creating less waste, saving more disposable income to give to others, and taking care of the goods you own. Pope Francis has called into question modern "throwaway culture" that shapes our minds around using up or consuming things (even so far as treating people as resources that can be used and tossed aside).[15] Keeping things beyond when they've gone out of style; repairing rather than replacing clothes, appliances, cars, etc.; buying second hand furniture, toys, and clothing; buying fewer items overall—all these practices help us reduce consumption and waste and help us appreciate the things we do choose to purchase and keep.

ADDITIONAL RESOURCES

- *Compendium of the Social Doctrine of the Church*
- *Catholic Social Teaching Collection,* Word on Fire
- *Connected: Catholic Social Teaching for This Generation,* Ascension Press
- *Catholic Social Teaching: Our Best Kept Secret,* Edward P. DeBerri and James E. Hug

DISCIPLESHIP PRACTICES
Love Your Neighbor

10 Tips for Better Conversations

1. **Ask questions!**
   This takes effort, thought, and intentionality.

2. **Make them the expert.**
   Everyone is an "expert" in something and loves to talk about it. Find it.

3. **Be genuinely curious, amazed, interested, and reverent toward people.**
   The Grand Canyon is a smaller miracle than each of us quirky humans.

4. **Seek first to understand.**
   Everyone has a deep desire to be known and understood—including you. Sacrifice some of your desire to be known, for a bit, while you give another the dignity of being truly listened to and the center of attention.

5. **Ask about the details.**
   "Tell me more about that." Who, what, when, where, why...? Lean away from questions that can be answered with "yes" or "no."

6. **Use differences as an aid to conversation, not a hindrance.**
   Don't worry if you don't have much in common. Differences present an easy opportunity to ask more questions. "I don't know the first thing about that! Tell me more about it..."

7. **Be fully present and truly listen.**
   No multi-tasking (bodily or mentally). Not half in, half out. The person in front of you is the most important thing right now. Even when you think of something you want to say in response, keep on listening. Avoid formulating questions and responses while the other person is talking. Let those thoughts come and go as you continue to listen.

8. **Watch your body language, and smile once in a while!**
   Convey warmth and care through your body. Relax your arms, smile, and show concern as appropriate.

9. **Earn the right to be heard.**
   People don't care what you know until they know that you care. Eventually, they may ask you some questions, especially if they trust you. Then you can share more of your thoughts.

10. **Don't jump to argue or defend.**
    Ask questions and seek to understand even when you disagree with what someone says. If they ask your opinion, share your thoughts and beliefs too, but keep a respectful tone and try not to get defensive.

Works of Mercy

Then the righteous will answer him and say, "Lord, when did we see you hungry and feed you, or thirsty and give you drink? When did we see you a stranger and welcome you, or naked and clothe you? When did we see you ill or in prison, and visit you?" And the king will say to them in reply, "Amen, I say to you, whatever you did for one of these least brothers of mine, you did for me."
– Matthew 25:37-40

The spiritual and corporal works of mercy are two traditional lists of prayer and action that remind us what it looks like to love like Jesus. They challenge us to remember our call to be salt, light, and leaven in the world.

Prayerfully review these lists on occasion. Think creatively: how are you drawn to live out one or more of these actions this week? This month? This year?

CORPORAL WORKS OF MERCY	SPIRITUAL WORKS OF MERCY
Feed the Hungry	Counsel the Doubtful
Give Drink to the Thirsty	Instruct the Ignorant
Shelter the Homeless	Admonish the Sinner
Visit the Sick	Comfort the Sorrowful
Visit the Imprisoned	Forgive Injuries
Bury the Dead	Pray for the Living and the Dead
Give Alms to the Poor	Bear Wrongs Patiently

ENDNOTES

1. Peter Kreeft, *Prayer for Beginners* (San Francisco: Ignatius Press, 2000), 20.

2. "[F]or God is love" (1 John 4:19).

3. See 1 Corinthians 13:1-3.

4. This list of the spiritual works of mercy is drawn from the USCCB at https://www.usccb.org/beliefs-and-teachings/how-we-teach/new-evangelization/jubilee-of-mercy/the-spiritual-works-of-mercy.

5. This list is of the corporal works of mercy is drawn from the USCCB at https://www.usccb.org/beliefs-and-teachings/how-we-teach/new-evangelization/jubilee-of-mercy/the-corporal-works-of-mercy.

6. As quoted in the *Catechism*, 2446.

7. St. John Paul II, *Evangelium vitae* (Vatican City, Vatican Press: 1995), sec. 19.

8. Thanks to our colleague, Peter Andrastek, for this sage advice.

9. See Romans 12:15.

10. Henri J.M. Nouwen, *Out of Solitude: Three Meditations on the Christian Life*, 1st Revised Edition (Notre Dame: Ave Maria Press, 2004), 40.

11. *Catechism*, 2635.

12. C. S. Lewis, *The Screwtape Letters: With Screwtape Proposes a Toast* (San Francisco: HarperSanFrancisco, 2001), 28.

13. St. Teresa of Calcutta, *Where there is Love, There is God: Her Path to Closer Union with God and Greater Love for Others* (New York: Doubleday, 2010), 190-191.

14. See *Compendium of the Social Doctrine of the Church*, chapter 4, for more information on the universal destination of goods.

15. See Pope Francis, *Laudato sí*, sec. 22, 106-108, 123.

WEEK 6
ENCOURAGE ONE ANOTHER

Encourage one another and build one another up.
– 1 Thessalonians 5:11

CONVERSATION SIX
Encourage One Another

OPENING PRAYER (2 MIN)
Select one person to open in prayer. Use the following prayer or your own words.

In the name of the Father, and of the Son, and of the Holy Spirit. Amen.

Heavenly Father, we remember your promise to be especially present "where two or three are gathered" in your name. Thank you for the ways you have met us and guided us this week. Help us continue growing in attentiveness to those you place in our lives. Shine your light through us into our families, neighborhoods, and workplaces. We invite you into our time together today. We pray this through Christ, our Lord, Amen.

CATCH UP (5 MIN)
Share highs and lows: one positive thing (a simple joy, gratitude, or blessing) and one challenge in your life since you last met.

REVIEW LOVE YOUR NEIGHBOR (10 MIN)
Discuss a few of the following questions.

- To whom did you send a hand-written note?
- What came to mind as you prayed about how to live one or more of the spiritual works of mercy?
- What about the corporal works of mercy?
- Which of the following passages from your prayer times stands out as most memorable and why?
  - St. Paul's chapter on the nature of Christian love in 1 Corinthians 13
  - Jesus identifying himself with "the least of these" in Matthew 25
  - The Lord's call for justice for the poor and afflicted in Isaiah 58
- Does anything from Balance and Boundaries, Care before Cure, or Intercessory Prayer stand out as particularly helpful or important to you?

ABOUT ENCOURAGE ONE ANOTHER (10 MIN)
Read aloud.

Scripture is full of exhortations to encourage one another. This means more than patting someone on the back and saying,

"You've got this." The word denotes a power to put *courage* into one another and build each other up. Through prayer, well chosen words that reflect the truth, and loving actions, we act as channels of God's own strength for one another.

By God's design, we all need the encouragement of others. We were never meant to follow Jesus alone. From the beginning, God created and called a community of believers, who would support, guide, and encourage each other.

In our modern Western worldview, we are lured into thinking that we need to go it alone, not ask for help, show up perfect. But what if Jesus were inviting us to a different way—a way where tax collectors learned from fishermen and where we need each other to keep forging the path ahead to our true Homeland?

Every member of the Church on earth is far from perfect. The same sins and weaknesses that beset the human race are found within the Church's walls and within her members. At the same time, you'd be hard-pressed to find another body on earth that has done more good together throughout the ages: feeding the poor, educating the masses, caring for the sick, and running into, not away from, the places most in need of justice and love. Still, the community of faith is not merely the sum of its collective strengths and weaknesses. Jesus himself, the source of our deepest encouragement, is present to the Church in a mysterious but real way; "For where two or three are gathered together in my name, there am I in the midst of them" (Matthew 18:20).

YOUR CHALLENGE THIS WEEK:

☐ Encourage one another by exchanging prayer intentions and praying for one another throughout the week. Write each others' stated intentions on notecards to carry as a reminder. Send a mid-week text to encourage each other and assure each other of your prayers.

☐ Reflect on the importance of intentional Christian community in living a Jesus-led life. The prayer guides will lead you to consider different aspects of this call to community, including the universal Church, the local parish, and a small network of holy friendships.

Discuss the following questions.

- Share the most life-giving experience of Catholic or Christian community you have known. What made it so special? How did it affect or change you?
- We grow the most when we're around others who inspire and build us up. Have you ever had the opposite experience of being negatively influenced by friends or community?
- Is it generally easy or difficult for you to make friendships?

READ AND DISCUSS (10 MIN)

Read aloud.

Hebrews 10:23-25, NRSV-CE

[23] Let us hold fast to the confession of our hope without wavering, for he who has promised is faithful. [24] And let us consider how to provoke one another to love and good deeds, [25] not neglecting to meet together, as is the habit of some, but encouraging one another, and all the more as you see the Day approaching.

Discuss the following questions.

- What reasons does the author of Hebrews give here for the Christian community to meet regularly?
- How is the experience of journeying together through the 10:10 Challenge an example of what the passage exhorts?
- Is there any other way you desire to "provoke one another to love and good deeds" and "encourage one another" besides your weekly meetings?

ENCOURAGE ONE ANOTHER (15 MIN)

Read aloud.

A theme running through the chapter you are about to begin is the need to "get real" with ourselves, with God, and with a few trusted friends. We need people in our lives who encourage us to live up to our commitment to following Jesus and who "provoke [us] to love and good deeds" (Hebrews 10:24, NRSV-CE). To truly encourage one another, we need relationships of trust where we are seen, known, and loved. You can intentionally build this kind of relationship with a few others.

The Second Vatican Council's document *Gaudium et spes* concerns the Church's role in the modern world. It begins with this paragraph:

> The joys and the hopes, the griefs and the anxieties of the people of this age, especially those who are poor or in any way afflicted, these are the joys and hopes, the griefs and anxieties of the followers of Christ. Indeed, nothing genuinely human fails to raise an echo in their hearts.[1]

Throughout the 10:10 Challenge you have shared with one another about your lives and about the ways you are growing in the Lord.

Take time now to ask each other about your joys and hopes and then your griefs and anxieties. Listen attentively, show compassion, and offer encouragement to one another.

- Each share about a joy or a hope in your life lately.
- Each share about a grief or an anxiety in your life lately.

CLOSING PRAYER (6 MIN)

Spend time intentionally praying for one another in your own words.

Pray in praise and thanksgiving for the joys and hopes shared and intercede for each other, asking for God's grace in the areas of grief and anxiety shared.

If there are two of you, each take a turn praying aloud for the other. If there are more than two of you, go around in a circle, praying for the person on your left.

In the name of the Father, and of the Son, and of the Holy Spirit. Amen.

(Pray for each person, both by giving thanks to God and by interceding on each person's behalf.)

Let us close in the Our Father together: Our Father, who art in heaven, hallowed be thy name; thy kingdom come; thy will be done on earth as it is in heaven. Give us this day our daily bread. And forgive us our trespasses, as we forgive those who trespass against us. And lead us not into temptation, but deliver us from evil. Amen.

NEXT MEETING (2 MIN)

Make sure you have your next discussion on the calendar.

PRAYER GUIDE
Encourage One Another

Day 1. Brighter Together

What came to be through him was life, and this life was the light of the human race; the light shines in the darkness, and the darkness has not overcome it.
— John 1:3-5

Every year, the Church begins the celebration of Easter with a simple and profound ritual: lighting a candle. After the betrayal of Holy Thursday, the suffering and death of Good Friday, the tomb of Holy Saturday—into the darkness of a world in need of a Savior—a small flame flickers into existence. "The light shines in the darkness, and the darkness has not overcome it."

Almost as soon as this candle is lit, it is shared. The Easter flame is passed from one candle to another until the whole church is awash in the gentle glow of light.

At Baptism, the priest says to the newly baptized: "Receive the light of Christ." We each hold this light and are given the grace and power of Christ to cut through the seemingly impenetrable darkness of our broken, sin-stained world. But when we're just one light shining alone, it seems like the darkness could easily suffocate or blot us out. Or even if the light of our faith feels secure, we can be tempted to hide it rather than let it shine before others.[2]

We need other believers who are also carrying the light of Christ to renew us, strengthen us, and build us up.

The Book of Ecclesiastes says "Two are better than one . . . If the one falls, the other will help the fallen one . . . Where one alone may be overcome, two together can resist. A three-ply cord is not easily broken" (4:9-10, 12). We each need deep Christian community and friendship with other disciples to sustain our faith in the midst of trials, doubt, and hardships. The joy of true fellowship uplifts our spirits and helps us to praise God. Like one candle lighting another, we rekindle each other and strengthen one another to shine like lights in the darkness.

OPEN TO GOD

Close your eyes and take a few deep breaths as you open to God.

In the name of the Father, and of the Son, and of the Holy Spirit. Amen.

Jesus, you are the light of the world. Come and shine your light into me as I give you this time in prayer today.

PRAY FROM THE HEART

Call to mind people who have stirred and strengthened your faith throughout your life. Use the questions below to jog your memory.

- Who first gave you the light of faith?
- Who helped light your way during a time in your life when the light of faith was particularly dim? Or who helped re-light your candle when it was nearly extinguished?
- Think of the person or people with whom you're journeying through this book. How do you see the light of Christ in them?
- Who have you been the light of Christ to? Who have you helped during a particularly dark or difficult stretch in their life?
- Who do you know whose light of faith seems to be dim or extinguished?
- The role of a godparent is to help keep the light of Christ burning brightly as the child is raised. Are you anyone's godparent?

Take some time now to give thanks for these people and intercede for them. As you did in Week 5, use the blessing below from St. Paul in Ephesians 1:17-19 (NRSV-CE) to aid your prayer. The pronouns have been changed so that the prayer addresses God and allows you to pray for the person or people you identified.

Just before this blessing, St. Paul writes, "I . . . do not cease giving thanks for you, remembering you in my prayers" (1:16). Begin your prayer by giving thanks for the people who have come to mind.

Heavenly Father, thank you for (name(s))_____.

I lift them up to you in prayer right now.

> *God of our Lord Jesus Christ, the Father of glory, . . . give [them] a spirit of wisdom and revelation as [they] come to know [you], so that, with the eyes of [their] hearts enlightened, [they] may know what is the hope to which [you] have called them, what are the riches of [their] glorious inheritance among the saints, and what is the immeasurable greatness of [your] power for us who believe, according to the working of [your] great power. Amen.*

What else do you want to bring to God today?

CLOSE

Take some deep breaths as you rest in God's presence for a few more minutes. Let him love you and dwell with you in this silence and solitude.

Thank you, Lord, for the light of faith. Send me to those who need the light you've given me. And continue sending to me those I need to keep my own light shining brightly.

In the name of the Father, and of the Son, and of the Holy Spirit. Amen.

Day 2. One, Holy, Catholic, and Apostolic

I believe in one, holy, catholic and apostolic Church.
— Nicene Creed

These four words are both true descriptions of the Church and what we must keep encouraging each other to be in every age. "The Church does not possess them of herself; it is Christ who, through the Holy Spirit, makes his Church one, holy, catholic, and apostolic, and it is he who calls her to realize each of these qualities" (*Catechism*, 811).

Think of how in baptism we have already died to sin and so live in Christ, yet we still need to turn away from sin and learn the ways of love until we are fully united with God in heaven. In the same way our whole Church is *already* one, holy, catholic, and apostolic and also *not yet* perfectly those things.

We are united as *one* Body of Christ and given life by *one* Holy Spirit. And yet, we experience the sadness of divisions in the Body of Christ. We are set apart and made *holy* by the power of Christ in the sacraments we receive. And yet, we are wounded by sin in ourselves and in our Church. We are grounded in the witness and teaching of Peter and the Apostles, handed down and proclaimed to each generation in an unbroken line of *apostolic* succession. And yet, we can struggle to know how to apply Jesus' teaching to our times. We are *catholic*, universal, embracing the whole world with Jesus' love and invitation to follow him into new life. And yet, many people have yet to encounter Jesus or the Church in a life-changing way.

As members of the Body who make up the Church, we all contribute to the Church's expression of these four attributes. In doing so, we benefit each other and become more credible witnesses to God's presence in our midst.

OPEN TO GOD

Close your eyes and breathe slowly and deeply as you open your-self to this time with God.

In the name of the Father, and of the Son, and of the Holy Spirit. Amen.

God, you are good; thank you for the gift of the Church. Open my eyes to see the beauty of your plan and open my heart to live as the disciple you're calling me to be.

PRAY FROM THE HEART

Since the Church (including you) is both *already* and *not yet* what it is called to be, the two responses of gratitude and lament, which we find readily in the Psalms, are appropriate when praying about the community of faith.

Start with gratitude.

> **Psalm 9:1-2, NRSV-CE**
> I will give thanks to the Lord with my whole heart;
> I will tell of all your wonderful deeds.
> I will be glad and exult in you;
> I will sing praise to your name, O Most High.

What are specific ways in which the Church is or has been a trea-sure and a blessing to you?

Spend some time thinking of specific people, experiences, places, or seasons in your life for which you are grateful. Take the time to thank God, once again, for each of these blessings.

Next, if you want, feel free to grieve and lament the ways the Church has not lived up to its calling—in your life or in the world.

> **Psalm 22:2**
> My God, my God, why have you abandoned me?
>   Why so far from my call for help,
>   from my cries of anguish?

What are specific ways you feel or have felt the imperfections, sins, shortcomings, and incompleteness within the Body of Christ on earth, the Church?

Cry out to God in lament and in supplication; invite Jesus into any feelings and thoughts that emerge.

End with an act of trust and any other prayers you wish to offer at this time.

Psalm 22:4-6
Yet you are enthroned as the Holy One;
  you are the glory of Israel.
In you our fathers trusted;
  they trusted and you rescued them.
To you they cried out and they escaped;
  in you they trusted and were not disappointed.

CLOSE

Rest in silence and solitude before your Maker, who both cele-brates and laments with you over the already and the not yet.

Jesus, you see all. I trust you, Lord; increase my trust. I love you; help me love you more. Thank you for receiving me just as I am, and for leading me on the everlasting path of life.

In the name of the Father, and of the Son, and of the Holy Spirit. Amen.

TIP: MEET NEW PEOPLE AT YOUR PARISH

Make an intentional effort to meet new people at your parish: whether before or after Mass, at social gatherings, through your kids' school, etc. Making these connections takes forethought and (for many of us) a bit of courage! If you notice someone at church who you'd like to meet, make an intentional effort to say hello and introduce yourself. While it may feel awkward to initiate a new relationship in this way, almost everyone delights in being seen and known by someone in their church community. It's as simple as reaching out your hand and saying, "Hi, I'm _____.
I don't think we've met." Then, use the Ten Tips for Better Conver-sations on page 164 to help you make conversation with new people you meet.

Day 3. Supply One Another's Needs

All who believed were together and had all things in common; they would sell their property and possessions and divide them among all according to each one's need.
— Acts 2:44-45

The Church has always banded together for the mutual benefit of all both spiritually and materially. Very early descriptions of the Mass even mention the custom of a collection for those in need during the celebration of the Eucharist: "Those who are well off, and who are also willing, give as each chooses. What is gathered is given to him who presides to assist orphans and widows, those whom illness or any other cause has deprived of resources, prisoners, immigrants and, in a word, all who are in need."[3]

While the Lord calls us to attend to the spiritual and material needs of others in our individual lives, we also do so together as a Church. Through the financial offerings of our community, we are able, together, to provide for the catechesis of children and adults, to sustain clergy and staff who build up the Body of Christ, to assist those without food or shelter, to maintain a clean and beautiful worship space that is attractive to newcomers and inspires reverence for God, to care for the sick and their families, and to support missionary efforts, among many other things.[*]

Giving financial offerings to the Church is rarely easy—we all have competing financial priorities to contend with; but when we can set aside a portion of our income as an offering to God in service of the Church, it helps us hold our belongings and material desires more loosely. We grow in appreciation that all we have is a gift from God, and we grow in godly love and concern for the people and causes that our gifts support. And when we are the beneficiaries of the gifts others have given, whether it be a sturdy roof to worship under or food on the table when money's run out, may we give thanks to God for the encouragement and support we have in one another.[†]

OPEN TO GOD

Turn your attention to God, who surrounds you and dwells within you.

In the name of the Father, and of the Son, and of the Holy Spirit. Amen.

Jesus, give me courage to pray about my relationship with money and my call to bless others with the financial resources you entrust to me. Come, Holy Spirit, I trust in you.

---

[*] "The Christian faithful are obliged to assist with the needs of the Church so that the Church has what is necessary for divine worship, for the works of the apostolate and of charity, and for the decent support of ministers. They are also obliged to promote social justice and, mindful of the precept of the Lord, to assist the poor from their own resources." *Code of Canon Law*, can. 222.

[†] See page 160 for more on our call to give.

PRAY FROM THE HEART

What concerns are you carrying into prayer today? Take a moment to entrust these into God's care.

Use the steps of *lectio divina* (read, reflect, respond, rest) to pray with the following passage. What is God's message for you in this passage today?

2 Corinthians 9:6-12, NRSV-CE

The point is this: the one who sows sparingly will also reap sparingly, and the one who sows bountifully will also reap bountifully. Each of you must give as you have made up your mind, not reluctantly or under compulsion, for God loves a cheerful giver. And God is able to provide you with every blessing in abundance, so that by always having enough of everything, you may share abundantly in every good work. As it is written,

> "He scatters abroad, he gives to the poor;
> his righteousness endures forever."

He who supplies seed to the sower and bread for food will supply and multiply your seed for sowing and increase the harvest of your righteousness. You will be enriched in every way for your great generosity, which will produce thanksgiving to God through us; for the rendering of this ministry not only supplies the needs of the saints but also overflows with many thanksgivings to God.

For help reflecting:

- When was the last time you prayed about and considered your financial giving?
- What percentage of your income are you currently able to give to the Church and other charities close to your heart? (Recall that supporting the local Church is one of the five precepts of the Church to which all baptized Catholics are called.[4])
- What virtues do you need in order to grow in freedom from worry over your finances and to bless others by sharing generously and joyfully? Courage, trust, decisiveness, greater communication with a spouse, detachment from certain luxuries, etc.?
- Do you need help in your financial planning that you aren't currently receiving? If so, who can you talk to? What next step would put you on a path to greater financial awareness, habits, or proactivity?

- Before you close, do a brief "notice, tell, invite" prayer with how you are feeling as you pray about your finances and the call to support the Body of Christ.

CLOSE

Rest in the love of God, who knows all the mixed feelings in you that might arise when thinking about money. Let him hold you in your gratitude, your worries, your imperfect trust, your open questions.

Jesus, you are King of kings and Lord of lords. Help me to be a cheerful giver. I give you permission to be the Lord of my life, my finances, my future, my present. Help me to follow your command to "store up treasures in heaven, where neither moth nor decay destroys, nor thieves break in and steal" (Matthew 6:20). May my treasure and my heart always be found in you.

In the name of the Father, and of the Son, and of the Holy Spirit. Amen.

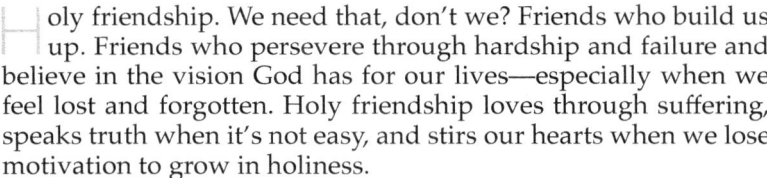

Day 4. Holy Friendship

In the world those who aim at a devout life require to be united one with another by a holy friendship, which excites, stimulates and encourages them in well-doing.[5]
– St. Francis de Sales

Holy friendship. We need that, don't we? Friends who build us up. Friends who persevere through hardship and failure and believe in the vision God has for our lives—especially when we feel lost and forgotten. Holy friendship loves through suffering, speaks truth when it's not easy, and stirs our hearts when we lose motivation to grow in holiness.

A holy friend is there when we need advice. They are a prayer warrior who will go to battle for us at the drop of a hat. They're someone with whom we have a regular and intentional practice of sharing our life in Christ.

"Iron is sharpened by iron; one person sharpens another" (Proverbs 27:17). Just as skilled athletes spur each other on to greater excellence, holy friendships spur us on to greater love of the Lord and pursuit of virtue. These relationships of trust both hold us accountable to a higher standard and offer a place for us to land when we fall.

Building a friendship like this takes time. We need to test the waters, dipping our toes into deeper vulnerability over time as trust is built. But when we finally let down our guard with the other person, then growth can happen. When we are truly known, we are able to give and receive the kind of love that calls us to live in a way that is worthy of the gospel.[6]

Whether you're introverted or extroverted, you won't regret pressing through the awkwardness or social pressure of making new connections. Giving time to making a new friendship or deepening an existing one is worth the investment. Truly, "faithful friends are beyond price; no amount can balance their worth" (Sirach 6:15).

OPEN TO GOD

Close your eyes and take some deep breaths as you open your heart to God.

In the name of the Father, and of the Son, and of the Holy Spirit. Amen.

Thank you, Lord, for the gift of friendship. When I experience authentic and holy friendship, let my heart be grateful beyond measure, and let my soul cling to you as my highest good. When I long for deeper friendships but do not see this gift in my life, help me cling to you all the more, trusting in your presence, your timing, and your love.

PRAY FROM THE HEART

Use the steps of *lectio divina* (read, reflect, respond, rest) to pray with the following passage.

Ecclesiastes 4:9-10, 12, NRSV-CE
Two are better than one, because they have a good reward for their toil. For if they fall, one will lift up the other; but woe to one who is alone and falls and does not have another to help . . . And though one might prevail against another, two will withstand one. A threefold cord is not quickly broken.

For help reflecting:

- How are you cultivating relationships with other disciples that support you in the ups and downs of life and faith? Pray about whether there are any friendships you could deepen by investing more time, opening up on a deeper level, or giving more attention to them. Ask God for any courage or initiative you need.
- If you currently feel disconnected, tell God about the sort of friendships you long to have. Ask him to bring the right

people into your life. Pray for both patience and persistence in this pursuit.

- If you already have deep and supportive friendships or relationships, pray for these people, especially for any struggles they are facing. How might you encourage them this week?
- Does this wisdom apply to your life in any other ways right now? Ask the Lord if there's something he is leading you to do in the near future in light of this passage.

CLOSE

Breathe deeply and rest in God's presence for a few moments before you close.

Holy Spirit, come and fill my heart, once again, with your goodness and love. Move me today and this week to be a good and encouraging friend to others, and to receive with gratitude those who you've placed in my life to encourage me. Grant me patience and perseverance always.

In the name of the Father, and of the Son, and of the Holy Spirit. Amen.

TIP: SHARE A WORD OF ENCOURAGEMENT

Encourage a fellow disciple by sending them a quick word of encouragement. If you're praying with a particular Scripture passage that you think would bless your friend, write it down on a note card to give to them or text them the passage. If you've both agreed to work on strengthening a discipleship habit and to keep each other accountable, send a quick message to remind one another to pray or get to Mass, etc. Touchpoints like these help you cheer each other on through your prayer and solidarity.

Day 5. Holy Conversation

What are you looking for?
— John 1:38

We can tell something about the nature of a friendship by looking at the types of conversations we typically have. Conversations are fueled by questions, whether implied or stated directly. For people we just like to have fun with, the implied questions behind our conversations might be: What made you laugh recently? What should we do (to avoid being bored) today?

For other relationships, perhaps at work or school, our conversations often center around shared projects. The questions behind these discussions are more utilitarian: How can we hit that deadline?

Relationships can also revolve around common interests and hobbies. Who do you think will win the Super Bowl? What are the best hiking trails around here?

Many of our relationships keep to these fun-focused or utilitarian types of conversations, and that's okay, but we need some relationships that go deeper. Deeper friendships include plenty of shared interests, practical matters, and fun, but they also have something more. At least occasionally they venture into sharing about the questions of the human heart.

In Scripture, the word "heart" refers to the deepest center of the person: one's core identity and true self. And every human heart is on a quest for meaning, purpose, truth, and goodness. It's one of the beautiful and unique gifts God gave humanity among other creatures on earth.

Jesus is the master of prompting questions of the heart. His questions cut through the noise and distractions. They're personal and deep.

"What are you looking for?" (John 1:38)

"What do you want?" (Matthew 20:21, NRSV-CE)

"Who do you say that I am?" (Matthew 16:15)

"What do you want me to do for you?" (Mark 10:51)

"Why are you afraid?" (Matthew 8:26, NRSV-CE)

Disciples of Jesus continually ask and answer not only the questions of Jesus, but also the deepest questions of their own hearts. And they long to share this quest with other disciples.

Before continuing your reflections on Christian community (which you'll do tomorrow), spend time in prayer today exploring some of the deeper terrain of your own heart.

OPEN TO GOD

Take a few deep breaths as you turn your heart to God.

In the name of the Father, and of the Son, and of the Holy Spirit. Amen.

Psalm 139:1-4, NRSV-CE
O Lord, you have searched me and known me.
You know when I sit down and when I rise up;

you discern my thoughts from far away.
You search out my path and my lying down,
    and are acquainted with all my ways.
Even before a word is on my tongue,
    O Lord, you know it completely.

Jesus, amid the noise and the activity of life, you alone know the depths of my heart. You know me better than I know myself. Guide me today in seeing more clearly the questions and longings of my heart.

PRAY FROM THE HEART

Peruse the following questions of the heart. Spend some time on whichever one or two your heart is drawn to ponder most. Or, feel free to write one of your own.

- What blessings from God are you savoring right now—or might you savor more of? What does it mean or look like for you to savor a blessing?
- Where or how are you being stretched or challenged? (Think of situations at work, health issues, family matters, etc.) Where is God for you in this?
- What do you feel the Lord asking you to trust him with right now?
- What decisions are you currently discerning or praying about? Or, what upcoming decisions do you desire to bring before the Lord?
- What negative emotions or thoughts do you find bubbling up from within yourself more often these days (fear, anger, resentment, jealousy, lust, etc)? How do you respond to them? Where is God in this for you?
- Is there a particular lie that you feel the enemy using to get under your skin and disturb your peace? If so, why do you think he chooses that specific lie? Is there a wound associated with that lie—some way you've been hurt, which made you more susceptible to believe it?

Next, imagine Jesus is sitting next to you. He looks at you with love in his eyes, and says, "What are you looking for? What do you want?"

What is your heart's response?

CLOSE

Rest in silence and solitude as God continues to work in the quiet of your heart.

Lord God, I trust you with the deepest question of my heart; increase my trust. I love you, Lord; increase my love. Lead me today to walk in your kindness, goodness, and truth.

In the name of the Father, and of the Son, and of the Holy Spirit. Amen.

TIP: AN OUTLINE FOR HOLY CONVERSATION

Whether you're meeting one-on-one with a close Christian friend or gathering with a small group for mutual encouragement in Christ, keep the following simple outline in mind to guide your conversations into holy and fruitful territory.

1. **Life:** Catch up briefly on what's happened since you last met.
2. **Growth:** Share what the Lord is up to in your lives, how prayer is going, and read some Scripture together.
3. **Mission:** Talk about whatever the Lord is calling you to do for others in this season of your life and share how it is going.

Encourage one another and follow the Spirit's lead as conversations flow from these topics. Bookend the discussion with opening and closing prayer, including interceding for one another, and you've got yourself a power-packed hour of holy conversation.

Day 6. Getting Real

Therefore, putting away falsehood, speak the truth, each one to his neighbor, for we are members one of another.
— Ephesians 4:25

Small talk is common courtesy and a part of life. Some people enjoy it, others endure it, others avoid it like the plague.

"How are you?"

"I'm fine. How are you?"

"Good."

"So, how about that weather?"

There's nothing wrong with small talk, of course, but it will never satisfy our deepest desires for relationship.

The Church is described as *one*, as *united*, as being in *communion* with each other and with God. It is a place where we should be able to find at least a few relationships that go beyond the surface level down to the deeper quests of our souls.

Yet for most of us, it can be difficult to find these kinds of relationships—in the Church or anywhere else. Being seen, known, and accepted by others is a fundamental human need, and we were created to receive and be received by others in these ways. So why is it so hard?

In a fallen, broken world being seen and known can be dangerous. What if others see my failures and imperfections and use them against me? What if they ridicule my dreams or the quirky things that make me, me?

There's no way around it, getting real with other people involves risk. They could hurt us. They could betray us. So, we conclude, perhaps it's safer to hide how we're *really* doing. Everyone else seems to be doing just fine, so that's how I'll act too. "I'm fine, how are you?" It seems safe, but eventually leaves us empty.

The risk could end in reward. They could receive us. They could strengthen us and build us up. They could understand us and even enjoy our quirks. Authentic discipleship invites us to interrupt the cycle of shallowness and "fine." It dares us to get real—not with everyone but with a trusted few. It challenges us to receive others' vulnerability with the compassion of Jesus and allow others to see and know our real selves.

OPEN TO GOD

Close your eyes and turn your attention to God.

In the name of the Father, and of the Son, and of the Holy Spirit. Amen.

Father, Son, and Holy Spirit, thank you for seeing me, for knowing me, and for loving me as I am. God, help me to find my deepest identity and security in your love for me. Please be with me during this prayer time and help me to be real with myself and with you.

PRAY FROM THE HEART

Relationship requires risk if it's going to get real. Be honest with God about any fears you may have of being real with the people in your life.

Use the steps of *lectio divina* (read, reflect, respond, rest) to pray with the following passage.

Philippians 2:1-11, NRSV-CE

If then there is any encouragement in Christ, any consolation from love, any sharing in the Spirit, any compassion and sympathy, make my joy complete: be of the same mind, having the same love, being in full accord and of one mind. Do nothing from selfish ambition or conceit, but in humility regard others as better than yourselves. Let each of you look not to your own interests, but to the interests of others. Let the same mind be in you that was in Christ Jesus,

who, though he was in the form of God,
did not regard equality with God
as something to be exploited,
but emptied himself,
taking the form of a slave,
being born in human likeness.
And being found in human form,
he humbled himself
and became obedient to the point of death—
even death on a cross.
Therefore God also highly exalted him
and gave him the name
that is above every name,
so that at the name of Jesus
every knee should bend,
in heaven and on earth and under the earth,
and every tongue should confess
that Jesus Christ is Lord,
to the glory of God the Father.

For help reflecting:

- St. Paul begins this passage with an exhortation to live united in one mind and heart. What gets in the way of you having that sort of close relationship with other disciples?
- What counsel does St. Paul give the Philippians about building community? How could you apply that counsel in your life?
- "We love because he first loved us" (1 John 4:19). Jesus initiated the relationship with us by humbling himself and making himself vulnerable to us. Is there someone in your life with whom you could initiate a deeper relationship by showing them respect, acceptance, or by being more vulnerable with them?

What else do you want to bring to God in prayer today? Share openly about whatever is on your mind and heart.

CLOSE

Receive God's love for you in a moment or two of quiet prayer.

God, you are my creator, savior, and friend. I praise you for knowing me better than I know myself and for loving me beyond what I can understand. Please help me to find real, true Christian friendships that show me your love and encourage me to live as the disciple you are calling me to be.

In the name of the Father, and of the Son, and of the Holy Spirit. Amen.

TIP: HAVE FUN TOGETHER! (IT'S SERIOUS BUSINESS)

Just because friendships are "holy" doesn't mean they have to be boring! Schedule time to have simple fun with your friends in the Lord. Do things you enjoy together whether that's playing a game of basketball, going bowling, sharing a meal or a drink, or seeing a concert together. It's *seriously* important to not be *serious* all the time. We need a healthy dose of fun in our relationships. It bonds us together in joy and is a taste of heaven.

Day 7. Bear with One Another

Bear with one another and, if anyone has a complaint against another, forgive each other; just as the Lord has forgiven you, so you also must forgive.
— Colossians 3:13, NRSV-CE

With all this talk of community and friendship, we might be tempted to concoct images of the perfect family, friends, Church community, or school. But real community isn't all sunshine and roses. It's hard. It's messy. It's made up of people, after all.

Our closest relationships can be the source of our deepest joy and our deepest pain. It's no wonder that many of the letters to early Church communities include instructions about how to live with each other—including living with others' faults and foibles. No two of us are created the same. God in his goodness decided to give us different skills, different strengths, different weaknesses. Sometimes these differences complement one another beautifully; sometimes they rub up against each other in painful, confusing, and terribly frustrating ways.

Jesus didn't sugarcoat his talk of community; he told us it would require forgiveness. And lots of it. "Then Peter approaching asked him, 'Lord, if my brother sins against me, how often must I forgive him? As many as seven times?' Jesus answered, 'I say to you, not seven times but seventy-seven times'" (Matthew 18:21-22). This doesn't mean that wrongs should go unaddressed—Jesus gives instructions about that, too. But he instructs us to forgive: restoring love for the other in our hearts and opening the possibility of reconciliation.

Intentionally withholding forgiveness hurts ourselves more than anyone else. So important is this command to forgive that Jesus spells out the harsh implications of ignoring it: "If you forgive others their transgressions, your heavenly Father will forgive you. But if you do not forgive others, neither will your Father forgive your transgressions" (Matthew 6:14-15). Strong words! Jesus gives us a solemn reminder of what it means to truly enter the stream of forgiving love that the Father lavishes upon us. Let us strive always to forgive each other as Christ has forgiven us.

OPEN TO GOD

Close your eyes and take some deep breaths as you open your heart to God.

In the name of the Father, and of the Son, and of the Holy Spirit. Amen.

Jesus, you prayed forgiveness over the very people who nailed you to the cross—while they were doing it. I cannot muster that kind of love on my own, Lord. Send me your Holy Spirit, that I might love more like you.

PRAY FROM THE HEART

Colossians 3:13, NRSV-CE
Bear with one another and, if anyone has a complaint against another, forgive each other; just as the Lord has forgiven you, so you also must forgive.

- Have you "had a complaint" against anyone recently? If so, pray for the grace to forgive them. Talk to God about any difficulties you have with this. Be honest. Ask for God's compassion and perspective.
- Is there anyone you have a hard time forgiving? Or someone you are consciously aware of not having forgiven? Trusting that he accepts you just as you are, tell Jesus how you feel as

you call this person to mind. Notice, tell, invite.*

- Have you hurt anyone and need to ask forgiveness? If so, ask the Lord to show you how to go about apologizing and seeking reconciliation.

Bring your desires to forgive and be forgiven to the Lord as you pray with the following passage. These are the words of Jesus' prayer to the Father after the Last Supper according to John.

John 17:11b, 20-23, NRSV-CE
Holy Father, protect them in your name that you have given me, so that they may be one, as we are one . . . I ask not only on behalf of these, but also on behalf of those who will believe in me through their word, that they may all be one. As you, Father, are in me and I am in you, may they also be in us, so that the world may believe that you have sent me. The glory that you have given me I have given them, so that they may be one, as we are one, I in them and you in me, that they may become completely one, so that the world may know that you have sent me and have loved them even as you have loved me.

CLOSE

Rest in the forgiving, healing, reconciling love of Jesus. Breathe deeply in his presence for a few minutes.

I need you, God. On my own I lack the strength to forgive those who have hurt me. But I believe with St. Paul, that "I have the strength for everything through him who empowers me" (Philippians 4:13). Grant me the grace I need to be a channel of your reconciling love today and this week.

In the name of the Father, and of the Son, and of the Holy Spirit. Amen.

---

*   Forgiveness is not always as simple as willing it, saying it, and moving on. Often we need time, healing, and the help of a counselor, spiritual director, or close friend to reach a point of letting go of our resentment and truly forgiving someone in our heart. If you're struggling with unforgiveness, talk to someone you trust about your desire and struggle to forgive. This could also include a struggle to forgive yourself or God.

MAKE IT A HABIT
Encourage One Another

Below, find tips and suggested readings for continuing to grow in intentional Chrisian community.

GATHER REGULARLY WITH OTHER DISCIPLES

Meet monthly with one or a few other disciples to build deeper friendships and support one another in life and discipleship. See page 192 for a basic outline to structure your conversations.

SEEK ONGOING FORMATION

Part of maturing in discipleship involves taking your need for ongoing formation seriously. One of the many gifts of the Church is that "we are surrounded by so great a cloud of witnesses" (Hebrews 12:1). The Church is a veritable treasure trove of some of the best minds, writings, speeches, teachings, and real-life stories of God in action. We all have an ongoing need to be re-inspired and re-evangelized by the gospel. We all have an ongoing need for deeper instruction and new pathways for understanding truth—about God, the world, others, and ourselves.

Who are your favorite people to learn from? Who inspires you to greater faith? What authors, contemporary or classic, make your heart beat faster for Jesus? What podcasts, YouTube subscriptions, or prayer guides help you to keep turning to Jesus and the Church for answers to your deepest questions? What local classes, workshops, or teachers are available to you that you might take more advantage of? What sacrifices of your time, money, or energy are you willing to make in order to ensure you are continually drawing deeply from the great cloud of witnesses that is the Church?

SERVE YOUR CHURCH COMMUNITY

Connect with other Catholics and support your community by participating in the ministries of your parish either at Mass (by lectoring/reading, as a Eucharist minister, ushering, etc) or in social or charitable activities sponsored by your parish. Getting to know other parishioners can help you experience the communal aspect of the Church and enrich your experience of worship. Investing your time and efforts into the health of your faith community can make it a better place for all to find and follow Jesus.

DEVELOP YOUR INTERESTS

One of the best ways to make new friendships is to invest time and energy cultivating your interests—not just religious interests, but hobbies, sports, and activities you enjoy. If you like art, take local painting classes to meet some new people who share this interest with you, or whatever your interest may be: playing soccer, sipping fancy bourbon, reading novels, learning a foreign language, etc. Do something you enjoy and meet new people in the process!

GET TO KNOW YOUR PARISH PRIESTS

Forming a good relationship with your pastor or any other priests serving at your parish can be a great blessing on both sides. Priests give their lives to service within the Church in a particular way, yet they are still very real human beings with likes, dislikes, and senses of humor! Start by inviting the priest(s) of your parish over to dinner to get to know them better. These men have taken particular vows to pray for, serve, and work for the good of the Church, including you! They are partners with the laity doing the work of God in the world.

ADDITIONAL RESOURCES

- *Catechism of the Catholic Church,* Part I, Chapter 3, paragraphs 811-835, 857-870
- *Transforming Discipleship,* Greg Ogden
- Small group discussion guides from the Evangelical Catholic. See the store page at *store.evangelicalcatholic.org*

DISCIPLESHIP PRACTICES
Encourage One Another

Discipleship Conversations

Aim for monthly life-growth-mission discipleship conversations with one or a few close Christian friends.

OPEN IN PRAYER

- One person opens in a brief prayer in their own words.

LIFE

- Spend a few minutes catching up with one another about how life has been since you last met.
- You might each share a high and a low (blessing and challenge).

GROWTH

- Each person shares an update on their relationship with God. For example:
  - How is prayer going?
  - What is God teaching or showing you lately?
  - How are you learning or growing?
- Recommended: read a short selection from Scripture or another trusted source and discuss how it applies to your lives.

MISSION

- Each person shares an update on their personal apostolate (the specific ways they are called to live and share the gospel).* For example, answer and discuss:
  - What does living and sharing the gospel look like for you right now?
  - How is it going? What joys and challenges are you experiencing?
  - What do you need this week or month to cling to Christ and to live your mission well?

---

* See the prayer times in Week 10 (starting on page 301), along with page 322 and following for help discerning your personal apostolate.

- What's your takeaway from the Scripture reading and discussion above? Is there anything to put into practice?

CLOSE IN PRAYER

- Intercede spontaneously for each other's needs and intentions.
- Perhaps close in a formal prayer such as the Our Father, Hail Mary, or Glory Be.

A Recipe for Intercession

Read through the following steps and examples, then pray.

1. **Talk directly to God**
   Use one of the names of God as you address him in prayer. Begin your prayer with "Jesus," "Heavenly Father," "Lord," "Holy Spirit," or "God."

2. **Be specific.**
   Pray for the person by name and be specific in your requests.

3. **Name the darkness.**
   What is broken or in need of help? What ought not to be? Where is sin or sickness causing fear, a lack of freedom, or pain? (For instance: "Jack doubts that you love him." "Lucia was diagnosed with cancer this week.")

4. **Ask for light in the name of Jesus.**
   What graces or virtues do you want God to impart? What could help the situation this person is in? What obstacles do you want God to remove? ("In Jesus' name, set loose faith in Jack's heart today." "Please give Lucia strength and heal her in the name of Jesus.")

5. **Make an act of trust or thanksgiving.**
   In the end, we trust God: that he is good, that he is able to fight for us, and that his will is the best answer to our prayer. ("Thank you for hearing my prayer, Lord." "I know you are always there for us, Jesus, I trust in you." "Your will be done, Father.")

PUT IT ALL TOGETHER

For example: "Heavenly Father, Lucia was diagnosed with cancer this week. Please give her your strength to fight, and please heal her in the name of Jesus. I trust you, God."

MAKE IT YOUR OWN

- Talk directly to God by name: _____
- Be specific: _____
- Name the darkness: _____
- Ask for light: _____
- Make an act of trust: _____

ENDNOTES

1. Second Vatican Council, "Pastoral Constitution on the Church in the Modern World, *Gaudium et spes*, 7 December, 1965," in *Vatican Council II: The Conciliar and Post Conciliar Documents*, ed. Austin Flannery (Collegeville, MN: Liturgical Press, 1975), sec. 1.

2. See Matthew 5:14-16.

3. St. Justin Martyr, *Apologia*, 1.67 quoted in *Catechism*, 1351. Justin wrote this in approximately 155-157 A.D.

4. See *Catechism*, 2043; *Code of Canon Law*, can. 222.

5. St. Francis de Sales, *Introduction to the Devout Life*, Vintage Spiritual Classics (New York: Vintage Books, 2002), 3.19.

6. See Philippians 1:27.

WEEK 7
FOLLOW GOD'S LEAD

My sheep hear my voice;
I know them, and they follow me.

– John 10:27

CONVERSATION SEVEN
Follow God's Lead

OPENING PRAYER (3 MIN)
Select one person to open in prayer. Use the following prayer or your own words.

In the name of the Father, and of the Son, and of the Holy Spirit. Amen.

Heavenly Father, we love you and we praise you today. Thank you for another opportunity to gather in your name, where you promised to be present. Thank you also for the ways you have met us and guided us this week. Holy Spirit, we invite you into our conversation today. You are welcome here; come and speak to us through one another and through your Word.

We pray this through Christ, our Lord, Amen.

CATCH UP (5 MIN)
Share highs and lows: one positive thing (a simple joy, gratitude, or blessing) and one challenge in your life since you last met.

REVIEW ENCOURAGE ONE ANOTHER (10 MIN)
Discuss a few of the following questions.

- The prayer times this week covered a number of topics including our experience of the Church, holy friendship, and forgiveness. Which prayer times affected you most?
- How do you feel about the call to support the Church and others with a portion of your finances? How can you grow in becoming a "cheerful giver" as 2 Corinthians 9:7 says?
- From day five: what is one of the "questions of the heart" you identified and prayed about, if you're willing to share?

ABOUT FOLLOW GOD'S LEAD (15 MIN)
Read aloud.

Any journey requires decisions: right or left, highway or low roads, drive-thru or sit down. Our adventure with Christ is no different. What to say to a grieving friend, whether to get married, how to correct a colleague, how much time to spend out with friends or home with family: our lives are full of decisions. So how do we make them?

God, the author of free will, gives us tools to help us sort through our options and choose well. We have our minds: both our logical, problem-solving skills and our empathetic, creative imaginations. We have our bodies: physical and emotional signals that can clue us in to deeper truths. We have our community: Scripture and the Church's teaching that give us wisdom and perspective from disciples across history, friends who know and care about us, spiritual mentors, advisors, or directors who can help us listen to God's leading. And we have the Holy Spirit dwelling within us, whom we can always call upon for guidance, wisdom, and strength.

Sometimes there is a clear choice between good and evil, but we still need courage to do what we know is right. But many times we need to decide between two (or more) *good* options with no obvious right or wrong way. Discernment helps us listen for God's voice and choose wisely. And even when we don't have perfect clarity, we're often nonetheless called to make the best choice we can. God will be there on the other side of the decision, come what may, to continue guiding us to him.

YOUR CHALLENGE THIS WEEK:

- ☐ Follow God's lead by practicing the skill of discernment. The daily prayer guides introduce the wisdom of St. Ignatius of Loyola,* whose Examen prayer and practical principles for discernment have guided millions of believers (over the course of five hundred years) to grow in responsiveness to God's promptings.

- ☐ Ask for the Holy Spirit's guidance in the midst of your daily activities. See the tip on page 204 for a few examples of how to do this.

Discuss a few of the following questions.

- Was there ever a time you felt clearly led by God in a decision? If so, how did you know God was speaking? What was that experience like?

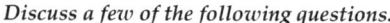

*   St. Ignatius of Loyola is the founder of the Society of Jesus, the Catholic religious order also known as the Jesuits. He lived from 1491 to 1556.

- Have you ever found it difficult to arrive at a big decision? Or perhaps just difficult to do what you knew God was calling you to? If so, how did you proceed, and what came of it?
- How do you typically make decisions? What role does God play in your decision making?
- What is a decision you're currently pondering or will be soon?

READ AND DISCUSS (20 MIN)

Read aloud.

The following selections from *Discernment: Reading the Signs of Daily Life* by Henri Nouwen focus on discernment as a way of listening.

> To discern means first of all to listen to God, to pay attention to God's active presence, and to obey God's prompting, direction, leadings, and guidance. . . .

> When we are spiritually deaf, we are not aware that anything important is happening in our lives. We keep running away from the present moment, and we try to create experiences that make our lives worthwhile. So we fill up our time to avoid the emptiness we otherwise would feel. When we are truly listening, we come to know that God is speaking to us, pointing the way, showing the direction. . . .

> The purpose of discernment is to know God's will, that is, to find, *accept*, and *affirm* the unique way in which God's love is manifest in our life. To know God's will is to actively claim an intimate relationship with God, in the context of which we discover our deepest vocation and the desire to live that vocation to the fullest. It has nothing to do with passive submission to an external divine power that imposes itself on us. It has everything to do with active waiting on a God who waits for us.

> Finding ourselves in a relationship with God is prerequisite to discernment of God's will and direction. As in any relationship, there will be feelings of rejection as well as attraction, resentment as well as gratitude, fear as well as love. There will be ups and downs in faithfulness as

we discover new things about ourselves and God. In our dynamic relationship with God, we can be sure of one thing: "If we are faithless, God is faithful still, for God cannot disown his own" (2 Timothy 2:13).

Acceptance of God's will does not mean submission or resignation to "whatever will be will be." Rather, we actively wait for the Spirit to move and prompt, and then discern what we are to do next.[1]

Discuss the following questions.

- What is your reaction to Nouwen's characterization of discernment as "a life of listening"?
- How does Nouwen describe our relationship to God's will? Does anything he writes surprise or challenge you?
- Do you take any comfort in Nouwen's honest description of a relationship with God in the second to last paragraph ("As in any relationship…")?
- Is there anything else in this excerpt you find meaningful or want to discuss?

NEXT MEETING (2 MIN)

Make sure you have your next discussion on the calendar.

CLOSING PRAYER (5 MIN)

Choose someone to lead the closing prayer time. Use the prompts below or your own words. Invite the other(s) to add their prayers when you prompt them.

In the name of the Father, and of the Son, and of the Holy Spirit. Amen.

God, thank you for the fellowship and conversation we are blessed to share here. Thank you for promising to dwell with us and to guide us always. With St. Paul we ask "that [we] may be filled with the knowledge of [your] will in all spiritual wisdom and understanding so that [we] may lead lives worthy of [you,] Lord" (Colossians 1:9-10, NRSV-CE). Help us tune into your Holy Spirit in the coming week, even more than we have in the past. Speak, Lord, your servants are listening.

We also lift up our petitions and intercessions to you. In particular we ask for _____, _____. What else should we pray for? (Allow time for others to share their prayers as well.)

Thank you for always hearing our prayers and for leading us along the path of life.

Let us pray together: Glory be to the Father, and to the Son, and to the Holy Spirit, as it was in the beginning, is now, and ever shall be, world without end. Amen.

PRAYER GUIDE
Follow God's Lead

Day 1. Noticing God's Presence

I am with you always.
— Matthew 28:20

In order to follow God's lead, we need to grow in awareness of his presence and movements in the regular events of our lives. Being a disciple isn't only for specific prayer times or sacramental moments. When St. Paul exhorts us to "pray without ceasing" (1 Thessalonians 5:17) he doesn't envision us locking ourselves in a church and never coming out! We can pray without ceasing by inviting God into every moment and learning to recognize his closeness at all times.

The French priest Jean Pierre de Caussade coined the phrase, the "sacrament of the present moment" to indicate the potential each moment holds as a place of encounter with the living God. Our defined times of prayer teach us to notice and get a feel for God's presence and character. If we've never seen someone before, it's hard to pick them out of a crowd. Likewise, getting to know Jesus through mental prayer, Scripture reading, and our experience of the sacraments allows us to notice him in other moments. But once we know him, we can recognize his Spirit dwelling with us even in the middle of a busy day.

One way to grow in awareness of God's presence in the moment is to reflect back over the day. A football coach watches game footage both to see opportunities for the team to improve and to understand their opponent better. Hindsight is twenty-twenty. In today's prayer, you'll use the Ignatian Examen, a method taught by St. Ignatius of Loyola, for reviewing the day with God. In this exercise, we allow God to pull us through our memory of the day—skipping through some moments quickly and slowing down at the ones he highlights to take a closer look. With a little distance, we can see what went well, what we missed, and the tactics of the enemy that tripped us up. This process helps us notice where God was present and how we responded to his invitations to follow him in the events of our lives. Over time, we become tuned in to Jesus' presence and invitations in real time and grow in responsiveness to his call.

OPEN TO GOD

Quiet your mind and body. Take a few deep breaths and settle into this time of prayer.

In the name of the Father, and of the Son, and of the Holy Spirit. Amen.

God, you have promised to be with me always. I place myself in your presence now.

PRAY FROM THE HEART

Use the steps of the Ignatian Examen[2] below to review the last twenty-four hours.

Give Thanks

What are you grateful for today? Give thanks for the big and small blessings of the last day.

Ask for Light

Invite the Holy Spirit to lead this prayer time. Ask for the grace to see your day from his perspective. Use the prayer below or your own words:

Come, Holy Spirit. Please lead this prayer time. Help me to see my day through your eyes. Protect me from self-condemnation and self-congratulation. Help me focus on what you want me to see.

Review the Day

Letting God lead you, review the last day going hour by hour. Skim over events or moments that don't seem significant. Slow down at any points that the Holy Spirit highlights. Try to recall the movements of your spirit in response to these significant moments.

- What do you notice about your spiritual and/or emotional state in those moments?
- Was Jesus inviting you to say/do/think/feel something?

- If so, did you respond to, ignore, or reject that invitation?

Give Thanks and Seek Forgiveness

Continue to give thanks for any blessings you notice as you review your day. Thank God for the times you were aware of his invitations in the moment and responded with generosity.

When you encounter moments in your day where you ignored or rejected God's invitations or sinned in any way, ask God for forgiveness.

Ask for Grace

Look ahead to your upcoming day:

- What graces or help do you need to follow God's lead more attentively?
- What resolutions or changes do you want to make?

Ask God for whatever you need to live according to his calling for your life.

CLOSE

Rest in God's presence for one or two minutes of silent prayer.

Holy Spirit, thank you for showing me your presence and action in my life. Help me grow in awareness of your presence. I want to follow you more closely today.

In the name of the Father, and of the Son, and of the Holy Spirit. Amen.

TIP: LOOK FOR THE SPIRIT'S PROMPTINGS

Try following God's lead in the little details of your day. For instance, when you enter a party or social event where you don't know many people, make a silent prayer asking God to lead you to the person he wants you to talk to. Follow any nudges you sense and see what happens! Sitting on a bus or plane? Ask the Holy Spirit to direct your attention to someone who needs your prayers and pray for that person, even if you don't know what they need.

Day 2. Desires

I delight to do your will, O my God;
your law is within my heart.

– Psalm 40:8, NRSV-CE

What role does *desire* play in the choices we make for our lives? Many of us have first-hand experiences of what can go wrong when we make choices based simply on what we *want* or *feel like* doing. But St. Ignatius believed that even though our desires can be disordered by sin, most desires are good at their root. Following God's lead entails looking at our varying desires in light of our deepest reason for being and our ultimate goal.

For instance, what could seem on the surface to be a desire for professional success may be—deeper down—a desire for security or a desire for the approval of parents who were never easy to please. Knowing our deeper desires frees us to re-ground ourselves in God's love and care. With that solid foundation in place, we can then sort out if greater success in our career would open up doors that would allow us to bring God greater glory (certainly possible!) or if it would lead us away from God into greater self-reliance.

Our deepest desires are God-given. God made us for joy! But it can take some work and practice to uncover these. Understanding our desires aids us in discerning the vocation(s) and missions he's calling us to undertake in life, which, in turn, lead us deeper into that joy for which we were created. This doesn't mean that life will ever be free from suffering and hardship, of course. This world, marred by sin and brokenness at every turn, is always, to some extent, a "valley of tears" compared with the glory of heaven. Yet, when we approach important decisions as opportunities to follow God's lead, we can learn the "peace . . . that surpasses all understanding" (Philippians 4:7), and the joy that endures even through pain, sadness, and hardship.

In today's prayer time, practice reflecting on the role of desire in your daily life by praying another Examen, this time paying attention to various desires you experienced in the last twenty-four hours.

OPEN TO GOD

Ready yourself for prayer in your usual way.

In the name of the Father, and of the Son, and of the Holy Spirit. Amen.

God, you are the author of my best and deepest desires. Thank you for putting these desires within my soul. Your love is better than life. Be with me during this time of prayer.

PRAY FROM THE HEART

Use the steps of the Ignatian Examen below to review the last twenty-four hours.

Give Thanks

What are you grateful for today? Give thanks for the big and small blessings of the last day.

Ask for Light

Invite the Holy Spirit to lead this prayer time. Ask for the grace to see your day from God's perspective, especially regarding your desires. Use the prayer below or your own words:

Come, Holy Spirit. Please lead this prayer time. Help me to see my day and my desires through your eyes. Help me focus on what you want me to see.

Review the Day

Letting God lead you, review the last day going hour by hour.

- What are some of the desires you experienced today? (They might be simple and surface level or deep and meaningful. They might be strong or weak. They might be healthy or unhealthy.)
- Pick one that stands out and reflect a bit more. Where does this desire come from? How deep or shallow is it? How strongly did you experience it?
- Does it align with God's purpose for your life or pull you away from it? Or is this cloudy or uncertain?
- How did you respond to it?
- Did you experience any holy inspirations or great desires today? (A person who inspired you, a sense of passion or deep longing for something good and holy, a daydream of being more loving, virtuous, or effective in some way?)
- Talk to God about any emotions or thoughts that emerge as you reflect on your experiences of desire over the last day. Is there anything for which you need his healing or help?

Give Thanks and Seek Forgiveness

Continue to give thanks for any blessings you notice as you review your day. If there are any moments when you ignored or rejected God's invitations or sinned in any way that come to light, ask God for forgiveness.

Ask for Grace

Look ahead to your upcoming day. Ask the Holy Spirit for whatever you need to live according to your deepest, God-given desires, and to grow in self-control over the shallow or unholy desires you may experience.

CLOSE

Rest in God's unending care for you in a minute or two of silence and stillness.

Father, I offer you all the desires of my heart—those that lead me to you, and those that lead me astray. Come and fill me once again with your love, that I may desire you more and more as my highest good and final goal.

In the name of the Father, and of the Son, and of the Holy Spirit. Amen.

Day 3. Principle and Foundation

Human beings are created to praise, reverence, and serve God our Lord, and by means of this to save their souls. . . . [Thus,] I ought to desire and elect only the thing which is more conducive to the end for which I am created.[3]
– St. Ignatius of Loyola

I n the "Principle and Foundation" of his *Spiritual Exercises,* St. Ignatius advises beginning with the end in mind. Knowing the goal of our lives puts things into perspective and helps us make decisions. We can judge the worth of all created things or potential decisions by the question: Is this helping me honor God and live with him forever in heaven?

When we face important decisions, certain options often attract us more than others at first glance. Keeping the goal in mind can help us detach from that initial judgment and take a step back to weigh our options according to our ultimate desire to follow Jesus. If we're closed off to any of the choices before us, then we're not really discerning. But when our deepest desire is to follow God's lead, we have what Ignatius calls "indifference." This doesn't mean that we don't care—not at all! It means we are "ready to serve God in any capacity God wishes."[4]

To use a common example: a young man finds himself attracted to elements of both priesthood and marriage and wants to discern his vocation. He may at first be somewhat afraid of the commitment of priesthood or religious life. If he ignores this path simply out of fear, his decision was not made in true freedom and discernment. In a better process, he would recall the ultimate goal of his life, open himself to both options as best he could, and trust that the path God called him along would ultimately be the best one for him. If he ends up choosing the lay vocation, he will have done so as a path to draw close to God and not merely out of fear or avoidance.

This certainly isn't easy. It requires faith in God's goodness and trust in his love for us. Yet following St. Ignatius's advice helps us approach any situation—big or small—with the heart of a disciple.

OPEN TO GOD

Take a few deep breaths and sit in silence as you open to God and prepare for prayer.

In the name of the Father, and of the Son, and of the Holy Spirit. Amen.

I was created to praise, reverence, and serve you both now and forever, Lord. So I begin this prayer today in praise. God, you are good beyond all things. You are _____ (fill in your own words of praise and honor. See page 108 for a list of ideas).

Free my heart, Lord, from preferring anything above or apart from you. Please guide my prayer today. Increase my love for you and my desire to be with you forever in heaven. Amen.

PRAY FROM THE HEART

Pray with this passage and with the points of reflection below.

Philippians 3:4-14, NRSV-CE

If anyone else has reason to be confident in the flesh, I have more: circumcised on the eighth day, a member of the people of Israel, of the tribe of Benjamin, a Hebrew born of Hebrews; as to the law, a Pharisee; as to zeal, a persecutor of the church; as to righteousness under the law, blameless.

Yet whatever gains I had, these I have come to regard as loss because of Christ. More than that, I regard everything as loss because of the surpassing value of knowing Christ Jesus my Lord. For his sake I have suffered the loss of all things, and I regard them as rubbish, in order that I may gain Christ and be found in him, not having a righteousness of my own that comes from the law, but one that comes through faith in Christ, the righteousness from God based on faith. I want to know Christ and the power of his resurrection and the sharing of his sufferings by becoming like him in his death, if somehow I may attain the resurrection from the dead.

Not that I have already obtained this or have already reached the goal; but I press on to make it my own, because Christ Jesus has made me his own. Beloved, I do not consider that I have made it my own; but this one thing I do: forgetting what lies behind and straining forward to what lies ahead, I press on toward the goal for the prize of the heavenly call of God in Christ Jesus.

St. Paul had done everything "right" in the eyes of his community, yet he came to realize that no identity, status, or accomplishment compared to "knowing Christ Jesus my Lord."

Think about what is most important to you, what you have worked hard to accomplish or what is most meaningful to you.

- How does knowing Christ Jesus surpass even these good things in your life? If you're not sure, tell Jesus you desire to know him more, that you might one day say these words along with St. Paul.
- What motivates St. Paul, according to this passage?
- Think again about those things that are most important in your life. In what ways do they help you "praise, reverence, and serve God" as St. Ignatius put it?

With great love, St. Ignatius and St. Paul both put knowing and being with Jesus as the most important goal in their lives.

- In what ways do you want to follow their example?
- If something comes to mind that you know is getting in the way of your relationship with Jesus, ask him for the grace and forgiveness you need to find freedom.

CLOSE

Jesus has claimed you and made you his own. Rest in his love for you for a couple of minutes.

Close with the following prayer of Thomas Merton:

My Lord God,
I have no idea where I am going.
I do not see the road ahead of me.
I cannot know for certain where it will end.
nor do I really know myself,
and the fact that I think I am following your will
does not mean that I am actually doing so.
But I believe that the desire to please you
does in fact please you.
And I hope I have that desire in all that I am doing.
I hope that I will never do anything apart from that desire.
And I know that if I do this you will lead me by the right road,
though I may know nothing about it.
Therefore will I trust you always though
I may seem to be lost and in the shadow of death.
I will not fear, for you are ever with me,
and you will never leave me to face my perils alone.[5]

In the name of the Father, and of the Son, and of the Holy Spirit. Amen.

TIP: DETERMINE WHAT IS IN YOUR CONTROL

An obvious, yet often forgotten truth is that not everything is within our power to control or change. Our freedom to respond to God in the ways we discern him calling us can be curtailed by other peoples' decisions (for instance, we discern we want a certain job, but our application is rejected). Or we may not have the freedom to change a decision we made in the past. Many saints and martyrs were imprisoned, tortured, and killed by people not acting in accord with God's desires. Even when external circumstances or situations are outside of our control, we still have the freedom to praise, reverence, and serve God there. Ask God how you can use your current disappointment or suffering to bring him glory. What decisions *are* within your control? How can you grow in faith, hope, and love even in the midst of hardship? How can this trial become fruitful for your salvation and that of others?

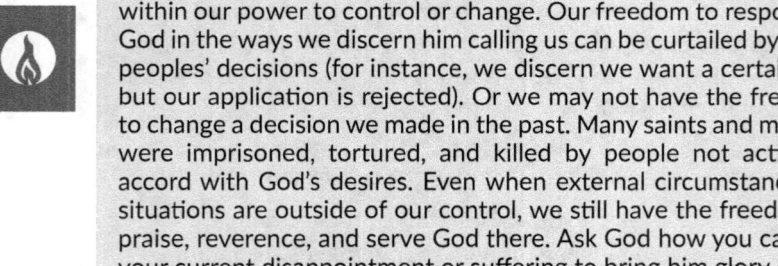

Day 4. Consolation and Desolation

Beloved, do not trust every spirit but test the spirits to see
whether they belong to God, because many false prophets have

gone out into the world.
–1 John 4:1

As he was recovering from a severe leg injury, Ignatius imagined two different lives for himself: one patterned after the knights of heroic tales and the other patterned after the lives of the saints. He noticed this difference:

> When he was thinking of those things of the world he took much delight in them, but afterwards, when he was tired and put them aside, he found himself dry and dissatisfied. But when he thought of going to Jerusalem barefoot, and of eating nothing but plain vegetables and of practicing all the other rigors that he saw in the saints, not only was he consoled when he had these thoughts, but even after putting them aside he remained satisfied and joyful. . . .
>
> . . . Little by little he came to recognize the difference between the spirits that were stirring, one from the devil, the other from God.[6]

Though both lines of thought pleased him in the moment, they had different effects on his spirit over time. The one brought only passing pleasure, while the other left a sustained gladness. Discernment allows us to notice how God and spirits contrary to God are at work in our inner selves. An increase in virtues (like faith, hope, and love) or the fruit of the Spirit (joy, peace, patience, kindness, generosity, faithfulness, gentleness, and self-control) are good indications of God's leading. The absence of them should cause us to stop and reconsider.

Ignatius calls these two movements "consolation" versus "desolation."[7]

Consolation may be experienced as:	**Desolation** may be experienced as:

• Increases in faith, hope, and love	• Decreases in faith, hope, and love
• Sadness over sin	• Turmoil and agitations of soul
• Desire to praise and serve God	• Temptations and downward impulses
• Interior joy that attracts one towards the things of heaven	• Feeling listless, tepid, unhappy
• Tranquility and peace in God	• Feeling separated from God

With practice and God's help, we too can discern these movements of our souls to follow the path that leads us to abundant life.

OPEN TO GOD

Settle into prayer in your usual way.

In the name of the Father, and of the Son, and of the Holy Spirit. Amen.

Holy Spirit, come to my aid. Please give me the gift of discernment of spirits. Help me to be more aware of the movements of your Spirit within me. I want to listen to the ways you are leading me. Give me the grace of awareness today.

PRAY FROM THE HEART

Begin by asking God to bring to mind an upcoming decision or opportunity you will need to discern soon. You'll pray about this decision over the next few days, using different discernment exercises from the Ignatian tradition. If nothing comes to mind, take this opportunity to pray about whether God is calling you to give some of your time or money to a charitable cause. Use that question as the subject of your discernment over the next few prayer times.

Clarify the Question at Hand

Do your best to articulate the pending decision clearly and simply. For instance:

- Should I talk to my colleague about that issue or not?
- Should I accept job A or job B?
- Which colleges should I apply to?

- How is God calling me to use my time outside of work?
- How should I use a portion of my finances to bless others?

Sometimes a decision can be worded as a yes or no question. Or you may have two clear options to choose between. Still other times, you need to sort through multiple options before you make a decision.

Write out the question you're discerning (here or in a journal).

_____

_____

_____

Desires: What's most important to you in this decision? Ask God to show you your deeper desires and hopes for your life that this decision affects.

_____

_____

_____

Principle and Foundation: Recall your deepest purpose: "Human beings are created to praise, reverence, and serve God our Lord, and by means of this to save their souls."[8] St. Ignatius teaches us to try to detach from our initial preferences and wishes (to achieve a level of initial detachment or "indifference"), so that we can better discern which paths most lead us to our ultimate goal.

Indifference: With respect to the question you are discerning, what initial desires and preferences might you need to suspend or step back from, for a bit, in order to truly consider the matter with freedom and openness? Write them down here or in a journal.

_____

_____

_____

Consolation/Desolation: Now imagine choosing one of the possible paths. Take a few minutes to sit quietly before God with this decision, paying attention to the movements deep within you. Do you notice anything that seems like either consolation or desolation as you imagine this particular path? (You might not be able to tell just yet, and any considerations should be tentative and provisional at this point. You're not looking for a definitive answer, but trying to begin noticing any movements toward or away from peace, love, virtue, etc.)

As time allows, do the exercise again with an alternative path in mind.

_____

_____

_____

CLOSE

Stay with Jesus for a few minutes more, resting silently in his presence.

Jesus, thank you for this time of prayer. Continue to enlighten my heart and mind. Help me to notice and pay attention to my deepest desires, where you speak to my soul. I desire you, Lord. Lead me along your path of peace, joy, and salvation.

In the name of the Father, and of the Son, and of the Holy Spirit. Amen.

TIP: NO MAJOR CHANGES IN DESOLATION

St. Ignatius advises against making any major changes when we're in a period of desolation. In such a state, the temptations of the devil seem easy and sweet, and we are not attracted to the freedom and life God offers. We can't trust our instincts. Guard against making bad decisions in desolation by persevering in spiritual practices and by relying on your community to hold you up.

Even though desolation tempts us to move away from God and our community, it is the time we need these supports the most. Ignatius writes that during desolation, "when the enemy of human nature turns his wiles and persuasions upon an upright person, he intends and desires them to be received and kept in secrecy."[9] Tell a priest, spiritual director, or fellow disciple about such thoughts and temptations to bring them into the light and to help you sift through the competing voices to find God's truth.

Day 5. Using Reason

Do not conform yourselves to this age but be transformed by the re-

newal of your mind, that you may discern what is the will of God, what
is good and pleasing and perfect.
– Romans 12:2

Making decisions with God's guidance involves using the natural resources he created us with, including our minds and intellects as well as the discernment of spirits within. Though we rarely know every detail and eventual outcome of a decision set before us, discernment invites us to give time to the process, dedicating space in our lives to think through and pray about the decision before making a choice.

Take for example a woman considering a job in a new city. She decides to use St. Ignatius' guidelines for making a decision. First, she defines the decision before her as clearly as possible: "Should I apply for the job or not?" Then, she reminds herself of her desire to praise, reverence, and serve God with her life. She considers whether it's a decision she has the freedom to make and determines she will certainly need to consult with her husband and family as she discerns the path ahead. Neither option seems like it would lead her away from God. She is discerning between two goods and trying to determine which would be *better* and give *greater* glory to God. She asks for the grace to be truly open to either option: applying for the job or passing it up.

Next, the woman has some work to do: she needs to gather information and understand as much as she reasonably can about the implications related to the decision. Doing so requires talking to the people affected and researching the job, area, and costs involved.

Then, she needs to bring all of these factors to prayer, asking the Holy Spirit to help her sift through and weigh them according to what is truly best for her, her family, and God's call on her life. She pays attention to the movements of her spirit, looking out both for consolation and desolation as she considers where the Lord is leading.

Today, continue praying with the decision you defined last time using Ignatian decision making techniques.

OPEN TO GOD

Center yourself on God, preparing yourself for prayer.

In the name of the Father, and of the Son, and of the Holy Spirit. Amen.

God, I come to you today in love and trust. Guide me according to your will. Help me notice how you are leading me in this decision making process.

PRAY FROM THE HEART

Recall the question you are discerning, which you defined yesterday. Today, use an Ignatian decision making technique you are likely familiar with: a pro and con list.[10] There are six points in the exercise, some of which overlap with what has been covered already.

1. Bring the decision in question before you, to call it to mind.

2. Recall the ultimate end for which you were created (to praise, reverence, and serve God for all eternity) and try to detach from what Ignatius calls "any disordered affection" for one particular option. This, once again, is called *indifference*. "I should find myself in the middle, like the pointer of a balance."[11]

3. Ask for God's guidance. In the words of St. Ignatius, "Beg God our Lord to be pleased to move my will and to put into my mind what I ought to do in regard to the matter proposed."[12] Take a moment now to ask for God's help in your own words.

4. Make the list of pros and cons for each alternative you are considering. What are the benefits and dangers of each option? For example:

Pros:

- What benefits would choosing this path bring to your life?
- What benefits would it bring to those closest to you?
- How would choosing this path allow you to honor God?
- How would it call you to greater faith, hope, or love?

Cons:

- How would this path cost you or cause hardship?
- What costs or hardships would it bring to those closest to you?
- How would choosing this path make it more difficult for you to honor God?

- What temptations would this path expose you to?

5. Look back at your lists. In order to avoid judging solely by emotion or feeling, try to "see to which side reason more inclines."[13] Keeping in mind your ultimate goal and your lists of pros and cons, which path seems to make the most sense? Ask God to help you see which of these factors is most important. Underline or circle one to three factors that stand out as especially weighty.

6. Seek confirmation. Once you have arrived at which option you think is best (this may not happen in one sitting), offer this decision and thought-process to the Lord, asking him to receive it and confirm it. The exercises we'll cover in the next few days can help in seeking clarity and confirmation.

CLOSE

What else do you want to talk to God about today?

Offer your decision making process to God once again, as you dwell for a few moments in silence with him.

God, again, I put my decision before you. Please help me notice the movements of your Holy Spirit. Help me to discern well and listen for your direction in this and every other decision.

In the name of the Father, and of the Son, and of the Holy Spirit. Amen.

Day 6. Using Imagination

May the eyes of [your] hearts be enlightened,
that you may know what is the hope that belongs to his call.
– Ephesians 1:18

maginative prayer can open a space for Jesus to reveal insights to us that rational thinking alone cannot always show us. It engages our physical, emotional, and interpersonal experiences, unlocking self-knowledge that can go deeper than words. We don't look to use our imaginations to overrule, contradict, or work completely separate from reason, but to complement it with insights that might otherwise go undiscovered.

St. Ignatius suggests three imaginative exercises to anyone seeking to make an important decision.[14]

1. Imagine someone you have never met before. You are im-

partial and desire only this person's true good—that they would choose whichever path would best allow them to glorify God and grow closer to him. This person is faced with the same decision you have before you. Imagine what advice you would give this person.

2. Imagine yourself at the end of your life, on your deathbed. Looking back on your life, and on the decision currently before you, which path will you have wished you had followed?

3. Imagine yourself on judgment day, standing before Jesus. In that moment, which decision will you have wished you had made?

In addition, a fourth can be done outside of your prayer times. Imagine that you have chosen one way or another, and then live with that decision for a set period of time, perhaps a few days or weeks. Through your imagination, you are, in essence, trying on the decision as you would a pair of shoes. Notice what feelings, thoughts, consolations, or desolations come to you as you walk around in this decision. Do you experience greater peace or anxiety? Are you more motivated to love God and others generously?

Next, "try on" and live with an alternative decision in the same manner, staying attentive to the movements of your mind and heart. Continue bringing all these experiences into prayer, asking God to help you come to a place of confidence in choosing well.

OPEN TO GOD

Ready yourself for prayer in your usual way.

In the name of the Father, and of the Son, and of the Holy Spirit. Amen.

Holy Spirit, I continue to bring before you the question I am discerning this week. I desire to put my imagination at your service. Come and fill my heart once more with your love; guide my thoughts and imaginings by the light of your truth.

PRAY FROM THE HEART

Give thanks to God for any blessings of the last twenty-four hours.

Recall the question you are discerning.

Choose one or more of the three imaginative exercises described above: advice to a stranger, your deathbed, or the day you meet Jesus face to face after death.

Spend several minutes imagining the scenario, and think about your pending decision from that vantage point. What advice do you give the stranger? Or what decision feels right from the perspective of those moments just before or after death?

CLOSE

Jeremiah 29:11-13 NRSV-CE
For surely I know the plans I have for you, says the Lord, plans for your welfare and not for harm, to give you a future with hope. Then when you call upon me and come and pray to me, I will hear you. When you search for me, you will find me; if you seek me with all your heart.

Rest for a few moments in the promise of the Lord's care over you and your future.

My Lord and my God, I trust in your promise to never leave me. Continue to guide my imagination, my reason, and my will into alignment with you. Grant me the courage and clarity to move forward with confidence.

In the name of the Father, and of the Son, and of the Holy Spirit. Amen.

Day 7. Make a Decision

He resolutely determined to journey to Jerusalem.
– Luke 9:51

Eventually, the process of discernment comes to an end: we need to make a decision. How do you know you're ready to make a decision?

Sometimes, we just *know*, deep in our bones, that one path is the way God is calling us. Further thought and prayer confirms this intuition and no other option even comes close to competing.

Often, however, we eventually notice a sustained sense of peace or "rightness" emerge as we think and pray with one option over the others. Once we have prayed and consulted with those involved and feel called to a certain path, it's time to make a decision, even if we are not entirely sure.

For many decisions, no option stands out as the obvious best choice. In these cases, we can only do our best to listen to God's guidance and choose the option that seems better than the rest.

We can trust that he will continue to guide us in the future this choice opens to us. He is always ready to lead us to himself, even if we regret a decision we've made in the past or have to live with difficult consequences.

Before fully committing to the decision, however, Ignatian practice advises making a *tentative* decision. Make the decision in your mind and heart (without making any outward changes or declarations) and live with that decision for a period of time (a few days or even more if your timeline permits). Ask God to confirm your intention through a consolation or sign during this time or, if this is not the path he wants for you, to alert you with experiences of desolation. If God confirms the decision in some way or nothing makes you question your decision, move forward in the path you have discerned.

OPEN TO GOD

Turn your mind and heart to God as you take a few deep breaths.

In the name of the Father, and of the Son, and of the Holy Spirit. Amen.

Jesus, you are the Way, the Truth, and the Life. I want to follow you, Lord. Lead me today and every day.

PRAY FROM THE HEART

Use the steps of the Ignatian Examen below. Today, instead of looking back over the last twenty-four hours, widen your view to take in the last few days as you have pondered a decision, paying attention to any movements of consolation, desolation, or clarity.

Give Thanks

What are you grateful for from your time of discernment? Give thanks for the big and small blessings you have experienced.

Ask for Light

Invite God to lead this prayer time. Ask for the grace to see your decision making process from his perspective. Use the prayer below or your own words:

Holy Spirit, you are so good to me. I trust you, God. I rely on you and need you. Be with me here, today. Guide my prayer time. Help me to see any decisions you are inviting me to make.

Review the Day

Allowing God to guide you, review the events of your last few days. Skim over events or moments that don't seem significant. Slow down at any points that the Holy Spirit highlights. Try to recall the movements of your spirit in response to these significant moments.

- What do you notice about your spiritual and/or emotional state in those moments?
- In what ways did you notice the Holy Spirit's prompts or guidance?
- What evidence of consolation or desolation do you notice?
- What events, thoughts, or interactions seemingly led to the consolation or desolation?
- How did you respond?

Give Thanks and Seek Forgiveness

Continue to give thanks for any blessings you notice as you review. Thank God for the times you were aware of his presence and guidance.

When you encounter moments where you ignored or rejected God's invitations or sinned in any way, ask God for forgiveness.

Ask for Grace

Ask God for whatever you need to live according to his calling for your life.

- What graces or help do you need to follow God's lead more attentively?
- What resolutions or changes do you want to make?
- What information or clarity do you need in order to make a decision?

Depending on the importance of the decision you are praying with, you may need to take more time than just these few days to gather information, weigh your options, and discern the movements of your spirit.

If, however, you are ready to come to a tentative decision, write that out here:

_____

_____

_____

CLOSE

Offer your decision to Jesus now. Be prayerfully attentive to him in one to two minutes of silence, listening for anything he wants to reveal to you in response.

God, I leave this decision in your hands. Give me the grace to want only what you want. If the decision I am leaning toward will bring you greater glory, Lord, please give me confirmation and peace about it. Protect me from making a decision that would draw me away from you.

In the name of the Father, and of the Son, and of the Holy Spirit. Amen.

MAKE IT A HABIT
Follow God's Lead

Below, find tips and suggested readings for continuing to grow in following God's lead.

SEEK GOD'S GUIDANCE DAILY

Following God's lead is not only for big, life-altering decisions. Bring your daily decisions and deliberations to prayer, talking with God about the situations of your life. As you have learned elsewhere in this book, God speaks to us through the Scriptures, the Sacraments, and the community of the Church. Be attentive, awaiting his word in answer to your prayers. "I wait for the Lord, my soul waits and I hope for his word. My soul looks for the Lord more than sentinels for daybreak" (Psalm 130:5-6).

PRAY A DAILY EXAMEN

Pray the Ignatian Examen you practiced in this chapter as part of your daily prayer routine. Many people find it particularly fruitful to pray the Examen in the evening or before bed to review their day. St. Ignatius proposes praying it twice a day: once midday and once in the evening. Whether you add it to your morning, midday, or evening prayer, praying the Examen daily can help you notice God's presence and action in your daily life and increase your readiness to respond to his invitations on a daily basis.

FIND A SPIRITUAL DIRECTOR

Spiritual directors receive special training to help others discern God's movements and direction in their lives. Meeting with a spiritual director regularly is helpful at any stage of life, but particularly during a period of important discernment. The spiritual director will pray with and for you and guide you to notice patterns or indications of God's leading that they see. Their perspective can help you unearth assumptions and look at your decision from a different point of view. Meeting monthly is a typical rhythm for spiritual direction, though some people meet more or less often. Talk to your parish priest or your local diocese for recommended spiritual directors in your area. Many directors will schedule a trial session with you so you can see if your pairing is a mutually good fit before setting regular appointments. Look for someone you resonate with, whose relationship with God is evident, and whose advice you trust and respect.

MAKE A RETREAT

Getting away for a few days or more to focus solely on your relationship with God can help you hear his voice more clearly. Retreats vary in length and content but the goal is to get away from the bustle of everyday life in order to spend longer stretches of time with the Lord in quiet prayer. Look up Catholic retreat centers in your area to see if there are any monasteries or centers nearby that offer guided or self-guided retreat accommodations for lay people. Many retreat centers offer three-, five-, eight-, or even thirty-day retreats guided by a spiritual director. Alternatively, create a self-directed retreat by reserving a quiet weekend in a cabin or space closer to nature (lake, mountain, forest, etc.) where you can have quiet alone time with God. If an overnight retreat isn't possible for you, consider getting away to a church, shrine, or other peaceful place within driving distance where you can spend three-to-four hours alone with God. Make retreats regularly (perhaps annually) for a set-apart time to connect with God and seek his direction. If you are discerning a particular vocation to the priesthood or religious life, contact the vocations office to find out about retreats specifically geared toward your vocational discernment.

ADDITIONAL RESOURCES

- *Discernment: Reading the Signs of Daily Life*, Henri Nouwen
- *God's Voice Within: The Ignatian Way to Discover God's Will*, Mark E. Thibodeaux, SJ
- *Reimagining the Ignatian Examen: Fresh Ways to Pray from Your Day*, Mark E. Thibodeaux, SJ
- *The Way of Discernment: Spiritual Practices for Decision Making*, Elisabeth Liebert
- *Reimagining the Examen* app

DISCIPLESHIP PRACTICES
Follow God's Lead

Ignatian Examen

Use the steps of the Ignatian Examen* below to review the last twenty-four hours.

GIVE THANKS

What are you grateful for today? Give thanks for the big and small blessings of the last day.

ASK FOR LIGHT

Invite the Holy Spirit to lead this prayer time. Ask for the grace to see your day from his perspective. Use the prayer below or your own words:

Come, Holy Spirit. Please lead this prayer time. Help me to see my day through your eyes. Protect me from self-condemnation and self-congratulation. Help me focus on what you want me to see.

REVIEW THE DAY

Letting God lead you, review the last day going hour by hour. Skim over events or moments that don't seem significant. Slow down at any points that the Holy Spirit highlights. Try to recall the movements of your spirit in response to these significant moments.

- What do you notice about your spiritual and emotional state in those moments?
- Was Jesus inviting you to say, do, think, or feel something?
- If so, did you respond to, ignore, or reject that invitation?

GIVE THANKS AND SEEK FORGIVENESS

Continue to give thanks for any blessings you notice as you review your day. Thank God for the times you were aware of his invitations in the moment and responded with generosity.

---

*   See St. Ignatius, *The Spiritual Exercises*, sec. 44. We also recommend Fr. Mark Thibodeaux S.J.'s useful book, *Reimagining the Ignatian Examen: Fresh Ways to Pray from Your Day* (Chicago: Loyola Press, 2015).

When you encounter moments in your day where you ignored or rejected God's invitations or sinned in any way, ask God for forgiveness.

ASK FOR GRACE

Look ahead to your upcoming day:
- What graces or help do you need to follow God's lead more attentively?

- What resolutions or changes do you want to make?

Ask God for whatever you need to live according to his calling for your life.

Rules for Discernment of Spirits

St. Ignatius developed the following (and more) ways to identify and tell the difference between interior movements in our souls.[*] These rules help us identify which of these movements is good (and thus to be welcomed and followed) or bad (and thus to be ignored or rejected). These movements can originate in ourselves, from a good spirit (God or an angel), or from an evil spirit.[†]

1. For a person moving away from God and going from one mortal sin to another, the evil spirit's suggestions feel sweet and desirable, while the promptings of the good spirit sting their conscience and bring remorse.

2. The person earnestly renouncing sin and moving progressively toward God experiences the opposite. For this person, the suggestions of the evil spirit typically cause anxiety, unsettledness, sadness, and obstacles. In contrast, the good spirit awakens courage, strength, devotion, consolations, inspirations, and peace of mind.

3. Remember the nature of spiritual consolation. Consolation moving within the soul stirs up a great love for God, even to tears. Consolation includes all increases of faith, hope, and

---

[*] The following paraphrased summary is based on sections 313-321 of St. Ignatius's *Spiritual Exercises*.

[†] See Fr. George E. Ganss, S.J., ed., "Notes for The Exercises, Discernment," 130-132 in Ignatius of Loyola's *Spiritual Exercises and Other Works*, (New York: Paulist Press, 1991), 424-425.

love and every interior joy that draws a person toward heavenly things and to desire the salvation of their soul, bringing joy, peace, and tranquility.

4. Remember the nature of spiritual desolation. Movements of desolation bring everything contrary to that of consolation such as darkness of soul, turmoil, downward impulses toward low and earthly things, agitation, and temptation. Desolation moves a person away from faith and leaves them without hope or love. The person is completely listless, lukewarm, and unhappy, and feels separated from God.

5. A person should not make changes during times of desolation. Instead, they should stay firm and constant in whatever inclinations and decisions they made before the desolation set in. The evil spirit seeks to give counsel in times of desolation, but a person can never find the way to a right decision by following his guidance.

6. While a person should not alter their life decisions while in desolation, they should make vigorous changes within themselves to fight against the desolation such as recommitting to prayer, meditation, self-examination, and other habits that reorient the person to God.

7. A person in desolation should exercise patience, remembering that consolation will return again. While in consolation, a person should savor and store up the strength received and make plans for how to deal with future desolations.

8. The enemy of human nature desires a person to keep the temptations and persuasions of the evil spirit secret and hidden. When a person reveals them to a spiritual director or other spiritual person the enemy is disappointed because his lies and wiles have been detected.

ENDNOTES

1. Henri J. M. Nouwen with Michael J. Christensen and Rebecca J. Laird, *Discernment: Reading the Signs of Daily Life* (New York: Harper One, 2013), 5, 8.

2. See St. Ignatius, *The Spiritual Exercises*, sec. 44. We also recommend Fr. Mark Thibodeaux S.J. 's useful book, *Reimagining the Ignatian Examen: Fresh Ways to Pray from Your Day* (Chicago: Loyola Press, 2015).

3. St. Ignatius, *The Spiritual Exercises*, sec. 23.

4. Thibodeaux, *Reimagining the Ignatian Examen*, 167.

5. Thomas Merton, *Thoughts in Solitude* (New York: Farrar, Straus and Giroux, 1956), 79.

6. St. Ignatius, *The Autobiography*, sec. 8 in *Ignatius of Loyola: Spiritual Exercises and Selected Works*, The Classics of Western Spirituality, trans. George E. Ganss (New York: Paulist Press, 1991).

7. See St. Ignatius, *The Spiritual Exercises*, sec. 316, 317.

8. Ibid., sec. 23.

9. Ibid., sec. 326.

10. See Ibid., sec. 181.

11. Ibid., sec. 179.

12. Ibid., sec. 180.

13. Ibid., sec. 182.

14. See Ibid., sec. 186, 187, 188.

WEEK 8
CALL ON MARY AND THE SAINTS

Pray for one another, that you may be healed. The fervent prayer of a righteous person is very powerful.

– James 5:16

CONVERSATION EIGHT
Call on Mary and the Saints

OPENING PRAYER (3 MIN)

Select one person to open in prayer. Use the following prayer or your own words.

In the name of the Father, and of the Son, and of the Holy Spirit. Amen.

Thank you for meeting us in our prayer times last week. Come and be with us in our conversation as we gather today. Lead us into a deeper appreciation for your Mother and for all the saints who point us to you and offer us their prayers. In your name we pray, Amen.

CATCH UP (5 MIN)

Share highs and lows: one positive thing (a simple joy, gratitude, or blessing) and one challenge in your life since you last met.

REVIEW FOLLOW GOD'S LEAD (15 MIN)

Discuss a few of the following questions.

- Did you remember to consciously ask for and follow the Holy Spirit's promptings this week? If so, what came of it? Share about any way you stepped out in faith or did something you wouldn't otherwise have done.
- What question did you pray about for your discernment exercises? Do you feel you made any progress towards a good decision?

- Which of the following concepts or prayer experiences stand out as most helpful and why?
  - The Examen prayer
  - Ignatius' principle and foundation and holy "indifference"
  - Consolation and desolation
  - Praying over pros and cons
  - Using your imagination to give advice to a stranger, consider your deathbed, or reflect on Judgment Day
  - "Trying on" a decision mentally for a while before committing to it

ABOUT CALL ON MARY AND THE SAINTS (15 MIN)

Read aloud.

The promise of Baptism is a mystical union with Christ that frees us not only from sin but from the consequence of sin—death itself. United to Jesus, we are invited to resurrection, to life ever-lasting. As St. Paul puts it: "If, then, we have died with Christ, we believe that we shall also live with him" (Romans 6:8). The people we call saints are those who responded to this invitation in their lives and who now share in Christ's resurrected life in Heaven.

We may be tempted to think saints are some special breed of people who float or glow or stay in prayer for hours on end. While it's true that many saints experienced God in supernatural ways, this is not at all a prerequisite for holiness. In fact, many saints would say with Pope Benedict XVI: "Holiness, the fullness of Christian life, does not consist in carrying out extraordinary enterprises but in being united with Christ, in living his mysteries, in making our own his example, his thoughts, his behaviour."[1] In truth, the Church teaches that *all* of us are called to this holiness and fullness of Christian life, following God faithfully however he leads us.

Since the early centuries of the Church, we have venerated and asked for the prayers of those disciples who did just that. Alive in God and purified of all sin, the saints exist in perpetual love of God and neighbor. They are praying for us to be completely united with Jesus (and all of them!) in heaven. Calling on Mary and the saints helps us follow Jesus as we are inspired by their example and strengthened by their prayers. Let's ask them to pray for our needs. God is pleased to answer their prayers on our behalf; indeed, "the fervent prayer of a righteous person is very powerful" (James 5:16).

YOUR CHALLENGE THIS WEEK:

- ☐ Call on Mary and the saints, reflecting on your life in light of their witness. The daily prayer guide will lead you through several ways of doing this.

- ☐ Pray the Angelus daily (See page 260). For seven days, set a reminder on your phone for noon or some other time when you can stop daily for two minutes to pray this traditional prayer and offer your day to the Lord through Mary's intercession.

Discuss a few of the following questions.

- What is your experience of Mary and the saints? What role have they played in your life of discipleship?
- There are some common misunderstandings about the Catholic practice of praying to Mary and the saints. For example, when we pray to the saints, we don't worship them; our worship is reserved *only* for God. But we do believe that, by God's design, they can hear us and intercede for us. What questions or struggles do you have about the practice of calling on Mary and the saints for their prayers?
- Do you have a favorite saint or two? If so, what about their life speaks to you? How or when do you call upon their help?
- What is your experience of praying the Angelus and the Rosary, if any?

READ AND DISCUSS (15 MIN)

Read the following excerpt from the document Lumen gentium *of the Second Vatican Council aloud.*

Until the Lord shall come in His majesty . . . some of His disciples are exiles on earth, some having died are purified, and others are in glory beholding "clearly God Himself triune and one, as He is"; but all in various ways and degrees are in communion in the same charity of God and neighbor and all sing the same hymn of glory to our God. For all who are in Christ, having His Spirit, form one Church and cleave together in Him. Therefore the union of the wayfarers with the brethren who have gone to sleep in the peace of Christ is not in the least weakened or interrupted, but on the contrary, according to the perpetual faith of the Church, is strengthened by communication of spiritual goods. For by reason of the fact that those in heaven are more closely united with Christ, they establish the whole Church more firmly in holiness, lend nobility to the worship which the Church offers to God here on earth and in many ways contribute to its greater edification. For after they have been received into their heavenly home and are present to the Lord, through Him and with Him and in Him they do not cease to intercede with the Father for us, showing forth the merits which they won on earth through the one Mediator between God and man, serving God in all things and filling up in their flesh those things which are lacking of the sufferings of Christ for His Body which is the Church. Thus by their brotherly interest our weakness is greatly strengthened.[2]

Discuss the following questions.

- The passage states that death does not weaken or interrupt the communion we have with those who have passed into heaven, but that our communion, in some ways, is actually *strengthened*. What do you think this means? Have you ever sensed the ongoing closeness, or perhaps a new kind of closeness, of a loved one after they have passed away?
- How does this picture of the one Church in different stages or places speak to you or encourage you?
- If you haven't shared already above, do you have any experiences of closeness with a particular saint you felt was in some way reaching out or getting your attention?
- What four or five different things does the passage say that the faithful in heaven do for us on earth?
- What else stands out to you from this excerpt?

NEXT MEETING (2 MIN)

Make sure you have your next discussion on the calendar.

PRAY TOGETHER (5 MIN)

Choose someone to lead the closing prayer time. Use the prompts below and add your own words. Invite the other(s) to add their prayers when you prompt them.

In the name of the Father, and of the Son, and of the Holy Spirit. Amen.

God we praise you for the amazing mystery of the Communion of Saints. Thank you for surrounding us with such a great cloud of witnesses, both in heaven and on earth. Help us call upon them and receive their help to follow you always, wherever life may bring us. Lead us to a deeper love for your Mother, and help us understand that she is our Mother too.

Mary our Mother, thank you for your prayers and protection; thank you for always leading us closer to your Son. We lay our petitions before you now, asking you to pray for us.

In particular, we pray for _____; _____; _____. What else should we pray for?

We close together with the Hail Mary: Hail Mary, full of grace, the Lord is with thee; blessed art thou among women, and blessed is the fruit of thy womb, Jesus. Holy Mary, Mother of God, pray for us sinners now and at the hour of our death. Amen.

PRAYER GUIDE
Call on Mary and the Saints

Day 1. A Cloud of Witnesses

Therefore, since we are surrounded by so great a cloud of witnesses, let us also lay aside every weight and the sin that clings so closely, and let us run with perseverance the race that is set before us, looking to Jesus the pioneer and perfecter of our faith.
– Hebrews 12:1-2, NRSV-CE

Imagine stepping out to compete in front of a crowd of total strangers—or worse! A crowd that is cheering *against* you. Isn't there a big difference between that and the feeling of having even a few friends or family members in the crowd cheering you on? Now imagine that everyone in the crowd is cheering *for* you and wants you to succeed. Wouldn't your confidence and joy soar as you realized a crowd of loving support surrounded you? There's a reason sports teams do better when they play at home.

Having the love and support of Christian friends gives us the confidence to stay true to our commitment to follow Jesus even when it's unpopular or we're among a crowd that stands against us. But even if we are physically alone in those spaces, the truth is, we are *always* surrounded by a crowd of people pulling for us.

The faithful who have gone before us into eternal life—the saints—are cheering us on in heaven, praying for us to have the strength of heart to receive all that God wants to give us. They are vying for us to be heroic in virtue, lavish in love and mercy, devoted to intimacy with Jesus.

Learning about the lives of the saints inspires and strengthens us to live as they lived, in our own way and circumstances. We don't worship the saints—worship is reserved only for God. But we can and should ask them to pray for us, just as we ask faithful friends to pray for us when we're struggling and in need of spiritual support. The saints are in our corner through every situation we face. "They do not cease to intercede with the Father for us. . . . Thus by their brotherly interest our weakness is greatly strengthened."[3]

OPEN TO GOD

Take a few moments to open to God in your usual way.

In the name of the Father, and of the Son, and of the Holy Spirit. Amen.

Come, Holy Spirit. Surround me with your presence. Surround me with your saints and angels. Strengthen my faith in the company of heaven, strengthen my hope that one day I will join them rejoicing in your presence.

PRAY FROM THE HEART

Do you have a saint who is associated with your name? If you were confirmed in the Catholic faith, who did you choose as your patron saint? Or, if neither of these apply, is there any saint that comes quickly to mind when you think of the saints?

Briefly ask for this saint's intercession for this prayer time and for whatever is on your heart or mind today.

St. _____, please pray for me, that I would draw close to Jesus as you did and hear his voice. I lift up my intentions and concerns today for your intercession. Please pray for. . .

Pray with this passage using *lectio divina*.

Hebrews 12:1-4, 11-13, NRSV-CE
Therefore, since we are surrounded by so great a cloud of witnesses, let us also lay aside every weight and the sin that clings so closely, and let us run with perseverance the race that is set before us, looking to Jesus the pioneer and perfecter of our faith, who for the sake of the joy that was set before him endured the cross, disregarding its shame, and has taken his seat at the right hand of the throne of God.

Consider him who endured such hostility against himself from sinners, so that you may not grow weary or lose heart. In your

235

struggle against sin you have not yet resisted to the point of shedding your blood. . . .

Now, discipline always seems painful rather than pleasant at the time, but later it yields the peaceful fruit of righteousness to those who have been trained by it.

Therefore lift your drooping hands and strengthen your weak knees, and make straight paths for your feet, so that what is lame may not be put out of joint, but rather be healed.

For help reflecting:

- Whose example of faithfulness inspires you and urges you to keep following Jesus? What about them do you want to imitate?
- The author of Hebrews says that Jesus endured his suffering knowing that beyond it lay the joy of sitting at the right hand of the throne of God in heaven. How does the promise of life with God in heaven motivate you in this life?
- This passage refers to some of the difficulties of fidelity to God. When have you been faithful to following Jesus even when doing so caused you pain, humiliation, or struggle? What fruit did this discipline yield in your life?
- Is there any area of your life that God is calling you to be more disciplined about or to seek healing in?

CLOSE

We are made to dwell in God's presence. Spend a minute or two now resting in the Father, Son, and Holy Spirit.

Jesus, you are the leader and perfecter of my faith. Lead me Lord, into a deep faith that overcomes any obstacle that would keep me from the joy of being with you forever in heaven. Unite me more and more to you, dear Jesus.

In the name of the Father, and of the Son, and of the Holy Spirit. Amen.

Day 2. Gloriously Different

There are different kinds of spiritual gifts but the same Spirit; there are different forms of service but the same Lord; there are different workings but the same God who produces all of them in everyone.
— 1 Corinthians 12:4-6

God is not a one-hit-wonder. Our marvelous Creator has breathed dust into life in billions of unique human beings since Adam. "Each of us is the result of a thought of God. Each of us is willed, each of us is loved, each of us is necessary."[4]

The saints have been all sorts of people: popes, farmers, young, old, desperately poor, royalty, extroverted, introverted, scholars, soldiers, slaves, and simple cooks. The saints exhibit different spiritualities and different vocations. They have lived and died in all corners of the world. They are united by having found their life in Christ. Beyond that, they are, as C.S. Lewis writes, "gloriously different."

> Until you have given up your self to Him you will not have a real self. Sameness is to be found most among the most 'natural' men, not among those who surrender to Christ. How monotonously alike all the great tyrants and conquerors have been: how gloriously different are the saints.[5]

We can be tempted to think of holiness as static, a place where we arrive and then remain. But the dynamism of the saints proves this thought wrong. Losing their lives in Christ, they have truly found their lives in him. Recreated in his image, the saints are mysteriously even *more* themselves. They are wonderfully unique, shining as a beautiful kaleidoscope that reveals God's splendor.

They are models for us, but not to copy in all the particulars. They show us that finding our life in Christ is both possible and worthwhile. They take joy in pointing us to the One they love beyond all else. When we imitate their commitment to Jesus, we, too, come alive in him and become uniquely who he created us to be.

OPEN TO GOD

Open yourself to God in a couple of minutes of silence.

In the name of the Father, and of the Son, and of the Holy Spirit. Amen.

God, you have created me in love and goodness. Help me trust you to make me into the person you have in mind for me to become. I believe, Lord, that you who began a good work in me will continue to complete it until the day I meet you in heaven.

PRAY FROM THE HEART

Reflect on the lives of the following saints from various backgrounds, experiences, and cultures. This is obviously a short selection—the Catholic Church recognizes over 10,000 saints! Read each short biography, and ask for that saint's intercession.

St. Joseph

St. Joseph was the husband of Mary, Mother of God, and adoptive father to Jesus. His constant care, companionship, and protection of Mary and Jesus shine through in the Scriptures. He is described as a carpenter and a righteous man who responded to the angel's instructions he received in his dreams. He is the patron saint of fathers, workers, and the universal church.

St. Joseph, patron of fathers and workers, pray for us.

St. Francis of Assisi

St. Francis of Assisi renounced his wealthy upbringing for an itinerant life of prayer, poverty, and care for the sick. He founded the Franciscan order in 13th century Italy. Francis saw the goodness of God mirrored in creation and even called animals and the earth his brothers and sisters. He is the patron saint of animals and ecology.

St. Francis, brother to the poor, the earth, and all creatures, pray for us.

St. Thérèse of Lisieux

St. Thérèse of Lisieux grew up in a very loving and faith-filled family in 19th century France. From an early age she desired to live her vocation as a religious sister and petitioned Pope Leo XIII to allow her to join the Carmelites at age fifteen. She died of tuberculosis at age twenty-four. Despite living a short, hidden life, the spirituality of her "Little Way" (recognizing her littleness and entrusting herself to Jesus to lift her up to heaven) has spread across the world.

St. Thérèse of Lisieux, Little Flower of Jesus and patron of missionaries, pray for us.

Blessed Miguel Pro

Blessed Miguel Pro was a Jesuit priest from Mexico at the turn of the twentieth century when anti-Catholic Mexican political entities engaged in a violent power struggle with the Catholic Church, killing and driving out many people of faith and religious leaders. Fr. Miguel Pro ministered to an "underground" church, secretly providing the Eucharist and other Sacraments to Catholics until he was falsely accused and executed without trial in 1927. As he faced the firing squad, he reportedly forgave his executioners and shouted, "¡Viva Cristo Rey!" "Long live Christ the King!"

Blessed Miguel Pro, example of persevering faith and courageous care for others despite persecution, pray for us.

St. Teresa of Avila

St. Teresa of Avila was a Spanish nun and mystic in 16th century Spain. She, along with St. John of the Cross, established a reformed version of the Carmelite order, traveling, advocating, and raising funds to found over a dozen convents and monasteries. She wrote descriptively of her experiences of God in prayer, both about her struggles through dry, distracted times and about the heights of mystical union with God.

St. Teresa of Avila, patron of those suffering headaches and great example of intimacy with Jesus, pray for us.

St. Augustine of Hippo

St. Augustine of Hippo lived in North Africa in the 4th century. He was an intellectual giant who struggled with lust and pleasure seeking. After his conversion to Christianity in his thirties, his writings and explanations formed a firm philosophical and theological foundation for the Christian faith that has informed centuries of Christian thought.

St. Augustine, help of those struggling with lust and intellectual doubts, pray for us.

St. Josephine Bakhita

St. Josephine Bakhita was born in Sudan around 1869 and kidnapped by slave traders when she was seven or eight years old. She spent over twenty years enslaved, in some cases by incredibly cruel owners. Josephine first encountered Christianity while staying with the Canossian sisters in Venice, Italy while her mistress was traveling. When her owner returned, Josephine refused to leave and, with the help of the Church community, petitioned for her freedom. After the Italian courts ruled she had been enslaved illegally her entire life, Josephine was baptized and subsequently joined the Canossian sisters with whom she lived, prayed, and served the local community for fifty years, until her death in 1947.

St. Josephine Bakhita, patron of victims of human trafficking and help of those suffering abuse and injustice, pray for us.

Sts. Louis and Zélie Martin

Sts. Louis and Zélie Martin were a married couple in 19th century France. Zélie gave birth to nine children, four of whom died in childhood. Both Louis and Zélie were career people: Louis as a watchmaker and Zélie as a highly skilled lacemaker in what was a competitive industry at the time. Zèlie managed a team of other lacemakers, and she and Louis ran her business from their home. They created a home environment where five daughters grew in love and devotion for Jesus, the youngest of whom was St. Thérèse of Lisieux (and all five lived lives of notable holiness). St. Zélie died of breast cancer in 1877 at age 45. St. Louis died in 1894 after suffering years of physical and mental deterioration from strokes.

Sts. Louis and Zélie Martin, patrons of married couples and parents, pray for us.

Give thanks to God for anything that stands out to you about these examples of faithful witness.

How do you feel inspired to grow in holiness today? Talk to God about any fears or obstacles in your way, and ask these or any other favorite saints to pray for you.

CLOSE

Rest in the sure faith that you are surrounded by God and all his angels and saints.

Jesus, you have inspired men and women throughout history to give their lives to you in faith and love. Thank you for the many ways these people have witnessed to the joy and peace of putting their trust in you alone. God, I am inspired by them and humbly ask you to make my life a witness to your goodness and mercy as well. Help me grow in faith and trust that those who lose their lives for you find their true lives in you.

In the name of the Father, and of the Son, and of the Holy Spirit. Amen.

TIP: BEFRIEND THE SAINTS

The great variety of the saints' personalities, strengths, and weaknesses is a great gift to us. Look up the stories of different saints to find one you can relate to. If you're not sure who to start with, try researching the story of a saint you are named after, your Confirmation saint, the saint whose feast falls on your birthday, or saints who share your national or cultural background. Put together a personal cadre of saints whom you connect with and ask for their prayers often.

Day 3. Mary, Our Mother

Turn then, most gracious advocate, thine eyes of mercy toward us, and after this our exile show unto us the blessed fruit of thy womb, Jesus.
— From the Hail, Holy Queen

The generosity of God cannot be outdone. Not only has he given us salvation through his Son, he gives us the help and solace of a mother who guides us to Jesus.[*]

Mary never competes with Jesus for the throne of our hearts. "For no creature could ever be counted as equal with the Incarnate Word and Redeemer."[6]

Instead, she rejoices to be "the handmaid of the Lord" (Luke 1:38). Everything about Mary's life shows her great love for and obedience to God. She cares for the child Jesus and encourages his mission of redemption, even following him to the Cross where, in her sorrow, she participates in his suffering. "She cooperated by her obedience, faith, hope and burning charity in the work of the Saviour in giving back supernatural life to souls. Wherefore she is our mother in the order of grace."[7]

It is an amazing fact that God involves us in his work of redemption, giving us roles to play in his kingdom. God has given Mary a

---

[*]   "There is but one Mediator as we know from the words of the apostle, 'for there is one God and one mediator of God and men, the man Christ Jesus, who gave himself a redemption for all'. The maternal duty of Mary toward men in no wise obscures or diminishes this unique mediation of Christ, but rather shows His power. For all the salvific influence of the Blessed Virgin on men originates, not from some inner necessity, but from the divine pleasure. It flows forth from the superabundance of the merits of Christ, rests on His mediation, depends entirely on it and draws all its power from it. In no way does it impede, but rather does it foster the immediate union of the faithful with Christ" (*Lumen gentium*, sec. 60).

singularly unique role. She becomes Mother of the Redeemer and of all who put their faith in him. As brothers and sisters of Jesus, we, too, receive her as a mother and advocate.

At the wedding that Mary, Jesus, and his disciples attend in Cana, Mary is the one who notices that the couple is running out of wine. A conversation ensues between Jesus and Mary as she encourages him to come to their aid. St. John Paul II writes that this shows "Mary's solicitude for human beings, her coming to them in the wide variety of their wants and needs."[8] In her position as his mother, she comes to Jesus with our needs. Yet, she is always aligned with his will, telling the servants, "Do whatever he tells you" (John 2:5). Mary's faithful intercession always leads us closer to Jesus.

OPEN TO GOD

Take a few deep breaths. Open to God in your usual way.

In the name of the Father, and of the Son, and of the Holy Spirit. Amen.

Jesus, Mary gave her life to you in the joyful moments, the mundane moments, the sorrowful moments. Thank you for giving us your mother as an example and intercessor who knows what we need and never tires to pray for us.

Mary, please pray for me to love Jesus with as much generosity and faithfulness as you do.

PRAY FROM THE HEART

John 19:25-27, NRSV-CE
Standing near the cross of Jesus were his mother, and his mother's sister, Mary the wife of Clopas, and Mary Magdalene. When Jesus saw his mother and the disciple whom he loved[*] standing beside her, he said to his mother, "Woman, here is your son." Then he said to the disciple, "Here is your mother." And from that hour the disciple took her into his own home.

For help reflecting:

- On the cross, Jesus gave his beloved disciple (John) to his mother, and his mother to John. This is traditionally understood as Jesus giving his mother to all of his followers. How do you relate to Mary as a spiritual mother? Is this difficult for you? A comfort?

---

*   In John's Gospel, the "beloved disciple" refers to John himself.

- Talk to Jesus and/or Mary about any thoughts, feelings, and desires you have about your relationship with Mary.

Pray a Decade of the Rosary

The Rosary is a powerful prayer to meditate on the events of Jesus' life and also to ask Mary's intercession. For some people it quickly feels like an accessible and helpful aid to prayer and meditation. For others, it can take a while to settle into its rhythms, feeling strange or monotonous at first. Regardless, for centuries the Rosary has been a profound way for individuals, families, and communities to call for heavenly help, to find protection from evil, and to access deeper levels of contemplative understanding around the central mysteries of the Catholic faith.

Before praying a decade of the Rosary (instructions below), use *lectio divina* to pray with this scriptural account of the wedding at Cana. This is the second Luminous Mystery of the Rosary (for more information about praying the Rosary, see page 258).

John 2:1-11, NRSV-CE

On the third day there was a wedding in Cana of Galilee, and the mother of Jesus was there. Jesus and his disciples had also been invited to the wedding. When the wine gave out, the mother of Jesus said to him, "They have no wine." And Jesus said to her, "Woman, what concern is that to you and to me? My hour has not yet come." His mother said to the servants, "Do whatever he tells you." Now standing there were six stone water jars for the Jewish rites of purification, each holding twenty or thirty gallons. Jesus said to them, "Fill the jars with water." And they filled them up to the brim. He said to them, "Now draw some out, and take it to the chief steward." So they took it. When the steward tasted the water that had become wine, and did not know where it came from (though the servants who had drawn the water knew), the steward called the bridegroom and said to him, "Everyone serves the good wine first, and then the inferior wine after the guests have become drunk. But you have kept the good wine until now." Jesus did this, the first of his signs, in Cana of Galilee, and revealed his glory; and his disciples believed in him.

For help reflecting:

- What do you notice about Mary in this passage? What qualities would you say she has?
- What does this passage tell you about the kind of person and God Jesus is?

- What needs or concerns (for yourself or others) do you want Mary to bring to Jesus on your behalf today?

Pray one decade of the Rosary, continuing to meditate on this event in Jesus' life. Pray one Our Father, ten Hail Marys, and one Glory Be. Use rosary beads if you have them or use your fingers if not.

CLOSE

Rest in one to two minutes of silence, entrusting your needs to Jesus through Mary.

Mary, thank you for being the help of Christians. As I move on with the rest of my day, please continue to bring my prayers to Jesus. Pray for me to grow in love for your Son and help me notice and pray for the needs of those around me.

In the name of the Father, and of the Son, and of the Holy Spirit. Amen.

TIP: PRAY THE ANGELUS

The Angelus is an ancient prayer based on the events of Luke 1 where Mary says "yes" to the angel's invitation to become the mother of God. Traditionally, church bells rang at 6:00 a.m., 12:00 p.m., and 6:00 p.m. as a reminder to pray the Angelus at these times (many still do!). Set a reminder or alarm on your phone for noon to remind you to pray this quick prayer honoring Mary's role in the Incarnation and asking for her intercession. See page 260 for instructions on how to pray the Angelus.

Day 4. Humility

True humility consists to a great extent in being ready for what the Lord desires to do with you and happy that He should do it.[9]
– St. Teresa of Avila

A common thread runs through the lives of the saints: they are deeply humble. Put simply, humility means knowing and living the truth about oneself. So why do most of us struggle to live true humility?

Humility requires us to keep our true identity at the forefront of our minds and hearts. In truth we are sinners—people who have turned away from God in disobedience and rebellion, people who have harmed others and broken the communion with God that we were created for. But also (and this must always be held together with the first truth), we are beloved sons and daughters of God, people he created fundamentally good and who are the subject of his love, mercy, and redemption.

Holding these together isn't always easy. On the one hand, we might be tempted to self-pity or anxiety over our perceived unworthiness. On the other hand, we might slip into thinking we are deserving of every good thing and are the authors of our charm, abilities, and achievements. In truth, both are forms of self-reliance. One uses self-condemnation and shame to disqualify us, the other uses self-righteousness and pride to qualify us. Instead, humility says with St. Paul: "Not that of ourselves we are qualified to take credit for anything as coming from us; rather, our qualification comes from God" (2 Corinthians 3:5 [NABRE]).

Many saints did, wrote, or said marvelous things through courage or intellect. But we don't honor them as saints because of their mighty deeds or wisdom. They are saints because they relied on God to make them into who they are. Diminishing ourselves out of a false sense of humility can be just as destructive as putting ourselves on a pedestal in pride. It is only in giving ourselves to God that we discover true humility and let him use the gifts he has given us to bring him glory.

OPEN TO GOD

Take a few moments to open to God in your usual way.

In the name of the Father, and of the Son, and of the Holy Spirit. Amen.

Father, I am fearfully and wonderfully made in your image. Thank you for the gifts you have given me to share with others. Thank you for my weaknesses that teach me to trust more in you than in myself. Give me the courage and humility to be the person you created me to be.

PRAY FROM THE HEART

1 Peter 5:6-7
So humble yourselves under the mighty hand of God, that he may exalt you in due time. Cast all your worries upon him because he cares for you.

- What do you need to ask forgiveness for today? Turn to God for mercy and help.

- What is causing you to worry? Cast your cares upon him in a few moments of petition.

Pray a Decade of the Rosary

Use *lectio divina* to pray with this scriptural account of the Annunciation. This is the first Joyful Mystery of the Rosary (for more information about praying the Rosary, see page 258).

Luke 1:26-38, NRSV-CE

In the sixth month the angel Gabriel was sent by God to a town in Galilee called Nazareth, to a virgin engaged to a man whose name was Joseph, of the house of David. The virgin's name was Mary. And he came to her and said, "Greetings, favored one! The Lord is with you." But she was much perplexed by his words and pondered what sort of greeting this might be. The angel said to her, "Do not be afraid, Mary, for you have found favor with God. And now, you will conceive in your womb and bear a son, and you will name him Jesus. He will be great, and will be called the Son of the Most High, and the Lord God will give to him the throne of his ancestor David. He will reign over the house of Jacob forever, and of his kingdom there will be no end." Mary said to the angel, "How can this be, since I am a virgin?" The angel said to her, "The Holy Spirit will come upon you, and the power of the Most High will overshadow you; therefore the child to be born will be holy; he will be called Son of God. And now, your relative Elizabeth in her old age has also conceived a son; and this is the sixth month for her who was said to be barren. For nothing will be impossible with God." Then Mary said, "Here am I, the servant of the Lord; let it be with me according to your word." Then the angel departed from her.

For help reflecting:

- How does Mary respond to the angel's greeting?
- How does Mary demonstrate humility? Courage? Trust in God? What else do you see in her?
- What virtues do you want to grow in? Ask for Mary's prayers for you in these areas and for any other needs on your heart today.

Pray one decade of the Rosary, continuing to meditate on this event in Jesus' and Mary's lives. Pray one Our Father, ten Hail Marys, and one Glory Be. Use rosary beads if you have them or your fingers if you don't.

CLOSE

Rest in God's life-giving presence.

Holy Spirit, create new life in me. Help me to have the faith and trust in you that Mary does. Let Jesus be born in me anew today, so that I, like Mary, can be a Christ bearer, bringing Jesus to the world.

In the name of the Father, and of the Son, and of the Holy Spirit. Amen.

Day 5. Loaves and Fishes

When it was evening, the disciples approached him and said, "This is a deserted place and it is already late; dismiss the crowds so that they can go to the villages and buy food for themselves." [Jesus] said to them, "There is no need for them to go away; give them some food yourselves." But they said to him, "Five loaves and two fish are all we have here." Then he said, "Bring them here to me."
– Matthew 14:15-18

t's easy to think of the saints as those who have done great deeds for God. Even St. Thérèse of Lisieux complained that she couldn't relate to the saints because they were like mountains in comparison to her.[10] And yet, she is now revered among the greatest of saints.

What makes a saint? When it comes down to it, what makes a saint is giving everything we are to God. Most of the time, we feel like the disciples—"Five loaves and two fish are all we have here." What good are five loaves and two fish for feeding over five thousand people? And yet Jesus says, "Bring them here to me." The disciples put their trust in Jesus and give him everything they have, to do with as he wishes.

In another place, Jesus praises a poor widow who contributed a mere two coins to the temple treasury: She "has put in more than all those who are contributing to the treasury. For all of them have contributed out of their abundance; but she out of her poverty has put in *everything she had*" (Mark 12: 43-44, NRSV-CE, emphasis added).

God is fully able. He doesn't need our help or our contribution. He could have fed the five thousand without the disciples' participation. But he didn't. He asks us to participate in his work of revealing the kingdom of heaven. You may look at your life and think, there's not much here to give. Fine. Give it anyway. Give Jesus your five loaves and two fish. Give him your two coins. Give all of yourself to him. And watch what he does.

OPEN TO GOD

Take a few moments to open to God in your usual way.

In the name of the Father, and of the Son, and of the Holy Spirit. Amen.

Lord, I come to you with all that I am. Receive me here, and turn your gaze upon me. I believe that you can and will do great things within me and through me as I say "yes" to you. Come, Holy Spirit. Fill me again with your light and your love.

PRAY FROM THE HEART

Use *lectio divina* to pray with this scriptural account of Jesus and Peter after the Resurrection. The Resurrection is the first Glorious Mystery of the Rosary (for more information about praying the Rosary, see page 258).

John 21:15-19, NRSV-CE
When they had finished breakfast, Jesus said to Simon Peter, "Simon son of John, do you love me more than these?" He said to him, "Yes, Lord; you know that I love you." Jesus said to him, "Feed my lambs." A second time he said to him, "Simon son of John, do you love me?" He said to him, "Yes, Lord; you know that I love you." Jesus said to him, "Tend my sheep." He said to him the third time, "Simon son of John, do you love me?" Peter felt hurt because he said to him the third time, "Do you love me?" And he said to him, "Lord, you know everything; you know that I love you." Jesus said to him, "Feed my sheep. Very truly, I tell you, when you were younger, you used to fasten your own belt and to go wherever you wished. But when you grow old, you will stretch out your hands, and someone else will fasten a belt around you and take you where you do not wish to go." (He said this to indicate the kind of death by which he would glorify God.) After this he said to him, "Follow me."

For help reflecting:

- This event happened just a few days after Peter denied Jesus three times, abandoning him in his darkest hour. Given this, how worthy do you imagine Peter felt to go out and serve God's people ("feed my sheep") in the name of Jesus?

- How does this Resurrection story speak to the power of God to "write straight with crooked lines," as the saying goes? What "crooked lines" in you or in the world do you want to bring to the God of Resurrection today?

- Imagine Jesus saying these words to you: "(Your Name), do you love me more than these?" What is the "these" Jesus is pointing to as he says this to you? Your career? Some material possessions? A hobby? The esteem of others? Some particular goal or aspiration? Something else?

- Even if we don't become martyrs as St. Peter did, life, for all of us, at times entails being taken "where [we] do not wish to go." How might Jesus' twofold invitation, "follow me" and "feed my sheep," guide you amid the inevitable painful circumstances of your life?

- Ask for Mary's intercession to carry your cross through to the Resurrection, and to entrust what you have—your five loaves and two fish—to Jesus.

Pray a Decade of the Rosary

Pray one decade of the Rosary, continuing to meditate on the Resurrection of Jesus. Pray one Our Father, ten Hail Marys, and one Glory Be. Use rosary beads if you have them or your fingers if not.

CLOSE

Imagine yourself walking on the beach with Jesus, just as Peter did. Rest for a few minutes in the company of your risen Savior and friend.

I love you, Jesus. I believe that you have risen from the dead. Lead me to live my life on earth by the power of your Resurrection. Teach me what it means to follow you today, and to lead others to you. Take my five loaves and two fish and make of them what you will.

In the name of the Father, and of the Son, and of the Holy Spirit. Amen.

Day 6. Perfect Love

We ought not to be weary of doing little things for the love of God,
who regards not the greatness of the work,
but the love with which it is performed.[11]
—Brother Lawrence of the Resurrection

ove for Jesus, love for God, when made perfect, is stronger than any other thing. It's love that says: "Jesus, I want you more than I want this temptation. Jesus, I love you more than money, more than pleasure, more than my own safety. Jesus, I love you more than life itself."

It's this sort of love that never fails,[12] and it's possible because God "first loved us" (1 John 4:19) with this fierce, irrevocable love. This kind of love gives everything to be with the beloved. It experiences even the smallest sins as an opportunity for repentance, healing, and growth. It "endures all things" and casts off the things of this world as "rubbish" in comparison with knowing Jesus.[13] It is love that leads people to suffer and die rather than turn away from the One they have given their hearts to; for "there is no fear in love, but perfect love drives out fear" (1 John 4:18).

When we surrender ourselves to the ocean of Christ's love, fear no longer has power over us. We live differently, face difficulties with the confidence of this love, sacrifice to be true to this love, even die to be faithful to this love. Because we have come to the same graced conviction as that of St. Josephine Bakhita: "I am definitively loved and whatever happens to me—I am awaited by this Love. And so, my life is good."[14]

In the words often attributed to Fr. Pedro Arrupe, S.J.:

> Nothing is more practical than finding God,
> than falling in Love in a quite absolute, final way.
> What you are in love with,
> what seizes your imagination,
> will affect everything.
> It will decide what will get you out of bed in the morning,
> what you do with your evenings,
> how you spend your weekends,
> what you read, whom you know,
> what breaks your heart,
> and what amazes you with joy and gratitude.
> Fall in Love, stay in love,
> and it will decide everything.

OPEN TO GOD

Settle your body and mind, opening yourself to God.

In the name of the Father, and of the Son, and of the Holy Spirit. Amen.

God you are Love itself. Draw me further into your love. Give me the courage to live my life for you, Lord. Help me know with a deep and sure knowledge that I am loved by you.

PRAY FROM THE HEART

Prayerfully consider these selections from *The Confessions of St. Augustine* and the questions for reflection. Contemplate with St. Augustine what it means to love God.

What is it then that I love when I love you? Not bodily beauty, and not temporal glory, not the clear shining light, lovely as it is to our eyes, not the sweet melodies of many-moded songs, not the soft smell of flowers and ointments and perfumes, not manna and honey, not limbs made for the body's embrace, not these do I love when I love my God.

Yet I do love a certain light, a certain voice, a certain odor, a certain food, a certain embrace when I love my God: a light, a voice, an odor, a food, an embrace for the man within me, where his light, which no place can contain, floods into my soul; where he utters words that time does not speed away; where he sends forth an aroma that no wind can scatter; where that satiety does not sunder us. This is what I love when I love my God.[15]

- St. Augustine is seeking to detach the pleasant experiences that have led him to God from his experiences of God himself. What experiences or environments have helped you love God?

- St. Augustine struggles to put into words how he has encountered God in the depths of his soul. Can you relate to what he describes? Meditate for a minute or two on what you love when you love God.

Continue reflecting with St. Augustine's *Confessions*:

Too late have I loved you, O Beauty so ancient and so new, too late have I loved you! Behold, you were within me, while I was outside: it was there that I sought you, and, a deformed creature, rushed headlong upon these things of beauty which you have made. You were with me, but I was not with you. They kept me far from you, those fair things which, if they were not in you, would not exist at all. You have called to me, and have cried out, and have shattered my deafness. You have blazed forth with light, and have shone upon me, and you have put my blindness to flight! You have sent forth fragrance, and I have drawn in my breath, and I pant after you. I have tasted you, and I hunger and thirst after you. You have touched me, and I have burned for your peace.

When I shall cleave to you with all my being, no more will there be pain and toil for me. My life will be life indeed, filled wholly with you.[16]

- St. Augustine's prayer both laments how long it took him to find God and praises God who "shattered [his] deafness" and "put [his] blindness to flight." Are there periods of your life when you were "blind" and "deaf" to God? How did he break through to you?

- Thank God for the ways he has loved you throughout your life, even if you didn't see it at the time.

- Express your devotion and love for God in your own words or by repeating St. Augustine's words of praise and longing for God.

- Is there anything else you want to say to God today? Speak openly with "him who we know loves us."[17]

CLOSE

Rest in silent, loving contemplation of the God who is closer to us than we are to ourselves.

When you are ready, close with the following prayer from St. John Vianney,

I love you, O my God, and my only desire is to love you until the last breath of my life. I love you, O my infinitely lovable God, and I would rather die loving you, than live without loving you. I love you, Lord, and the only grace I ask is to love you eternally. . . . My God, if my tongue cannot say in every moment that I love you, I want my heart to repeat it to you as often as I draw breath.[18]

In the name of the Father, and of the Son, and of the Holy Spirit. Amen.

Day 7. Heaven

The throne of God and of the Lamb will be in it, and his servants will worship him. They will look upon his face, and his name will be on their foreheads. Night will be no more, nor will they need light from lamp or sun, for the Lord God shall give them light, and they shall reign forever and ever.
— Revelation 22:3-5

At the Last Supper, Jesus tells his disciples that he is about to leave them and go to the Father where he will prepare a place for them. He tells them, "If I go and prepare a place for you, I will come back again and take you to myself, so that where I am you also may be. Where [I] am going you know the way" (John 14:3-4). Thomas, asking the question many of us would have on our minds, responds: "Master, we do not know where you are going; how can we know the way?" Jesus said to him, "I am the way and the truth and the life. No one comes to the Father except through me. If you know me, then you will also know my Father" (vv. 5-7).

Our friendship with Jesus is just beginning. This life is only the start. But knowing him, following him, ushers us into the fullness of life that he promises, together with all the communion of saints who seek and find the way, the truth, and the life. We experience just a taste of that now, a taste that makes us long for the fulfillment of our desires. The things of this world—even the best, purest things—they always fail to satisfy us because we are "strangers and foreigners" on this earth, people who "are seeking a homeland," who "desire a better country . . . a heavenly one" (Hebrews 11:8-16, NRSV-CE).

Jesus is the way, the truth, and the life. He bears "the name that is above every name" (Philippians 2:9), and he leads us home. In a real sense, he is our home. Eternal life begins now; for "this is eternal life, that they may know you, the only true God, and Jesus Christ whom you have sent" (John 17:3, NRSV-CE).

OPEN TO GOD

Take a few moments to open to God in your usual way.

In the name of the Father, and of the Son, and of the Holy Spirit. Amen.

Jesus, help me to reflect on my true home today, which is found only in you. But with you is also the company of your Mother and all the saints and angels. These are my siblings, my friends, my people, those with whom I belong. Because of you, Lord, I'm invited to this banquet, the feast of eternal life. Thank you for such an unimaginable gift. I receive it; I receive you with a humble and contrite heart.

PRAY FROM THE HEART

Begin today's prayer time by doing a brief examination of conscience. Where do you need the Lord's forgiveness, mercy, and help today to become more fit for the company of heaven?

What are your hopes or fears about life after death? Take a moment to notice, tell, invite.

Pause to offer thanks to God for his saving help and for anything else you are grateful for today.

Reflect slowly and prayerfully on the following poem "My Hope" from St. Thérèse of Lisieux. Add your own daydreams about "the endless joys of heaven." Talk to God about whatever comes to mind, or sit in contemplative silence.

> Though in a foreign land I dwell afar,
> I taste in dreams the endless joys of heaven.
> Fain would I fly beyond the farthest star,
> And see the wonders to the ransomed given!
>
> No more the sense of exile weighs on me,
> When once I dream of that immortal day.
> To my true fatherland, dear God! I see,
> For the first time I soon shall fly away.
>
> Ah! give me, Jesus! wings as white as snow,
> That unto Thee I soon may take my flight.
> I long to be where flowers unfading blow;
> I long to see Thee, O my heart's Delight!
>
> I long to fly to Mary's mother-arms, —
> To rest upon that spotless throne of bliss;
> And, sheltered there from troubles and alarms,
> For the first time to feel her gentle kiss.
>
> Thy first sweet smile of welcoming delight
> Soon show, O Jesus! to Thy lowly bride;
> O'ercome with rapture at that wondrous sight,
> Within Thy Sacred Heart, ah! let me hide.
>
> O happy moment! and O heavenly grace!
> When I shall hear Thee, Jesus, speak to me;
> And the full vision of Thy glorious Face
> For the first time my longing eyes shall see.
>
> Thou knowest well, my only martyrdom
> Is love, O Heart of Jesus Christ! for Thee;
> And if my soul craves for its heavenly home,
> 'Tis but to love Thee more, eternally.
>
> Above, when Thy sweet Face unveiled I view,
> Measure nor bounds shall to my love be given;
> Forever my delight shall seem as new
> As the first time my spirit entered heaven.[19]

CLOSE

Rest for a few minutes longer in the unfathomable promise that "What no eye has seen, nor ear heard, nor the human heart conceived, what God has prepared for those who love him'—these things God has revealed to us through the Spirit" (1 Corinthians 2:9-10, NRSV-CE).

Heavenly Father, Holy Spirit, Jesus my Lord, Savior, and Friend, I worship you. I long to be forever united to you and all your family. Blessed Virgin Mary, Queen of Heaven and Mother of my Lord, my Mother, pray for me and all my loved ones, that we may glorify God in our joys and sufferings, and never turn away from the heavenly help we are granted through Christ, through the Church, and through your prayers for us. All you saints and angels, pray for us.

In the name of the Father, and of the Son, and of the Holy Spirit. Amen.

MAKE IT A HABIT
Call on Mary and the Saints

Below, find tips and suggested readings for continuing to grow in calling upon Mary and the saints.

CULTIVATE A DAILY DEVOTION TO MARY

Continue to deepen your love and devotion to Mary, the Mother of God, by making a daily commitment to some form of Marian prayer. This could take the form of praying the Angelus, a decade or all of the Rosary, a Hail Mary to start the day, or singing a Marian song before bed.

MEDITATE ON THE MYSTERIES OF THE ROSARY

The rhythmic nature of praying the Rosary allows us the inner space to meditate on what are known as the Mysteries of the Rosary. These twenty events correspond to different events in the life of Mary and Jesus. They are divided into four categories: the Joyful, Luminous, Sorrowful, and Glorious Mysteries. You prayed with one of each of these four sets of mysteries in this chapter. In order to pray with all twenty events over the course of a week, many people pray certain mysteries on particular days of the week: Glorious on Sundays and Wednesdays, Joyful on Mondays and Saturdays, Sorrowful on Tuesdays and Fridays, and Luminous on Thursdays.*

PRAY A NOVENA

A novena (derived from the Latin word for "nine") is a customary way to pray to a saint for a particular intention over nine days. This practice has its roots in the nine days that Mary and the disciples waited for the Holy Spirit to descend on them after Jesus' Ascension into heaven. You can pray a novena to a favorite saint or a saint known for helping people with your particular need at any time. Many people also pray novenas in the nine days preceding a saint's feast day. Find special novena prayers for your favorite saints online or in novena prayer books, or simply ask for a saint's intercession each day for nine days.

CELEBRATE FEAST DAYS

While we're accustomed to celebrating birthdays, the Catholic Church typically celebrates saints on the day of their death, celebrating their birth into *eternal* life. This day of celebration is called a saint's feast day. Every day of the year marks at least one saint's feast. How can you celebrate your favorite saint's feast day? Go to Mass to celebrate them in the Eucharist, make a special meal to honor their culture or some facet of their life, or pray a novena leading up to their special day. Have fun with your celebration—like getting Hawaiian pizza in honor of St. Damian of Molokai, or be extra creative—like making chicken soup with dumplings that rise to the surface in honor of St. Teresa of Avila's experience of levitating in prayer! Food and festivities aside, use the feast days of the Church to get to know different saints and ask for their intercession each day.

READ THE SAINTS

Read the writings of the saints to get to know them better and to learn from their lives and teachings. Many saints wrote autobiographies or put their theological or practical spiritual wisdom down on paper. Or if they didn't, look to other sources for biographical and historical data on the saints.

---

*   Find the full list of the mysteries of the Rosary on page 259.

PRAY FOR SOULS IN PURGATORY

We believe that those who have put their faith and hope in the Lord are saved from hell through the death and resurrection of Jesus. Yet, unless we fully allow ourselves to be conformed to Christ in this life, approaching God's glory in heaven may be an overwhelmingly painful experience, for a time. The pain isn't so much a punishment as an experience of purification where every attachment and sin is removed. Scripture describes this experience using the metaphor of gold ore being refined by incredibly hot fire in order to burn away the impurities and reveal the gold within. We pray for people in purgatory for the same reason we would pray for anyone else: that they would have the grace to receive all that God wants to give them. In the case of the people in purgatory, we pray that they would be purified and refined of all their sins so that they can rejoice with the saints living in full communion with God in heaven. The Church prays for all the souls in purgatory on All Souls Day (November 2) each year, but you can pray for people in purgatory at any time. Pray for loved ones who have passed away, call your parish to request a Mass to be prayed for someone who has died, pray for your ancestors (both those you can name and those you can't), or walk around a cemetery and pray for the people buried there.

ADDITIONAL RESOURCES

- *The Confessions of St. Augustine*, St. Augustine of Hippo
- *Story of a Soul*, St. Thérèse of Lisieux
- *Introduction to the Devout Life*, St. Francis de Sales
- *St. Thomas Aquinas & St. Francis of Assisi*, G. K. Chesterton
- *Where There Is Love, There Is God*, Mother Teresa of Calcutta
- *Pray for Us: 75 Saints Who Sinned, Suffered, and Struggled on Their Way to Holiness*, Meg Hunter-Kilmer
- *33 Days to Morning Glory: A Do-It-Yourself Retreat In Preparation for Marian Consecration*, Michael E Gaitley

DISCIPLESHIP PRACTICES
Call on Mary and the Saints

Pray the Rosary

The prayer of the Rosary helps you deepen your relationship with Jesus through Mary. This classic devotional prayer uses the words and rhythms of repeated vocal prayers like the Our Father and Hail Mary to draw us into meditation. Each of the five large beads on a rosary represents the start of a "decade," a set of ten small beads on the rosary. Over the years, the faithful have identified events in Christ's life and salvation history to meditate on while praying the Rosary. These are known as the Mysteries of the Rosary, and they are organized into four sets of five mysteries according to different themes.

Below, find instructions for praying the Rosary as well as a list of each of the Mysteries. Familiarize yourself with the Mysteries by using the Scripture verses cited below.

HOW TO PRAY THE ROSARY

1. Make the Sign of the Cross.

2. Holding the Crucifix, say the Apostles' Creed.

3. On the first bead, say an Our Father.

4. Say one Hail Mary on each of the next three beads. It is common to ask for an increase of the virtues of faith, hope, and love with these three beads.

5. Say the Glory Be.

6. Pray the five decades. For each one, follow these steps.

   ◦ Announce the Mystery then say the Our Father.
   ◦ Say ten Hail Marys, counting them by moving your fingers along the small beads.
   ◦ Meditate on the Mystery while you do this.
   ◦ Then say a Glory Be.
   ◦ After finishing each decade, some say the following prayer requested by Mary at Fatima: *O my Jesus, forgive us our sins, save us from the fires of hell; lead all souls to Heaven, especially those in most need of your mercy.*

7. After saying the five decades, say the Hail, Holy Queen, followed by this dialogue and prayer:

Pray for us, O holy Mother of God.

That we may be made worthy of the promises of Christ.

Let us pray: O God, whose Only Begotten Son, by his life, Death, and Resurrection, has purchased for us the rewards of eternal life, grant, we beseech thee, that while meditating on these mysteries of the most holy Rosary of the Blessed Virgin Mary, we may imitate what they contain and obtain what they promise, through the same Christ our Lord. Amen.

8. Close with the Sign of the Cross.

THE MYSTERIES OF THE ROSARY

The Joyful Mysteries
Typically prayed on Mondays and Saturdays

1. **The Annunciation** The angel Gabriel announces the Incarnation to Mary. *Luke 1:26-38*
2. **The Visitation** Mary visits her cousin Elizabeth. *Luke 1:39-56*
3. **The Nativity** Jesus Christ is born in Bethlehem. *Luke 2:1-20*
4. **The Presentation** Joseph and Mary present the infant Jesus in the Temple. *Luke 2:22-40*
5. **The Finding in the Temple** Joseph and Mary find Jesus in his Father's house. *Luke 2:41-52*

The Luminous Mysteries
Typically prayed on Thursdays

1. **The Baptism of the Lord** John the Baptist baptizes Jesus in the Jordan. *Matthew 3:13-17*
2. **The Wedding Feast at Cana** Jesus turns water into wine at Mary's request. *John 2:1-11*
3. **The Proclamation of the Kingdom** Jesus preaches and heals. *Matthew 4:23-5:12*
4. **The Transfiguration** Jesus reveals his glory to Peter, James, and John. *Matthew 17:1-7*
5. **The Institution of the Eucharist** Jesus gives his disciples his Body and Blood. *Luke 22:14-20*

The Sorrowful Mysteries
Typically prayed on Tuesdays and Fridays, also on Sundays during Lent

1. **The Agony in the Garden** Jesus prays on the night before his death. *Mark 14:32-42*
2. **The Scourging at the Pillar** Pontius Pilate has Jesus beaten. *Mark 15:6-15*
3. **The Crowning with Thorns** The soldiers mock, strip, and beat Jesus. *Matthew 20:27-31*
4. **The Carrying of the Cross** Jesus carries his Cross up Calvary. *Luke 23:26-31*
5. **The Crucifixion** Jesus is hung on the Cross and dies. *Luke 23:32-49*

The Glorious Mysteries
Typically prayed on Sundays and Wednesdays

1. **The Resurrection** Jesus rises from the dead on the third day. *John 20:1-18*
2. **The Ascension** Jesus ascends into heaven. *Acts 1:6-12*
3. **The Descent of the Holy Spirit** The Spirit falls on Mary and the disciples. *Acts 2:1-21*
4. **The Assumption of Mary** Mary receives the first fruits of Jesus' Resurrection. She is taken up into heaven, body and soul, at the end of her life. *Acts 2:22-33*
5. **The Coronation of Mary** Mary is crowned as queen of heaven and earth. *Revelation 12:1-5*

The Angelus and Regina Coeli

The Angelus combines Hail Marys and short verses to outline the pivotal moment in salvation history when the angel Gabriel came to Mary and she said "yes" to becoming the Mother of God. The prayer honoring the Incarnation is traditionally said three times a day: in the morning, at noon, and in the evening. It is a way to honor Mary and to remember God's saving love for us throughout the day. If you have heard church bells ring at noon or 6pm, it's probably to remind all within hearing to pray the Angelus! During the Easter season, the Regina Coeli ("Queen of Heaven") is said in place of the Angelus in celebration of the Resurrection.

If you are praying these prayers on your own, pray all the parts below, or if you are praying them with others, the leader prays the "versicle" (V/.) and the others the response (R/.).

THE ANGELUS

V/. The angel of the Lord declared unto Mary,

R/. And she conceived of the Holy Spirit.

Hail Mary . . .

V/. Behold, the handmaid of the Lord,

R/. Be it done unto me according to thy word.

Hail Mary . . .

V/. And the Word was made flesh, [genuflect or bow]

R/. And dwelt among us.

Hail Mary . . .

V/. Pray for us, O holy Mother of God,

R/. That we may be made worthy of the promises of Christ.

Let us pray. Pour forth, we beseech thee, O Lord, thy grace into our hearts: that we, to whom the Incarnation of Christ thy Son was made known by the message of an angel, may by his Passion and Cross be brought to the glory of his Resurrection. Through the same Christ our Lord. Amen.

REGINA COELI ("QUEEN OF HEAVEN")

V/. Queen of Heaven, rejoice, alleluia!

R/. For he whom you merited to bear, alleluia!

V/. Has risen, as he said, alleluia!

R/. Pray for us to God, alleluia!

V/. Rejoice and be glad, O Virgin Mary, alleluia!

R/. Because the Lord is truly risen, alleluia!

O God, who by the Resurrection of your Son, our Lord Jesus Christ, granted joy to the whole world, grant, we beseech you, that through the intercession of the Virgin Mary, his Mother, we may enjoy the happiness of eternal life, through the same Christ Our Lord. Amen.

ENDNOTES

1. Pope Benedict XVI, "General Audience, St. Peter's Square, Wednesday, 13 April 2011" (Vatican Website).

2. *Lumen gentium*, sec. 49.

3. Ibid., sec 49.

4. Pope Benedict XVI, "Mass, Imposition of the Pallium and Conferral of the Fisherman's Ring for the Beginning of the Petrine Ministry of the Bishop of Rome, Homily of His Holiness Pope Benedict XVI, St. Peter's Square, Sunday, 24 April, 2005" (Vatican website).

5. C. S. Lewis, *Mere Christianity* (New York: HarperCollins, 2001), 226.

6. *Lumen gentium*, sec. 62.

7. Ibid., sec. 61.

8. St. John Paul II, *Redemptoris mater* (Vatican City: Vatican Press, 1987), sec. 21.

9. St. Teresa of Avila, *Way of Perfection* (Ontario: Devoted Publishing, 2018), ch. 17.6.

10. St. Thérèse of Lisieux, "Manuscript C: Chapter X," *Story of a Soul: The Autobiography of Saint Thérèse of Lisieux,* Study Edition, trans. John Clarke, O.C.D. (Washington, D.C.: ICS Publications, 2005), 328.

11. Brother Lawrence, "The Fourth Conversation," *The Practice of the Presence of God with Spiritual Maxims,* trans. Fleming H. Revell (Grand Rapids: Baker Book House Company, 2003), 27.

12. See 1 Corinthians 13:8.

13. See 1 Corinthians 13:7-8; Philippians 3:7-9.

14. Quoted in Pope Benedict XVI, *Spe Salvi,* 3. St. Josephine Margaret Bakhita was born in Sudan in about 1869. She spent over twenty years as an enslaved person. After she petitioned for and won her freedom, she was baptized and entered the Canossian sisters in Venice, Italy where she lived until 1947.

15. St. Augustine, *The Confessions of St. Augustine,* translated by John K. Ryan (New York: Doubleday, 1960), X.6.8.

16. Ibid., V.27-28.38-39.

17. St. Teresa of Avila, *The Book of Her Life,* 8, 5 sec. I, 67 in *The Collected Works of St. Teresa of Avila,* trans. K. Kavanaugh, O.C.D., and O. Rodriguez, O.C.D. (Washington DC: ICS, 1976).

18. St. John Vianney, quoted in *Catechism,* 2658.

19. St. Thérèse of Lisieux, "My Hope," *Poems of St. Teresa, Carmelite of Lisieux, known as the 'Little Flower of Jesus,'* accessed December 4, 2023, https://www.clerus.org/bibliaclerusonline/en/gxg.htm.

WEEK 9
ENTRUST YOUR LIFE TO JESUS

For whoever wishes to save his life will lose it, but whoever loses his life for my sake will find it.

– Matthew 16:25

CONVERSATION NINE
Entrust Your Life to Jesus

OPENING PRAYER (3 MIN)
Select one person to open in prayer. Use the following prayer or your own words.

In the name of the Father, and of the Son, and of the Holy Spirit. Amen.

Come, Holy Spirit. We welcome you into our hearts today, and into our conversation as we gather here. Thank you for the gift of faith, and for calling us your children and your friends. Guide our discussion as always, and speak to us through your Word and one another. In Jesus name, Amen.

CATCH UP (5 MIN)
Share highs and lows: one positive thing (a simple joy, gratitude, or blessing) and one challenge in your life since you last met.

REVIEW CALL ON MARY AND THE SAINTS (10 MIN)
Discuss a few of the following questions.

- What was your overall experience of Week 8: Call on Mary and the Saints?
- What saints caught your attention, whether because of their life story or an excerpt you read from their writings?
- Did you pray the Angelus every day or on some of the days? What was that experience like?
- What prayer session was particularly helpful or meaningful, and why?
- What questions came up for you this week?

ABOUT ENTRUST YOUR LIFE TO JESUS (15 MIN)
Read aloud.

Trust is among the most important elements of any relationship. When we trust someone, we can be ourselves around them, open and honest. We can delight in their company, learn from them, and collaborate in effective ways.

When trust is lacking in a relationship, however, all kinds of debilitating patterns develop. We might hide our true thoughts and feelings, worry excessively about what the other person thinks of us, constantly question their motives, or defend ours. It's hard to get anything done in a relationship that lacks trust. And it's exhausting.

The prayer guides this week lead you to reflect on what we might consider *the* ultimate discipleship challenge: to entrust our lives completely to Jesus. At some point or another, we awaken to the reality that Jesus compels a choice. Is he who he said he was or not? Is he, or is he not, the Alpha and Omega, the Lamb of God, the King of kings, the Savior of the world? Do we aspire to trust him with everything or not? Do we choose to seek and find our life's meaning and sustenance in him, or to look elsewhere?

The call to trust Jesus with all our hearts beckons us daily, from our first thoughts in the morning to our last ones at night; from how we use our time to where we spend our money; from how we respond to the small inconveniences of the day to where we turn when tragedy strikes. We can practice entrusting small matters to Jesus as we grow in the ability to entrust large matters—even our whole life and inevitable death—to his care and guidance. As we give him access to more places in our hearts and lives, we journey toward becoming single-heartedly his.

YOUR CHALLENGE THIS WEEK:

☐ Entrust more of your life to Jesus as you pray through the reflections and exercises in the daily prayer guide. If you have been skimping on some of your prayer times throughout this journey, don't miss any this week!

☐ Pray "Jesus, I trust in you" as your first and last words of each day this week.[*] To remind yourself, write the prayer on a notecard and keep it on your pillow during the day and on your nightstand while you sleep.

Discuss the following questions.

- Have you experienced some of the differences between human relationships of high trust and low trust? What's it like to be in each type?

---

* This simple, powerful prayer comes from St. Faustina Kowalska, a nun in the Congregation of Sisters of Our Lady of Mercy in Poland during the 1930s. She received numerous messages from Jesus about his Divine Mercy which he asked her to share with the world.

- Do you ever wrestle with the question of God's trustworthiness in your life? Or with Jesus as "the way and the truth and the life" (John 14:6)? If so, share a little bit about that struggle (to the degree you are comfortable).
- Have you ever made an explicit decision to follow Jesus and entrust your life fully to him, at least as a firm intention or hope? If so, how did (or do) you express that intention to the Lord?
- How has this book so far helped you say "yes" to God in new ways?

READ AND DISCUSS (20 MIN)

The following passages from Matthew's Gospel are a few examples of Jesus inviting people (including us) to make a clear and decisive choice to follow him. Read them aloud and discuss your thoughts and reactions with the questions below.

Matthew 16: 24-26, NRSV-CE

24 Then Jesus told his disciples, "If any want to become my followers, let them deny themselves and take up their cross and follow me. 25 For those who want to save their life will lose it, and those who lose their life for my sake will find it."

Matthew 7:24-29, NRSV-CE

"Everyone then who hears these words of mine and acts on them will be like a wise man who built his house on rock. 25 The rain fell, the floods came, and the winds blew and beat on that house, but it did not fall, because it had been founded on rock. 26 And everyone who hears these words of mine and does not act on them will be like a foolish man who built his house on sand. 27 The rain fell, and the floods came, and the winds blew and beat against that house, and it fell—and great was its fall!"

28 Now when Jesus had finished saying these things, the crowds were astounded at his teaching, 29 for he taught them as one having authority, and not as their scribes.

Matthew 11:28-30, NRSV-CE

28 Come to me, all you that are weary and are carrying heavy burdens, and I will give you rest. 29 Take my yoke upon you,

and learn from me; for I am gentle and humble in heart, and you will find rest for your souls. [30] For my yoke is easy, and my burden is light.

Discuss the following questions.

- Take a few minutes to look back over all three passages. Which of the three speaks to you the most as you do this?
- Underline words or phrases in these passages that you find challenging. Circle those you find comforting.
- Reflect on the relationship between challenge and comfort by thinking about other relationships you have had with children (like in parenting, coaching, or teaching). What role do challenge and comfort each play in the healthy growth and maturity of the child or student? What does this say to you about your life as a child of God and student/follower of Jesus?
- It's been said that Jesus comforts the afflicted and afflicts the comfortable. How do you see this in the passages above? How have you experienced this in your life or in your journey through this book?

NEXT MEETING (2 MIN)

Make sure you have your next discussion on the calendar.

CLOSING PRAYER (5 MIN)

Choose someone to lead the closing prayer time. Use the prompts below or your own words. Invite the other(s) to add their prayers when you prompt them.

In the name of the Father, and of the Son, and of the Holy Spirit. Amen.

Jesus, you are the way, the truth, and the life. You alone are the Alpha and the Omega, the beginning and the end, the author and perfecter of our faith. Increase our faith, Lord. Give us the grace to entrust you with more of our lives. Help us to follow you above everything else vying for our attention and wills. Meet us in our prayer times this week, and lead each of us wherever you want us to go—in both prayer and action.

Thank you for our conversation today. We lift up our intentions to you now, in particular for _____; _____; _____. I invite you to share your own prayers now as well.

*Thank you, Lord, for hearing our prayers and for your high call of disciple-
ship. We say "yes" to life with you.*

*Together, we pray: Glory be to the Father, and to the Son, and to the Holy
Spirit, as it was in the beginning, is now, and ever shall be, world without
end. Amen.*

PRAYER GUIDE
Entrust Your Life to Jesus

Day 1. God is Faithful

*For in [Christ] every one of God's promises is a "Yes." For this reason
it is through him that we say the "Amen," to the glory of God.*
– 2 Corinthians 1:20, NRSV-CE

God's word to us is "yes." Not to every whim we might have.
Not to the conflicted desires of our egos. But "yes" to *us*.
Another word for a firm, unalterable "yes" is "covenant." It's
the word God has used throughout history to communicate his
"yes" to all who seek him. In Baptism, God's covenantal "yes" to
humanity becomes a personal, intimate "yes" to each of us—his
beloved children. What, then, does a covenant say?

> A covenant says, I love you. I will never leave you. I will
> never forsake you. I am not going anywhere. I am here for
> you. No matter what happens, I will not reject you. I love
> you as you are, and I desire your ultimate good. I give
> myself to you completely and I receive you completely. You
> do not have to hide anything. You do not have to pretend.
> You can bring anything to me and I will be with you in it,
> bear it with you, and speak the truth to you about it in love.[1]

How are we to respond to such a gift? How about by giving
God our "yes" in return? God's "yes" is perfect; ours isn't yet. But
as we say "yes"—again and again—to find our life in him, our
"yes" grows in integrity. We mature in holiness through grace and
effort (and much failure) over a lifetime of learning to say "yes."

Throughout the process, let us trust in Jesus; when we feel
worthy and when we feel anything but; when we're filled with
faith, or when we're clinging to the crumb we hope is as big as
a mustard seed. Jesus does the heavy lifting. God always moves

first. "God is faithful" (1 Corinthians 1:9). "He remembers forever his covenant" (Psalm 105:8). "If God is for us, who can be against us?"(Romans 8:31).

OPEN TO GOD

Take a minute of silence to open interiorly to God.

In the name of the Father, and of the Son, and of the Holy Spirit. Amen.

Heavenly Father, I praise you today for your strong, unbreakable, covenant love. Thank you for communicating this love to your people in ways we can understand. Please help me to know, deep in my soul, that your covenant is not just words in an ancient text, but is true, and real, and includes me—here, now, and forever.

PRAY FROM THE HEART

What are a few ways the Lord has been faithful to you, whether in small ways in the past few weeks or in big ways over the course of your lifetime? Name a few specific examples of God's faithfulness and give him thanks.

God, you are faithful and generous. Help me to call to mind some of the ways I have experienced your faithfulness.

Thank you, Lord, for your faithfulness in _____; _____; and _____.

Mindful of God's covenantal "yes" to you, read the following passage in which St. Paul exhorts believers to place all their trust in the love that God has for us.

Romans 8:31-35, 37-39, NRSV-CE

What then are we to say about these things? If God is for us, who is against us? He who did not withhold his own Son, but gave him up for all of us, will he not with him also give us everything else? Who will bring any charge against God's elect? It is God who justifies. Who is to condemn? It is Christ Jesus, who died, yes, who was raised, who is at the right hand of God, who indeed intercedes for us. Who will separate us from the love of Christ? Will hardship, or distress, or persecution, or famine, or nakedness, or peril, or sword? . . . No, in all these things we are more than conquerors through him who loved us. For I am convinced that neither death, nor life, nor angels, nor rulers, nor things present, nor things to come, nor powers, nor height, nor depth, nor anything else in all creation, will be able to separate us from the love of God in Christ Jesus our Lord.

271

Take a few minutes to sit in silence and stillness, letting this word penetrate your soul.

How do you want to respond? Consider giving God your own "yes" in return for his covenant love for you in Christ. Use one or more of the following prompts if you find them helpful.

- Utter a silent "yes" to God in the depths of your soul, taking a few minutes to be still and know that he is God.
- Repeat the words, "I am yours, Lord, and you are mine" a few times, slowly and prayerfully. That's the language of love; the fragrance of family.
- "I believe in you, Jesus of Nazareth, as the meaning of the world and of my life."[2]

CLOSE

Don't rush out of this special prayer time. Take a few more minutes to linger silently in God's covenantal love for you.

Jesus, thank you for coming into this world, for bearing the sins of our broken world on your innocent shoulders, for dying out of love for us— for me. In you, the covenant of the Father's love for me is made visible and tangible. Thank you. I love you, Lord. I receive your covenant love. Jesus, I trust in you.

In the name of the Father, and of the Son, and of the Holy Spirit. Amen.

Day 2. The Cross

If anyone wishes to come after me, he must deny himself and take up his cross daily and follow me. For whoever wishes to save his life will lose it, but whoever loses his life for my sake will save it.
— Luke 9:23-24

What can we say of suffering? Of pain, loss, and grief? That it will all one day work out "for good for those who love God" (Romans 8:28)? Yes, we *do* say this; we cling to this promise as our faith and hope because of Jesus' Death and Resurrection. Still, suffering is the most profound challenge we all must endure. At some point, we all feel its sting.

Even the most compassionate words and deft arguments fail to sufficiently answer the "problem of suffering." Nothing can. Suffering is not a theoretical problem that requires an answer, but a reality that must be endured by all, in this world filled with weeds and wheat. "In the world you will have trouble," says Jesus, "but take courage, I have conquered the world" (John 16:33).

Rather than answer or remove this mystery for us, our God walked through it himself, so that we wouldn't have to walk through it alone. The testimony of countless saints and everyday believers is that the crosses of pain and suffering in their lives, somehow, eventually, drew them into a deeper intimacy with God and a firmness of character that they wouldn't have traded for the world. Though we would never have asked for our crosses, learning to bear them "with the strength that comes from God" (2 Timothy 1:8) (which can, at times, feel more like weakness than strength, see 2 Corinthians 12:9) is part of the awesome paradox of grace.

Learning to trust God in and with our pain is part of the high call of discipleship. It's part of our journey of transformation in and into Christ, as we accept what we cannot change, cry out to God for our daily bread, and unite our sufferings to his. Jesus goes before us, behind us, and within us in all things, including the Cross.

OPEN TO GOD

Take a minute of silence to open yourself to God and this time of prayer.

In the name of the Father, and of the Son, and of the Holy Spirit. Amen.

Here I am, Lord. I give you this time that I have set aside to be with you in prayer. I give you my distractions, my desire to get on with my day, and any fears or reluctance I have to reflect on my painful crosses in life. Give me your courage and compassion today, God. Teach me that it's okay to be weak because your love is strong. Jesus, even in the midst of suffering, I trust in you.

PRAY FROM THE HEART

- Gently call to mind a cross of pain or suffering that you are currently carrying.
- Close your eyes, take several deep breaths. Speak the name of Jesus interiorly as you inhale.
- Picture Jesus carrying this cross with you, just as Simon of Cyrene carried Jesus' cross with him.
- Spend several minutes with Jesus in this space. Perhaps you just sit with him in silence. Perhaps, in your prayerful imag-

ination, you see him do something or hear him speak. Perhaps you talk with him.

When you are ready, read the following excerpts and ponder the questions that follow.

Romans 5:2-5

[W]e boast in our hope of sharing the glory of God. And not only that, but we also boast in our sufferings, knowing that suffering produces endurance, and endurance produces character, and character produces hope, and hope does not disappoint us, because God's love has been poured into our hearts through the Holy Spirit that has been given to us.

Catechism of the Catholic Church 1505

By his passion and death on the cross Christ has given a new meaning to suffering: it can henceforth configure us to him and unite us with his redemptive Passion.

Reflect

- Re-read each selection slowly. Does any idea, word, or phrase stand out to you or draw you into further reflection? If so, take a few minutes to prayerfully reflect.
- What new emotions or reactions emerge from reading these passages? Whether they seem "good" or "bad" to you at first, simply note them and tell Jesus what you are thinking and feeling.
- Consider prayerfully: how is this suffering a new invitation to trust God, or to become more intimately united with Jesus? What does it look like for you to follow Jesus in or with this cross?
- Declare your trust in God, even if it feels imperfect or incomplete. Invite Jesus into any pain or emotions you feel. Pray for whatever you need.

CLOSE

Rest in silence for another minute before you wrap up.

Close with this prayer from St. Charles de Foucauld, a Trappist monk who was killed in 1916. The words are written as though Jesus were speaking them to the Father from the Cross, but are meant for us to make our own as well. This prayer is a profound expression of entrusting our lives to God.

Father, I abandon myself into your hands, do with me what you will.
Whatever you may do, I thank you: I am ready for all, I accept all.
Let only your will be done in me and in all your creatures.
I wish no more than this, O Lord.
Into your hands, I commend my soul;
I offer it to you with all the love of my heart;
For I love you, Lord, and so need to give myself:
To surrender myself into your hands without reserve and with boundless confidence. For you are my Father.[3]

In the name of the Father, and of the Son, and of the Holy Spirit. Amen.

TIP: LEAN ON COMMUNITY

In times of doubt or suffering we need the support of Christian community even more than usual. In these times of weakness we are susceptible to the enemy's lies and distortions of the truth. If you are struggling with doubt, pain, or God's plan for your life, confide in a Chrisitan friend, seek out guidance from a spiritual advisor, or find a counselor who can walk with you through your difficulties. These supports will help you continue to find the freedom and healing of Jesus amid your trials.

Day 3. Maturing Our Desires

One does not live by bread alone, but by every word that comes forth
from the mouth of God.
– Matthew 4:4

Catholics are well-known for giving up meat on Fridays in Lent. We might wonder: life is hard enough; struggling against sin is hard enough; why make it harder by giving up things that aren't even sinful?

Abstaining from meat is just one small way to practice "asceticism." You may have heard of the great "ascetics" of the early church who fled to the desert for lives of radical simplicity, prayer, and self-denial amidst a corrupt world. However, some practice of asceticism is an essential ingredient in all Christian discipleship. Drawn from two Greek words meaning "practice" or "exercise" and "work," asceticism is simply "the exercise, the effort, the labor expended to attain a goal."[4] It's the effort we put into our union with God.

As a result of original sin, we all have disordered and conflicted appetites. Just as we might prefer candy to vegetables, we don't always immediately love what is best for us or others. The priorities of the Kingdom (humility, worship, repentance, generosity, forgiveness, etc.) can thus be acquired tastes. We might muster up the strength to choke them down at first, but our desires, our soul-appetites revolt. Yet with grace, disciplined practice, and repeated exposure, appetites mature. We learn to love what God loves. We entrust our life to God as we embrace what will help us find our true life in him.

As athletes train their bodies to achieve their goals, so discipleship involves discipline, as the word suggests. Fasting for a time, going without TV or some other pleasure for Lent, offering up little (or big) inconveniences and sufferings as prayer for others; these are just a few ways to practice asceticism. By doing this, we bring ourselves more fully under the reign of Christ—who also fasted! Sometimes our stomachs, our senses, or our calendars must be emptied a bit of the things of this world, so that we can learn at greater depths that God alone is life.

OPEN TO GOD

Take a few moments to open to God in your usual way.

In the name of the Father, and of the Son, and of the Holy Spirit. Amen.

Heavenly Father, thank you for your relentless, refining love. Teach me your ways, Lord. For you have the words of everlasting life.

PRAY FROM THE HEART

1 Corinthians 9:24-27, NRSV-CE
Do you not know that in a race the runners all compete, but only one receives the prize? Run in such a way that you may win it. Athletes exercise self-control in all things; they do it to receive a perishable wreath, but we an imperishable one. So I do not run aimlessly, nor do I box as though beating the air; but I punish my body and enslave it, so that after proclaiming to others I myself should not be disqualified.

For help reflecting:

- What stands out to you upon reading this passage a few times?
- What does Jesus highlight for you as you ponder the phrase, "run in such a way that you may win"?

- What is an area in which you need or desire to grow in self-control?
- Is there any sin here to confess? If so, express your contrition now to God. Make plans to go to confession soon if it has been a while or if you sense a particular need for it.
- What is something small that is weighing down your love of God or neighbor that you could make a concerted effort to abstain from for a time? A bad habit of getting to bed too late? A tendency to turn to gossip or a drink when you have a bad day? An incessant checking of email, news, or social media?
- Pause to write down any practical resolution you desire for a brief period of abstinence, fasting, or self-denial with regard to this weight. What will you go without? Or, what good but hard thing will you take up? Why? When? For how long?
- Ask God for the graces and help you need to follow through on your good intentions.
- Talk to God about anything you need in this, or anything else on your mind today.

CLOSE

Rest in God's perfect and enduring love for you, which purifies your intentions and grounds your very being. Dwell for a few minutes in the peace of knowing you do not need to earn God's love or prove anything to him.

Jesus, I trust in you—more than in the comforts of this world. I trust your love for me even in my slowness at times to run the race you have set before me. I trust your good and perfect will to free me, more and more, to love like you, to walk (and run) with you, and to lead me on the pathway of joy.

In the name of the Father, and of the Son, and of the Holy Spirit. Amen.

TIP: TAKE UP A SMALL ASCETICAL PRACTICE

Each year during Lent, Catholics fast from something and make sacrifices as a form of penitence and asceticism. Making sacrifices and fasting at other times of the year can be a rich opportunity to pray for others or to grow in detachment from the things of this world. Ideas are endless, but could include fasting from lunch once a week, taking a colder shower than usual, giving up sugar in your coffee once a week, allowing your spouse, roommate, or sibling to pick what movie to watch, etc. Talk to a spiritual director or mentor to discern which sacrifices are right for you and do not lead you to pride or interfere with your vocation. Let these opportunities of fasting and sacrifice draw you into prayer for others, deeper reliance on God's strength, and hope for the even better things to come.

Day 4. Becoming Jesus

I have been crucified with Christ; yet I live, no longer I,
but Christ lives in me.
– Galatians 2:19-20

The goal and purpose of our existence, according to Christian faith, is deeper than our typical understanding of closeness with God, happiness, or heaven. It's more glorious than the promise of a God who stays faithful through thick and thin, or of a final resting place with no more suffering. Including but exceeding all these, it's an invitation "to share in the divine nature" (2 Peter 1:4). The *Catechism* further explains: "Christ enables us to live in him all that he himself lived, and he lives it in us."[5]

It's worth pausing to let it sink in. Consider a provocative phrase repeated by many early Church fathers, meant to jolt us into pondering such an unfathomable mystery: "for the Son of God became man so that we might become God."[6]

The relationship described here goes beyond that of teacher to student, parent to child, even friend to friend or spouse to spouse. It reaches into a sort of shared identity between us and God, which the fathers called "theosis" or "divinization." We don't become divine in the sense of losing our own identity or replacing God, of course, but we are privileged to become sharers and participants in God's own life. To be a Christian, after all, means to be a part of the mystical Body of Jesus himself. Jesus shares with us his own relationship to the Father. The offer is to become *by grace* (with our willful participation) what Jesus is *by nature*: pure, unquenchable, radiant, splendorous, eternal, divine love.

We don't become this kind of creature overnight. It's a grace-filled process of learning to let God's love come to characterize us completely. But, thanks be to God, if we continue clinging to Christ, we can have the same confidence that St. Paul declared to the Philippians: "I am confident of this, that the one who began a good work in you will continue to complete it until the day of Christ Jesus" (Philippians 1:6).

OPEN TO GOD

Take a few moments to open to God in your usual way.

In the name of the Father, and of the Son, and of the Holy Spirit. Amen.

Lord, I praise you today. And I confess that your ways are too high for my full understanding. Yet, I ask you to give me a glimpse of what the precious promises of faith mean for me. Open my eyes to see a bit more from your perspective today. Come, Holy Spirit.

PRAY FROM THE HEART

What is your understanding of the idea of participating, here and now, in God's own life and nature? How does it go beyond imitation and even beyond relationship?

How does God continue to live his divine life in the details of your life? In your sufferings? In your victories? In what other ways?

Pause for a few minutes to ponder the union God invites you to.

To help us try to fathom the process of continual conversion into divine, eternal creatures fit for heaven, C.S. Lewis used the analogy of renovating a house. Read it slowly and pray with the prompts that follow.

> Imagine yourself as a living house. God comes in to rebuild that house. At first, perhaps, you can understand what He is doing. He is getting the drains right and stopping the leaks in the roof and so on: you knew that those jobs needed doing and so you are not surprised. But presently he starts knocking the house about in a way that hurts abominably and does not seem to make sense. What on earth is He up to? The explanation is that He is building quite a different house from the one you thought of- throwing out a new wing here, putting on an extra floor there, running up towers, making courtyards. You thought you were going to be made into a decent little cottage: but He is building a palace. He intends to come and live in it Himself . . .

> If we let Him—for we can prevent Him, if we choose—He will make the feeblest and filthiest of us into a god or goddess, a dazzling, radiant, immortal creature, pulsating all through with such energy and joy and wisdom and love as we cannot now imagine, a bright stainless mirror which reflects back to God perfectly (though, of course, on a smaller scale) His own bound-

less power and delight and goodness. The process will be long and in parts very painful; but that is what we are in for. Nothing less. He meant what He said.[7]

- What is your reaction to this analogy? Consider using Notice, Tell, Invite to talk to God about it.
- From your experience, how is growth in faith or in virtue both a wonderful and, at times, painful process?
- Give thanks to God for one way you are more free and loving than you used to be.
- Talk to Jesus, your Divine Builder and Great Renovator. Do you give him the building permit of your soul and life? Declare your trust in him to make you into a palace.

CLOSE

Spend another minute or two in contemplative silence before God.

Jesus, I run to you with all that I am and all that I am not. Thank you for your enduring love, and for your invitation to share in your freedom and life. Jesus, I trust in you as the Master Builder and Renovator of my soul. Continue your work in me, until every fiber of my being is pure love, as you are love. I say yes to whatever you are building both in and through me.

In the name of the Father, and of the Son, and of the Holy Spirit. Amen.

TIP: PRAY FOR GROWTH IN A SPECIFIC VIRTUE

While we can make progress in virtuous living through determination and intentionality, in reality it is always God who is shaping us in his image. In addition to striving to live virtuously and avoid sin, ask God for the particular graces you need to be more like him. You might focus on a particular area where you want to see growth (e.g. to be more patient with a spouse or child) or for a grace that extends to all areas of your life (e.g. to be more courageous). Give God greater permission to build out this part of your life by asking for the grace to grow in these areas. The fruit of the Spirit (love, joy, peace, patience, kindness, generosity, faithfulness, gentleness, and self-control)[8] and the gifts of the Spirit (wisdom, understanding, counsel, fortitude, knowledge, piety, and fear of the Lord)[9] are two lists of wonderful graces to ask for more of from the Lord.

Day 5. Have to or Get to?

Teacher, what must I do to inherit eternal life?
— Luke 18:18

Discipleship is best understood through the lens of *participation* (what we *get to* do with God) rather than mere *obligation* (what we *have to* do).* It's about joining God in what he is doing. We can look at the various discipleship habits through this illuminating lens.

Why do we *have to* pray? We don't. But we *get to* join the loving, stimulating, life-giving conversation that's been going on since before time and will never end. It includes God himself and the greatest people to ever live. Who are *we* to sit at this table?!

We don't *have to* go to Mass; but we *get to* travel back in time to the foot of the cross, add our prayers to Jesus' great act of intercession for the world, sing with choirs of angels, and receive the Lord himself as heavenly food. Is sleeping in or that event on the calendar really more important?

We don't *have to* confess our sins; but we *get to* jump headlong into the stream of God's reconciling work to restore love as the keynote of all creation. We even get to join him in sharing the good news as co-reconcilers, agents of mercy and grace in a hurting world. Could there be a more meaningful vocation?

We don't *have to* care for the poor; but it's what Jesus is always doing. In serving them we *get to* encounter him and acquire his tastes for compassion, justice, generosity, sacrifice, and solidarity. Do we really want to miss out on this?

There's only one thing we all *have to* do, and that is to die. And here, perhaps, lies the greatest news of this promise of participation. Look what we *get to* do when death finally comes: "If the Spirit of the one who raised Jesus from the dead dwells in you, the one who raised Christ from the dead will give life to your mortal

---

*   Don't misunderstand: the Christian life, along with any life of goodwill and maturing love, entails many duties and obligations. To truly love anyone is to submit, willingly and joyfully, to a series of demands and obligations that are inherent to love itself. Love is no mere feeling of infatuation or warm-heartedness; it's a way of decisive action and commitment for and with another. Still, questions built on a premise of obligation aren't always the best questions we can ask. To really understand the "logic" of grace—to put on "the mind of Christ"—it is helpful to think in terms of participation in God's own life (*a la* 2 Peter 1:4) rather than merely of obligation.

bodies also, through his Spirit that dwells in you" (Romans 8:11).

We don't *have to* find the abundant life, both now and forever. But because of Jesus, we *get to*.

OPEN TO GOD

Take a few moments to open to God in your usual way.

In the name of the Father, and of the Son, and of the Holy Spirit. Amen.

Lord God, open my eyes to see the absolute privilege of grace. Help me see more as you see, beyond bare minimums or dutiful obligations only, and into the richness of participating in your abundant life.

PRAY FROM THE HEART

For prayer today, try to articulate your own list of what you *get to* do because of Jesus and the gifts of faith and discipleship.

Start with an open-ended reflection, then move on to each of the ways covered in this book. The following prompts guide you through this, but use a journal for adequate space to put into words what is in your heart.

Jesus, because of who you are and what you have done for the world, and for me, by your life, Death, Resurrection, and sending of the Holy Spirit, I am immeasurably blessed. I believe, and desire to believe even more firmly, that in you I get to _____.

Thank you Lord for the gift of prayer. Through this gift, I get to share in your abundant life by _____.

Thank you for the gift of your Word. Through this gift I get to share in your abundant life by _____.

Thank you for the gift of growing in freedom from sin and freedom for love. Through this gift I get to share in your abundant life by _____.

Thank you for the gift of worship. Through this gift I get to share in your abundant life by _____.

Thank you for the sacraments of the Church. Through this gift I get to share in your abundant life by _____.

Thank you for the call to love my neighbor as I love myself. Through this gift I get to share in your abundant life by _____.

Thank you for the gift of Christian community and the Church. Through this gift I get to share in your abundant life by _____.

Thank you for the ability to follow your lead, discerning the paths that are good for me. Through this gift I get to share in your abundant life by _____.

Thank you for your Mother and the Communion of Saints. Through this gift I get to share in your abundant life by _____.

Thank you for the call to spread your good news in the world. Through this gift I get to share in your abundant life by _____.

CLOSE

Linger in God's presence for two more minutes. Quiet your thoughts and let the reality of God's love envelop you.

Jesus, you truly are the way, the truth, and the life. You are the good shepherd who leads me to green pastures and to streams of abundant life. I'm honored and privileged to call you by name, to believe in you by faith, and to follow you forever. Jesus, I trust in you.

In the name of the Father, and of the Son, and of the Holy Spirit. Amen.

Day 6. Nothing Less Than Everything

The kingdom of heaven is like a merchant searching for fine pearls.
When he finds a pearl of great price,
he goes and sells all that he has and buys it.
– Matthew 13:45-46

"You only get out of it what you put in." This common phrase applies to a number of situations in life. The gospel is decidedly not one of them. The gospel is far less fair than that, which is great news for us.

Scripture speaks of our rescue from evil and our status as heirs of the Kingdom as the free gift of God. It's a gift we can never earn, but only receive with humble and grateful hearts. Yet it does cost us to receive it. Grace is free, but not cheap.[10] It cost Jesus his own life to give this gift. What does it "cost" us to receive it?

Saying "yes" to Christ means saying "no" to sin and selfish inclinations, even if it takes our actions, habits, and appetites a long time to catch up with our intentions. It also means saying "no" to some good things (like this or that career, relationship, or possession) if we're not called to pursue them. It might mean saying "no" even to preserving one's own life. Ultimately, according to the Gospels, the free gift of grace costs us nothing less than *everything*. Because truly accepting this gift means letting it transform us into someone who, like Mary, can receive the gift *in full*: a being fit for heaven. It's a refining process that takes our whole life, and even continues after death. But it's one which we joyfully accept, as the merchant happily sells all he has to gain the pearl of great price.

In the long run, there simply are no half-measures. We either become fully "yes" or fully "no" to God's offer and promises.

Thus, the great paradox: the gospel is free, yet costs us everything. What we receive, however, is also nothing less than *everything*. And God's *everything* far outshines and outlasts our own. Thank heavens the gospel is far better than "fair."

OPEN TO GOD

Open to God with a minute or two of silence and stillness.

In the name of the Father, and of the Son, and of the Holy Spirit. Amen.

I give you praise and honor, Lord. Send me your Holy Spirit today. Breathe your breath of life in me now. Open my eyes to see more clearly the preciousness of your gifts of salvation and grace. Open my heart to joyfully choose you, your Kingdom, your will over all else. Jesus, I trust in you.

PRAY FROM THE HEART

Pray with the following points of reflection.

- Jesus told his followers to count the cost of discipleship (Luke 14:25-33), even as he reassured them that what they would gain would far outweigh anything given up. What is your cost of discipleship? What have you already given up to follow Jesus?
- Do you ever worry there might be a higher "cost" you aren't sure you have the strength or willingness to endure? If so, be honest with God about your fears, doubts, and worries. Perhaps pray Notice, Tell, Invite with any feelings that emerge as you ponder this.
- Reflect briefly on the "cost of non-discipleship."[11] If you were to choose not to follow Jesus in your life, what would be the cost? What would you miss out on?

Read the following excerpt from the inaugural homily of Pope Benedict XVI:

> If we let Christ enter fully into our lives, if we open ourselves totally to him, are we not afraid that He might take something away from us? Are we not perhaps afraid to give up something significant, something unique, something that makes life so beautiful? Do we not then risk ending up diminished and deprived of our freedom? . . . No! If we let Christ into our lives, we lose nothing, nothing, absolutely nothing of what makes life free, beautiful and great. No! Only in this friendship are the doors of life opened wide. Only in this friendship is the great potential of human existence truly revealed. Only in this friendship do we experience beauty and liberation. And so, today, with great strength and great conviction, on the basis of long personal experience of life, I say to you . . . Do not be afraid of Christ! He takes nothing away, and he gives you everything. When we give ourselves to him, we receive a hundredfold in return. Yes, open, open wide the doors to Christ – and you will find true life. Amen.[12]

How do Pope Benedict's words strike you?

Talk to God about anything that emerges in you as you take in this exhortation.

CLOSE

Dwell in silence and stillness for a minute or two more, resting in God's goodness.

Close with the following prayer of surrender by St. Ignatius of Loyola called the Suscipe. Ask God for the grace, and St. Ignatius for his prayers, to conform your heart to its meaning.

Take, Lord, and receive all my liberty,
My memory, my understanding, my entire will,
All that I have and call my own.
You have given it all to me.
To you, Lord, I return it.
Everything is yours; do with it what you will.
Give me only your love and your grace.
That is enough for me.[13]

In the name of the Father, and of the Son, and of the Holy Spirit. Amen.

> ## TIP: OFFER SUFFERING AS PRAYER FOR OTHERS
>
> Most of us don't have to look too hard to find our crosses. Life in a broken world includes suffering. But because of Jesus' solidarity with us in the Incarnation, each encounter with suffering and hardship in this world includes a choice: Will we face it on our own (whether gracefully or complainingly) or will we offer it to God as an opportunity to unite our suffering with Christ's? Uniting our suffering with Jesus' gives at least some meaning to our hardships on this side of heaven. St. Paul writes that this overflows to the benefit of the rest of the Body of Christ, the Church: "I rejoice in my sufferings for your sake, and in my flesh I am filling up what is lacking in the afflictions of Christ on behalf of his body, which is the church" (Colossians 1:24). St. Paul speaks of a great mystery. Somehow, as we share the pains of this imperfect world with him who suffered for us, his divine life flows even more freely into the Church and the world.

Day 7. Never Outdone

Then Peter said to him in reply, "We have given up everything and
followed you. What will there be for us?"
— Matthew 19:27

et's admit it; as much as we might tell ourselves that the Kingdom of God is worth anything it may demand of us, we find ourselves asking the same question as Peter. "What will there be for us?" Will we have enough? Will we be happy? Is God going to demand something of me that is too much for me to give?

Perhaps we feel these questions rise to the surface when facing a big vocational decision, or when we read such stern passages as those found in the fourteenth chapter of Luke:

> If any one comes to me without hating his father and mother, wife and children, brothers and sisters, and even his own life, he cannot be my disciple (v. 26).

> Everyone of you who does not renounce all his possessions cannot be my disciple (v. 33).

Who can live up to such a high call? Do we even want to?

Jesus does not intend for his followers to hate, or to never own anything, but this strong language makes it abundantly clear who ought to be the lord of our lives: not family, nor possessions, but only the Lord himself.

Jesus' answer to Peter ought to reassure all of us. He explains that God is never outdone in generosity. "At the renewal of all things . . . everyone who has left houses or brothers or sisters or father or mother or children or fields, for my name's sake, will receive a hundredfold, and will inherit eternal life" (Matthew 19:28-29, NRSV-CE).

Could it be that all the good we have had to let go of—whether through voluntary renunciation or through a forced detachment (as in the deaths of loved ones), will one day be restored in super-abundant measure? Could it be that everything good in this world, which we love so much, is but a foretaste of what will be in "the renewal of all things"? Could it possibly be that "the sufferings of this present time are *as nothing* compared with the glory to be revealed for us" (Romans 8:18, emphasis added)?

Yes! All God's promises are "yes" in Jesus.

OPEN TO GOD

Take a few minutes of silence and stillness to open your heart to God.

In the name of the Father, and of the Son, and of the Holy Spirit. Amen.

Come, Holy Spirit. I give you this time for prayer. Thank you for the ways you have met me, spoken to me, and nurtured me so far. Continue doing a good work in me, Lord. I love you. I invite you. I give myself to you today.

PRAY FROM THE HEART

Whether you were baptized as a child or last week, you took up, with the help of the community of faith, a new identity as a child of God and heir to the eternal Kingdom. If you are not yet baptized, consider this prayer time a look ahead at what you may enter into if you choose.

The identity bestowed upon you in Baptism is a grace, purchased by the Death and Resurrection of Jesus for the forgiveness of sins and the freedom of the children of God. To embrace this identity means saying a fundamental "yes" to God and all he has revealed to us in Christ, which entails saying a fundamental "no" to Satan, evil, and sin.

The baptismal promises are not a promise to be perfect or never to struggle with sin, doubt, or surrendering to God. They are, rather, a declaration of what we're agreeing to become as we live in the family of God and grow in grace. They are a statement of our decisive choice to live as branches on the vine of Jesus within the garden of the Church, which he established on earth and will never abandon. They are the verbal expression of our fundamental "yes" to the new covenant Jesus established with us by his blood, by which we learn to love like him.

If, after all the prayers and reflections of this chapter and book, and despite any (very common) feelings of weakness or doubt or unworthiness, you are ready to reaffirm your choice to follow Jesus in the Catholic Church, pray your own renewal of baptismal promises below. You can do this once or several times over the next few days. You can do it at home, or perhaps in front of a tabernacle, or in Eucharistic adoration.

Declare each promise slowly and intentionally, pausing for a few deep, prayerful breaths in between each one.

Renewal of Baptismal Promises[14]

Heavenly Father, by the power of the Holy Spirit and in the name of Jesus Christ my Lord, Savior, Teacher, and Friend,

- *I renounce sin, so as to live in the freedom of the children of God.*
- *I renounce the lure of evil, so that sin may have no mastery over me.*
- *I renounce Satan, the author and prince of sin.*
- *I believe in God, the Father almighty, Creator of heaven and earth.*
- *I believe in Jesus Christ, his only Son, our Lord, who was born of the Virgin Mary, suffered death and was buried, rose again from the dead and is seated at the right hand of the Father.*
- *I believe in the Holy Spirit, the holy catholic Church, the communion of saints, the forgiveness of sins, the resurrection of the body, and life everlasting.*

CLOSE

Remember that God's "yes" to you is perfect and strong; it's not broken by any gaps that remain in you. He is yours and you are his. Rest now for a few minutes longer in that unshakeable love.

Jesus, I trust in you.

Jesus, I trust in you.

Jesus, I trust in you.

In the name of the Father, and of the Son, and of the Holy Spirit. Amen.

MAKE IT A HABIT
Entrust Your Life to Jesus

Below, find additional tips and suggested readings to continue entrusting your life to Jesus.

TRUST IN THE MIDST OF DOUBT

You might worry what kind of Christian it makes you if you ever doubt God's existence, character, or closeness. Or perhaps you're more prone to doubting the Church. Or yourself. But some level of doubt is a normal part of the Christian life, in part because "at present we see indistinctly, as in a mirror" (1 Corinthians 13:12). The mere presence of doubt does not signal a failure on our part or on God's. Faith and doubt can be understood more like two sides of the same coin than as enemies. If we could see and easily trust in everything good, we wouldn't need the virtue of faith at all. We wouldn't need the Christian community to carry us when we find it difficult to believe. Many of the saints experienced lengthy seasons of darkness, doubt, and struggle that, in the end, assured them even more of God's closeness. Indeed, growing in spiritual maturity almost always entails learning to love God and others even in the absence of good feelings or assurances. In these absences, God is often teaching us a deeper language of love. Next time you find yourself struggling to believe something important to the Catholic or Christian faith, pray the words found in Mark's Gospel, on the lips of a father asking Jesus to heal his son: "I do believe, help my unbelief!" (9:24). What a refreshingly honest prayer!

READ APOLOGETICS

The study of the reasons for believing something is called apologetics (one meaning of the word "apology" is a rational defense). If you experience doubt or have a burning curiosity to better understand our faith, read some good articles and books on Catholic and Christian apologetics. They can solidify your own faith while helping you become more conversant in explaining it to others. It's a great way to strengthen the habit of trusting in Jesus and the Church.

Check out Peter Kreeft and Ronald Tacelli's *Handbook of Christian Apologetics* (IVP Academic, 1994) and Alan Schreck's *Catholic and Christian: An Explanation of Commonly Misunderstood Catholic Beliefs* (Blue Sparrow Books, 2004).

PRAY THE LITANY OF TRUST

Pray the Litany of Trust, a beautiful prayer composed by Sr. Faustina Maria Pia, SV. The prayer asks Jesus to deliver us from those things that bind us or hold us back from him. It encourages us to greater trust in his promises. For example, here are a couple of lines: "From disbelief in Your love and presence: *Deliver me, Jesus*. From the fear of being asked to give more than I have: *Deliver me, Jesus*." Find the prayer for free by visiting the Sisters of Life website: *sistersoflife.org/litany-of-trust*.

PRAY THE SURRENDER NOVENA

Pray nine days of greater surrender to Jesus with the prayers from Servant of God Don Dolindo Ruotolo's Surrender Novena which you can find online. Each day, the novena ends with the refrain *O Jesus, I surrender myself to you, take care of everything!* prayed ten times. In addition to doing the novena, you can make this short refrain a daily prayer by writing it on a sticky note in a place you see every day or setting it as a recurring reminder on your phone.

ADDITIONAL RESOURCES

- *Catechism of the Catholic Church*, paragraphs 456-460, 519-521, 1030-1032, 1987-1995
- *The Great Divorce*, C.S. Lewis
- *The Problem of Pain*, C.S. Lewis
- *Making Sense of Suffering*, Peter Kreeft
- *The Cost of Discipleship*, Dietrich Bonhoeffer

DISCIPLESHIP PRACTICES
Entrust Your Life to Jesus

Act of Trust and Commitment

God's love, word, and promises are perfect and irrevocable. God has promised himself to us in an everlasting covenant, and while we may strive to return his love with our own complete commitment and faithfulness, in the end we can only do so by entrusting ourselves to Jesus.

Turn to the Lord often, recommitting your life to Jesus and asking for the grace to entrust more and more of your life to him. This God who "first loved us" (1 John 4:19) never ceases to come to our aid and to sustain us with his grace.

EXAMINE

What do you need to invite the Lord into in greater surrender, trust, and commitment?

Past	Present	Future
Regrets	Painful	Fears, worries
Shame	circumstances	Tightly held plans
Anger	A particular sin,	Vocational
Grudges,	attachment, vice	uncertainty
unforgiveness	Doubts	Financial security
Injustices suffered	Envy	Unknowns
"If only"	Difficulties with	Eternity
	marriage, divorce,	
	family	
	Finances	

PRAY

Present what you need to surrender to God by saying a prayer of surrender, trust, and commitment. Use one of the following suggestions or create your own.

- "O Jesus, I surrender myself to you, take care of everything!"*

---

*   From the Surrender Novena by Servant of God Don Dolindo Ruotolo.

- "In the morning let me hear of your mercy, for in you I trust. / Show me the path I should walk, for I entrust my life to you. / Rescue me, Lord, from my foes, for I seek refuge in you. / Teach me to do your will, for you are my God. / May your kind spirit guide me on ground that is level. / For your name's sake, Lord, give me life" (Psalm 143:8-11).

- "The Lord is my shepherd; there is nothing I lack" (Psalm 23:1).

- St. Charles de Foucauld's Prayer of Abandonment (p. 275)

- St. Ignatius' Suscipe prayer (p. 285) or simply, "Take, Lord, and receive _____."

- Visualize placing what you want to entrust to Jesus at the foot of the Cross.

- Write your own.

Renewal of Baptismal Promises

The renewal of baptismal promises is a formal liturgical act performed at the Easter Vigil, but you can also do this at home at any time. Consider doing so on the Feast of the Baptism of the Lord in January or the anniversary of your own baptism.

RENEWAL OF BAPTISMAL PROMISES

Through the Paschal Mystery we have been buried with Christ in Baptism, that we may walk with him in newness of life. And so, let us renew the promises of Holy Baptism, by which we once renounced Satan and his works and promised to serve God in the holy Catholic Church. And so I ask you:

V. Do you renounce sin, so as to live in the freedom of the children of God?
R. I do.

V. Do you renounce the lure of evil, so that sin may have no mastery over you?
R. I do.

V. Do you renounce Satan, the author and prince of sin?
R. I do.

V. Do you believe in God, the Father Almighty, Creator of heaven and earth?
R. I do.

V. Do you believe in Jesus Christ, his only Son, our Lord, who was born of the Virgin Mary, suffered death and was buried, rose again from the dead and is seated at the right hand of the Father?
R. I do.

V. Do you believe in the Holy Spirit, the holy Catholic church, the communion of saints, the forgiveness of sins, the resurrection of the body, and life everlasting?
R. I do.

V. And may almighty God, the Father of our Lord Jesus Christ, who has given us new birth by water and the Holy Spirit and bestowed on us forgiveness of our sins, keep us by his grace, in Christ Jesus our Lord, for eternal life.
R. Amen.

All are sprinkled with holy water.

---

* From the *Roman Missal*, 3rd Edition from 2011.

ENDNOTES

1. Sr. Miriam James Heidland, SOLT, *Restore: A Guided Lent Journal for Prayer and Meditation* (Notre Dame: Ave Maria Press, 2022), 35.

2. Joseph Cardinal Ratzinger, *Introduction to Christianity* (San Francisco: Ignatius Press, 2004), 81.

3. Charles de Foucauld, "Prayer of Abandon," Spiritual Family, Charles de Foucauld, accessed December 4, 2023, https://www.charlesdefoucauld.org/en/priere.php.

4. David Fagerberg, "Between Heaven & Earth, C.S. Lewis on Asceticism & Holiness," Touchstone, accessed December 4, 2023, https://www.touchstonemag.com/archives/article.php?id=17-03-030-f&readcode=&readtherest=true.

5. *Catechism*, 521, emphasis added.

6. St. Athanasius, quoted in *Catechism*, 460.

7. Lewis, *Mere Christianity*, 205.

8. See Galatians 5:22.

9. See Isaiah 11:2.

10. See Dietrich Bonhoeffer, *The Cost of Discipleship*, ch. 1.

11. See Dallas Willard, *The Spirit of the Disciplines: Understanding How God Changes Lives* (New York: Harper Collins, 1991), 1.

12. Pope Benedict XVI, "Mass, Imposition of the Pallium and Conferral of the Fisherman's Ring for the Beginning of the Petrine Ministry of the Bishop of Rome, Homily of His Holiness Pope Benedict XVI, St. Peter's Square, Sunday, 24 April, 2005." (Vatican Website).

13. St. Ignatius, *The Spiritual Exercises*, sec. 234. This readily available wording of St. Ignatius' prayer is an adaptation of the 1951 translation by Fr. Louis J. Puhl, S.J.

14. Adapted from the commonly used renewal of baptismal promises found in the *Roman Missal*.

WEEK 10
SHARE THE GOOD NEWS

Go, therefore, and make disciples of all.
– Matthew 28:19

CONVERSATION TEN
Share the Good News

OPENING PRAYER (2 MIN)
Select one person to open in prayer. Use the following prayer or your own words.

In the name of the Father, and of the Son, and of the Holy Spirit. Amen.

Jesus, we trust in you. You are the source and center of our lives, and we desire to build our lives on the rock, not the sand. Lead us to joyfully share the good news of your love with the world. We give you this time that we have set aside to gather, and ask you to be at the center of it. Guide our minds, our hearts, and our conversation to what is pleasing to you and helpful for us. Thank you, Lord. In Jesus' name, Amen.

CATCH UP (5 MIN)
Share highs and lows: one positive thing (a simple joy, gratitude, or blessing) and one challenge in your life since you last met.

REVIEW ENTRUST YOUR LIFE TO JESUS (15 MIN)
Discuss a few of the following questions.

- What was your overall experience of Week 9: Entrust Your Life to Jesus?
- What prayer session was particularly helpful or meaningful, and why?
  - The covenant faithfulness of God
  - The Cross
  - Asceticism
  - Theosis (becoming fully one with Jesus even in his divinity)
  - The privilege of participation in divine life
  - Give all to gain all
  - The renewal of baptismal promises
- Which of the prayers or excerpts in this chapter stand out as most memorable or inspiring?
  - St. Faustina's prayer, "Jesus, I trust in you"
  - St. Charles de Foucauld's Prayer of Surrender
  - C.S. Lewis' analogy of the house under construction
  - St. Ignatius of Loyola's *Suscipe* prayer
- What questions came up for you this week?

ABOUT SHARE THE GOOD NEWS (15 MIN)
Read aloud.

magine you're in heaven, and someone you know comes to find you. They've been eager to tell you something. Here's what they say:

> Friend, I want to thank you from the bottom of my heart for pointing me to Jesus. You played an important role in my story. I know now just how *much* you prayed for me. And even when I was running hard away from God and the Church, I knew something of the love of Jesus because of your attentiveness and compassion for me. You didn't preach at me or judge me. You just kept on praying and loving. And when I was ready to hear more, when my heart was finally starting to soften, you shared more of your life in Christ with me. You taught me the ways of eternal life. *Thank you.*

Could there be any greater honor than hearing words like this? Perhaps hearing "well done, my good and faithful servant" (Matthew 25:21) from the King of kings himself would take the cake. But second only to this might be the testimonies of those who we had the privilege of loving, serving, witnessing, and accompanying further into the Kingdom of God.

The good news of God's Kingdom and love, made known to us in Jesus, is too good not to share with the world. And Jesus himself commissioned us to spread the gospel to all: "Go, therefore, and make disciples of all nations, baptizing them in the name of the Father, and of the Son, and of the holy Spirit, teaching them to observe all that I have commanded you" (Matthew 28:19-20).

In Week 5: Love Your Neighbor, you considered the call of Jesus to love others as he has loved us. This tenth and final week, Share the Good News, deeply connects with and builds upon the fifth.

YOUR CHALLENGE THIS WEEK:

- ☐ Reflect on various ways to share the good news, as directed by the prayer guide.

- ☐ Ask someone about their experience of faith. See the tip on page 308.

> ☐ Consider who else might enjoy and benefit from the 10:10 Challenge.

Discuss the following questions.

- What associations—good, bad, or otherwise—do you have with the word "evangelization"? What images come to mind? How does the concept make you feel?
- What makes you hesitate to share your faith with others?
- Do you have any experiences you can share about particularly effective or ineffective evangelization efforts?
- How might you summarize in your own words the "good news" that disciples of Jesus seek to pass on to others in word and deed?

READ AND DISCUSS (15 MIN)

Read aloud.

These selections from the apostolic exhortation, *The Joy of the Gospel,* by Pope Francis describe what he calls "Spirit-filled evangelizers."[1]

264. The primary reason for evangelizing is the love of Jesus which we have received, the experience of salvation which urges us to ever greater love of him. What kind of love would not feel the need to speak of the beloved, to point him out, to make him known? If we do not feel an intense desire to share this love, we need to pray insistently that he will once more touch our hearts. We need to implore his grace daily, asking him to open our cold hearts and shake up our lukewarm and superficial existence. Standing before him with open hearts, letting him look at us, we see that gaze of love which Nathaniel glimpsed on the day when Jesus said to him: "I saw you under the fig tree" (Jn 1:48). How good it is to stand before a crucifix, or on our knees before the Blessed Sacrament, and simply to be in his presence! How much good it does us when he once more touches our lives and impels us to share his new life! What then happens is that "we speak of what we have seen and heard" (1 Jn 1:3). The best incentive for sharing the Gospel comes from contemplating it with love, lingering over its

pages and reading it with the heart. If we approach it in this way, its beauty will amaze and constantly excite us. But if this is to come about, we need to recover a contemplative spirit which can help us to realize ever anew that we have been entrusted with a treasure which makes us more human and helps us to lead a new life. There is nothing more precious which we can give to others.

[265.] Jesus' whole life, his way of dealing with the poor, his actions, his integrity, his simple daily acts of generosity, and finally his complete self-giving, is precious and reveals the mystery of his divine life. Whenever we encounter this anew, we become convinced that it is exactly what others need, even though they may not recognize it: "What therefore you worship as unknown, this I proclaim to you" (Acts 17:23). Sometimes we lose our enthusiasm for mission because we forget that the Gospel responds to our deepest needs, since we were created for what the Gospel offers us: friendship with Jesus and love of our brothers and sisters. If we succeed in expressing adequately and with beauty the essential content of the Gospel, surely this message will speak to the deepest yearnings of people's hearts: "The missionary is convinced that, through the working of the Spirit, there already exists in individuals and peoples an expectation, even if an unconscious one, of knowing the truth about God, about man, and about how we are to be set free from sin and death. The missionary's enthusiasm in proclaiming Christ comes from the conviction that he is responding to that expectation". Enthusiasm for evangelization is based on this conviction. We have a treasure of life and love which cannot deceive, and a message which cannot mislead or disappoint. It penetrates to the depths of our hearts, sustaining and ennobling us. It is a truth which is never out of date because it reaches that part of us which nothing else can reach. Our infinite sadness can only be cured by an infinite love.

Discuss the following questions.

- What parts or phrases of this excerpt stand out to you and why?
- What is the primary motivation Pope Francis insists upon for spreading the gospel? What do you think about this?

- How does he speak to the connection between prayer and evangelization in these paragraphs? What is your own experience of this connection?
- What is your reaction to Pope Francis' insistence in paragraph 265 that the gospel corresponds to people's deepest yearnings and hopes, even if they're currently unaware of this?
- In paragraph 264, the Pope says, "The best incentive for sharing the Gospel comes from contemplating it with love, lingering over its pages and reading it with the heart." How has your experience of the first nine weeks of the 10:10 Challenge helped you to contemplate the gospel with love, linger over its pages, and read it with the heart? Has your experience so far led you to greater enthusiasm to share with others what you have experienced in Christ?
- What questions do you have about sharing faith with others? What fears or hesitations do you have?

PLAN YOUR FINAL MEETING (3 MIN)

Your next discussion will be your final meeting for the 10:10 Challenge. Consider making it more celebratory or special in some way! You will take time to look back over your whole experience and make plans for the future.

CLOSING PRAYER (5 MIN)

Choose someone to lead the closing prayer time. Use the prompts below and add your own words. Invite the other(s) to add their prayers when you prompt them.

In the name of the Father, and of the Son, and of the Holy Spirit. Amen.

Lord Jesus, we take you at your word today—that you have called, equipped, and anointed us for mission with you in the world. Calm any fears we may have as we ponder this Great Commission of yours in the upcoming weeks, and inspire us in new ways to be salt and light to those you put in our paths. Help us continue to discover the treasure that you are to us, that we might joyfully share this treasure with others. Come, Holy Spirit; fill us and fuel us for mission.

In particular, we pray for _____; _____; _____. I invite you to add your own prayers now as well.

We close together with the Glory Be: Glory be to the Father, and to the Son, and to the Holy Spirit, as it was in the beginning, is now, and ever shall be, world without end. Amen.

PRAYER GUIDE
Share The Good News

Day 1. Three-Dimensional Evangelization

Above all, the gospel must be proclaimed by witness.[2]
– St. Paul VI

St. Paul VI said three forms of evangelization work together to offer a compelling witness to the world: the witness of life, of word, and of community. First, the witness of life. By the simple goodness, generosity, and holiness of their lives, Christians offer a "wordless witness" and "stir up irresistible questions in the hearts of those who see how they live: Why are they like this? Why do they live in this way? What or who is it that inspires them?. . . Such a witness is already a silent proclamation of the Good News and a very powerful and effective one."[3]

Next is the witness of word. Even though the witness of life is essential, we cannot neglect the importance of occasionally using words. By itself, the witness of life always remains insufficient, because "even the finest witness will prove ineffective in the long run if it is not explained, justified . . . and made explicit by a clear and unequivocal proclamation of the Lord Jesus. The Good News proclaimed by the witness of life sooner or later has to be proclaimed by the word of life."[4]

Finally, there is the witness of community. Though we each have a unique role to play, we don't evangelize in isolation. The supernatural love that is meant to exist among Christians *itself* gives witness to the Kingdom of God. Nor do we break up the world into neat categories of those who are "in" and "out" of the club, or who is "saved" and "not saved." The community of faith is constantly re-evangelizing itself, and it is in the witness of community that we truly learn to make the gospel a *way of life*. This "adherence [to the gospel], which cannot remain abstract and unincarnated, reveals itself concretely by a visible entry into a community of believers."[5]

301

Love does. Love speaks. Love unites. This three-dimensional witness is the reason we know Jesus today and continue living by his Spirit. More people await the discovery of this priceless treasure.

OPEN TO GOD

Open to God with a few deep breaths, turning your attention to him. As you do this, give any immediate cares or worries over to God, who cares for you.

In the name of the Father, and of the Son, and of the Holy Spirit. Amen.

Father, thank you for the ways you have captured my attention through the witness of your followers. Grant me the grace, today, to see how you have drawn me to yourself through the witness of life, word, and community.

PRAY FROM THE HEART

How have you been the beneficiary of each of the three types of witness St. Paul VI described (life, word, and community)? Pause to give God thanks for each person or experience that comes to mind.

Which of the three types of witness are you most comfortable with? Least comfortable?

While this chapter will focus largely on the skill of the witness of word, the other nine chapters in this book have aimed to strengthen you in both the witness of life and the witness of community.

Think back to the previous chapters. How has growing in each of these discipleship practices allowed you to live as a more authentic witness of Jesus?

- Pray from the Heart
- Dwell in God's Word
- Grow in Freedom
- Worship the Lord
- Love Your Neighbor
- Encourage One Another
- Call on Mary and the Saints
- Entrust Your Life to Jesus

Pray with the following two passages. Ask God to give you greater insight for how to live as an authentic witness that stirs up curiosity in others. How can you avoid the common pitfalls of hiding faith or showing it off?

Matthew 5:14-16, NRSV-CE
You are the light of the world. A city built on a hill cannot be hid. No one after lighting a lamp puts it under the bushel basket, but on the lampstand, and it gives light to all in the house. In the same way, let your light shine before others, so that they may see your good works and give glory to your Father in heaven.

Ephesians 2:8-10, NRSV-CE
For by grace you have been saved through faith, and this is not your own doing; it is the gift of God—not the result of works, so that no one may boast. For we are what he has made us, created in Christ Jesus for good works, which God prepared beforehand to be our way of life.

Talk to God about anything else on your mind today. Ask him for your daily bread.

CLOSE
Rest in the love of God for a few minutes of silence and stillness.

God of life, you have drawn me to yourself in many ways. Thank you for the gift of faith and the channels through which you have reached me. Continue your saving work in me, and lead me to those who need my witness of life, word, and community.

In the name of the Father, and of the Son, and of the Holy Spirit. Amen.

TIP: CALL ON THE HOLY SPIRIT
Each of us has a way of sharing the gospel that we're most comfortable with, and other ways that might feel out of reach. Beginning (and continuing) evangelization in prayer helps us follow Jesus out of our comfort zones to say or do what he's calling us to. "The Holy Spirit is the protagonist, 'the principal agent of the whole of the Church's mission.' It is he who leads the Church on her missionary paths."[6] There will be times we need to say a strong word of challenge or correction to another and times when we need to keep quiet. Ask for wisdom from the Holy Spirit to understand what is needed in each situation and for each person. And remember to pray for others, too, for it is the Holy Spirit who "in the depths of consciences causes the word of salvation to be accepted and understood."[7]

Day 2. The Good News

The angel said to them, "Do not be afraid; for behold, I proclaim to you good news of great joy that will be for all the people. For today in the city of David a savior has been born for you who is Messiah and Lord.
— Luke 2:10-11

At the center of our Christian faith lies an announcement of the good news that God has not abandoned us to the brokenness and sin of the world. Instead, in Jesus, God has entered into our humanity and given us a path back to the loving communion we were created to experience in him. This message of hope, freedom, purpose, and salvation is just as good now as when it was first proclaimed by the angels at Jesus' birth.

The Church uses the Greek word *kerygma* to refer to this core message and central proclamation of the gospel. In a Church with as long a history and as many streams of theological discussion as ours, it can be easy to get lost in the wideness of it all. The *kerygma* always brings us back to what our faith is all about at its core: Jesus.

There isn't just one way to state the *kergyma*, but it is often expressed with four essential elements, which can be summarized as creation, fall, redemption, and response. Here is one description of these four elements by Bishop Donald Hying.

> [Creation] "God created us in His image and likeness with a will, heart, soul, mind, and body, so that we can enter into an intimate relationship with Him."

> [Fall] "The effects of sin and death, both in our personal lives and the entire human race, have pushed us into a state of alienation and brokenness."

> [Redemption] "Never giving up on us, Jesus Christ offers us new life through the mercy and forgiveness flowing from the Paschal Mystery."

> [Response] "When we accept the Lord's gracious offer, we become a new creation and are called to witness the love and truth of Christ to others as missionary disciples."[8]

OPEN TO GOD

Center yourself and turn to God in your usual way. Entrust any daily concerns you have to him as you settle into your prayer time.

In the name of the Father, and of the Son, and of the Holy Spirit. Amen.

Lord God, I believe that you are here; that you see me, and hear me, and love me more than I'll ever understand. I ask you today for the grace to see more clearly the good news upon which I stand as your beloved child. Open my heart to know who you are, what you have done for my salvation and for the salvation of the world.

PRAY FROM THE HEART

Pray with Bishop Hying's articulation of the four elements of the *kerygma* by pausing for some brief reflection and prayer after each sentence.

"God created us in His image and likeness with a will, heart, soul, mind, and body, so that we can enter into an intimate relationship with Him."

- Pause for silent reflection. How do you experience this truth?
- What thoughts or feelings emerge?
- What do you say to God in response?

"The effects of sin and death, both in our personal lives and the entire human race, have pushed us into a state of alienation and brokenness."

- How do you experience this truth? What thoughts or feelings emerge?
- What do you say to God in response?

"Never giving up on us, Jesus Christ offers us new life through the mercy and forgiveness flowing from the Paschal Mystery."

- How do you experience this truth? What thoughts or feelings emerge?
- What do you say to God in response?

"When we accept the Lord's gracious offer, we become a new creation and are called to witness the love and truth of Christ to others as missionary disciples."

- How do you experience this truth? What thoughts or feelings emerge?
- What do you say to God in response?

CLOSE

Behold the goodness of God in a minute of silence and stillness. Invite him to speak the truth of the *kerygma* to your innermost being.

Jesus, thank you for your saving, healing, guiding love. May I always find my true identity in you. Jesus, because you are _____, I am _____. (Fill this prayer in however you feel led.)

In the name of the Father, and of the Son, and of the Holy Spirit. Amen.

Day 3. The Power of Your Experience

People today put more trust in witnesses than in teachers, in experience than in teaching, and in life and action than in theories.
— St. John Paul II[9]

Imagine if someone were to ask you, point blank, "Why are you Catholic?" or "Why are you a Christian?" Perhaps they are asking because they are politely curious about you and your life, but perhaps it's something more. Maybe they're thinking: "What motivates a person like you to believe in something as old-fashioned, judgmental, and irrelevant as Christianity?"

Putting the common misconceptions aside, what *does* motivate you to profess and practice Catholic discipleship? Why *are* you willing to go against the tide, give time to prayer and worship, love those who hate you, serve those in need, and give your life to Jesus?

Sharing the good news is not only about sharing the facts of the *kerygma*. It is also about witnessing to how those facts have impacted our lives. When we are able to share with others in meaningful, relevant ways about our lived experience of the *kerygma*, we become powerful witnesses to God's living presence and action in the world, not only two-thousand years ago, but *today*.

As St. John Paul II (quoted above) pointed out, people more readily trust and respect witnesses who have "been there." Sharing our experience proposes the facts of faith in disarming and compelling ways that feel relevant to the listener's life because they are facts that feel "lived in"—not dry and dusty.

Speaking of our friendship with Jesus helps others imagine what it might be like if Jesus were part of their lives, too. Even if you're never asked, "Why are you Catholic?" plenty of opportunities arise where you could appropriately share a short story of

God working in your life. These stories proclaim your personal experience that the gospel is not merely a theory, but that Jesus lives and makes all the difference.

OPEN TO GOD

Take a few deep breaths and settle into prayer in your usual way.

In the name of the Father, and of the Son, and of the Holy Spirit. Amen.

Heavenly Father, I know you are here with me, that you love me, and that you know me. Thank you for my life and for leading me to where I am now. Please bring to mind meaningful moments or relationships in my life that have formed my faith in you.

PRAY FROM THE HEART

Reflect today on your experience of the gospel. What are the unique ways God has worked in your life? While we often think of our lives on a day-to-day level, take some time to "zoom out" and consider the whole picture from a 30,000-foot perspective. What high points or low points, people, or important seasons of growth stand out? Write down some events or people that come to mind as you look over the following prompts. You don't need to be thorough and record everything; just focus on what seems most important to you now.

- High points
- Low points
- Defining moments
- Influential relationships
- Times you felt God's presence or apparent absence
- Seasons of growth/discovery

_____

_____

_____

Read through the following prompts. Choose one or two that apply to you and use them to prompt your prayer. Pray with whatever stands out to you:

- What is one way you have changed for the better because of your relationship or an encounter with God? Relish in this blessing, giving thanks.
- How was God present to you in good times and in bad?

- How does this exercise affect your view of the past? Your experience of the present? Your feelings about the future?

Share with God any thoughts or emotions that came up as you made your list. Use Notice, Tell, Invite.

CLOSE

Close with a few moments of wordless presence with your Creator.

You know me better than I know myself, Lord. Give me eyes to see your faithfulness and love everywhere I turn. Use my past, present, and future for your glory.

In the name of the Father, and of the Son, and of the Holy Spirit. Amen.

TIP: ASK ABOUT OTHERS' EXPERIENCES OF FAITH

Everyone believes in something, whether they can articulate it or not. Ask people with whom you have a solid foundation of trust good questions about what they believe. From time-to-time, turning conversations to spiritual topics and listening compassionately to others' experiences of God, faith, and the Church can deepen your relationship and open up new pathways of conversation. Be non-judgmentally curious about them and seek to understand their stories and experiences. Sometimes they may ask you about your experiences in return. Whether or not they ask you what you believe, listening to someone with curiosity, love, and attention is a rare gift that shows them the love of God.

Day 4. Always Be Ready

Always be ready to give an explanation to anyone who asks you for a reason for your hope, but do it with gentleness and reverence.
– 1 Peter 3:15-16

Some situations demand more than the quiet witness of life: like when we're asked a direct question about faith or when the Spirit prompts us with a timely word for someone. There's no script for responding when these opportunities come, but reflecting on how you might share your story of faith in a few short sentences can help prepare you for those moments. It's a powerful and practical exercise to go deeper in your own understanding, and to "always be ready to give . . . a reason for your hope."

Every believer has a story of faith and lives as a unique expression of the story of salvation that God is still bringing about in our world. The U.S. Bishops strongly affirm this:

> Whether you were baptized as a child or joined the Church as an adult, you have a story of faith.Whether you sincerely live your faith in quiet or have a great public ministry, you have a story of faith. Whether you have a grade-school knowledge of the Catechism or have a theological degree, you have a story of faith. We all have—and are—stories of faith. . . We can understand evangelization in light of these stories of faith: namely, how we have been changed by the power of Christ's word and sacraments and how we have an essential role in sharing that faith through our daily lives as believers.[10]

Some people's stories include moments of dramatic conversion, others feature the quiet power of choosing Jesus again and again over a lifetime of faith. No matter how God has worked in your life, you have—and are—a story of faith worth sharing.

OPEN TO GOD

Prepare for prayer in your usual way.

In the name of the Father, and of the Son, and of the Holy Spirit. Amen.

Heavenly Father, "You formed my inmost being; you knit me in my mother's womb" (Psalm 139: 13). You know every second of my story and have been with me through it all, whether I knew it or not. Help me see where and how you're calling me to be and share your good news.

PRAY FROM THE HEART

Consider again the significant moments and experiences you prayed with yesterday. Pick a moment, season, or experience that reveals an encounter with Jesus that changed you or made a difference in your life.

What three to five words describe what you were like *before* this moment, season, or experience?

What three to five words describe how you changed as a result of this encounter with Jesus? How were you different *after* this moment, season, or experience?

Now put these three pieces of "before," "encounter with Jesus," and "after" into a mini story of your experience of the good news. Aim to write it in fewer than ten sentences. Ask for God's help as you begin.

_____

_____

_____

_____

_____

Look at your story again. How is God the protagonist or main player in your story? Rewrite it, if needed, with Jesus as the star of the story.

_____

_____

_____

_____

_____

1 Peter 3:15-16
Always be ready to give an explanation to anyone who asks you for a reason for your hope, but do it with gentleness and reverence.

Imagine sharing some part of your story with someone who might be encouraged or helped by hearing it. Does any person or any situation come to mind? What might you say if you had an opportunity to share?

Pray for the Lord to open pathways of deeper communication and witness in your life.

Talk to God about anything else on your mind. What do you want or need to entrust to him today?

CLOSE

Rest silently in God's saving love for a minute or two.

Jesus, thank you for seeking me out and for giving me new life. Continue to give me eyes that see the ways you are working in my life. I want to be able to share your good news with others at the right time *and in a loving way. Help me witness to how good you are and all you have done for me.*

In the name of the Father, and of the Son, and of the Holy Spirit. Amen.

TIP: PRACTICE YOUR 1-MINUTE STORY

With a fellow disciple, practice sharing a story of one of your important faith experiences. Try to share the crux of the story in just three minutes—or even one minute! Most of the time, when someone asks you about your faith, they are not looking for a twenty-minute or even a five-minute answer. Practice saying something compelling about your journey with Christ in ways that are short enough to share in the course of a normal conversational environment. If, after your brief story, someone wants to know more, you can always answer their questions.

Day 5. A Unique Witness

At the sight of the crowds, his heart was moved with pity for them because they were troubled and abandoned, like sheep without a shepherd. Then he said to his disciples, "The harvest is abundant but the laborers are few; so ask the master of the harvest to send out laborers for his harvest."
— Matthew 9:36-38

When considering the Great Commission, our call to draw the whole world into a relationship with Christ,[11] St. John Paul II wrote that each of us has a "unique task which cannot be done by another."[12] Let that sink in for a moment.

We are each created and known by God; a unique expression of his image and likeness. And God is pleased to use our uniqueness to proclaim his goodness. "God calls the individual in Jesus Christ, each one personally by name. In this sense, the Lord's words 'You go into my vineyard too' (Matthew 20:4), directed to the Church as a whole, come specially addressed to each member individually."[13] Evangelization is the work of the whole Church, but it is also the joyful responsibility of each one of us.

With a vineyard as large as the Lord's, it is no wonder that Jesus tells his disciples, "The harvest is abundant but the laborers are few" (Matthew 9:37). None of us can evangelize the world alone, and yet we're often tempted into all-or-nothing thinking.

"I can't be a great preacher or missionary in a foreign land," we might think. Instead, God calls each of us to labor in a particular corner of his vineyard. For most of us, that corner includes the places and people we already walk among each day.

There are some ways to spread the Kingdom that are unique *only to you*. There are some people that will be brought into a relationship with Christ *only through you*. No one else is in the exact mix of relationships and secular arenas as *you*. No one else has the same personality, skills, gifts, scars, and idiosyncrasies as *you*. This doesn't mean everything is up to you; you aren't the savior of the world, and the community of faith complements both your gifts and your weaknesses. Just remember this: no one else can be salt, light, and leaven in just the same way or place as *you*.

OPEN TO GOD

Prepare for prayer in your usual way.

In the name of the Father, and of the Son, and of the Holy Spirit. Amen.

Holy Spirit, surround me with your presence. Thank you for creating me as uniquely me. Thank you for my life and the purpose you give it. Help me see the unique opportunities in my life where you are calling me to shine your light.

PRAY FROM THE HEART

If we start to think about all the crowds of people in the world in need of God's care, the magnitude of the need can overwhelm our good intention. Instead, let's start with the unique corner of the vineyard that Jesus has given you to tend.

Prayerfully consider people you know—family, friends, neighbors, acquaintances—to start identifying the people in your vineyard. Use the lists and questions below to prompt your memory.

Household Members/Family

- Immediate family
- Extended family
- Roommates
- Hall or dorm mates

Friends and Acquaintances

- People you see regularly
- Friends you haven't talked to in a while
- Neighbors
- Co-workers/classmates
- Someone you recently met
- People you see at church

Ask the Holy Spirit to highlight one to three people he might be calling you to "tend" or "cultivate" in his vineyard right now.

- How can you build or strengthen your relationship with this person? What do they need?
- Which people on this list do you have the most trust or influence with?
- Who would be most receptive to talking with you about matters of faith?
- Sometimes, the people we love the most and who we most want to see transformed by God's love are not open to hearing about Jesus from us. What are some ways you can love them well and show them your witness of life rather than your witness of words?

Pray for the people who came to mind during today's reflections. Ask God to give you opportunities to share his love with these people through your witness of life, word, and community in appropriate and fruitful ways.

CLOSE

Rest silently in the presence of God.

Father, thank you for giving me a place to work in your vineyard. I praise you that you have entrusted me with a unique life and unique purpose. Please help me notice opportunities to witness to your goodness in my friendships and relationships. Give me wisdom to know when to speak and what to say and courage to do so when the time is right. Thank you for calling me to take part in your work of evangelization.

In the name of the Father, and of the Son, and of the Holy Spirit. Amen.

Day 6. The Divine Pedagogy

With such affection for you, we were determined to share with you not
only the gospel of God, but our very selves as well,
so dearly beloved had you become to us.
— 1 Thessalonians 2:8

When God the Son came into this messy world, he left behind the comforts of heaven to enter into solidarity with a world lost in the darkness of suffering and sin. By this great act of the Incarnation and all that would follow, Jesus not only provided us a way to eternal life, he also modeled the way to serve, teach, and influence others in his name. It's never *from afar*. God's way, and therefore our way, is not to sit back and hurl out advice, instructions, or sermons from a safe, detached distance. It is to dive deeply into the messiness of life with others: to walk *with* them, not just say things *to* them or do things *for* them.

St. Paul expressed this way of life, this divine pedagogy, insisting, "We were determined to share with you not only the gospel of God, but our very selves as well" (1 Thessalonians 2:8). Just as Jesus did (and does), St. Paul took a *relational* and *incarnational* approach to evangelization, sharing his *very life* with the people he served and ministered to.

As relational beings made for genuine friendship and love, people can smell inauthenticity or "salesy" agendas a mile away. Witnessing to the gospel is not a sales pitch or an agenda. It's an act of authentic self-giving we approach with reverence, prayer, and discernment. From small acts of service, to extending a listening ear, to praying for and with others, to prompting timely conversations, the Lord moves in and through us to extend his compassion to others.

Relational, incarnational evangelization isn't clear-cut or swift. Accompanying others as they discover the good news of Jesus takes patience, prayer, and "apostolic endurance."[14] Sometimes we get beat up or bruised by others' fear and rejection in the process. But it teaches us to love other people with the enduring love of Jesus. It teaches us not to give up hope and to believe in Jesus' power to change hearts.

OPEN TO GOD

Open your mind and heart to God by speaking your favorite name or title for God while taking a few deep breaths.

In the name of the Father, and of the Son, and of the Holy Spirit. Amen.

Thank you Jesus for crossing the threshold of sin and death to give me the gift of yourself. Thank you for dwelling with me now, even making yourself available in the quiet gift of the Eucharist. Move my heart to beat with yours, as St. Paul's did, out of love for your people.

PRAY FROM THE HEART

Read the broader context of St. Paul's words to the Thessalonians and pray with the questions that follow.

1 Thessalonians 2:5-12

Nor, indeed, did we ever appear with flattering speech, as you know, or with a pretext for greed—God is witness—nor did we seek praise from human beings, either from you or from others, although we were able to impose our weight as apostles of Christ. Rather, we were gentle among you, as a nursing mother cares for her children. With such affection for you, we were determined to share with you not only the gospel of God, but our very selves as well, so dearly beloved had you become to us. You recall, brothers, our toil and drudgery. Working night and day in order not to burden any of you, we proclaimed to you the gospel of God. You are witnesses, and so is God, how devoutly and justly and blamelessly we behaved toward you believers. As you know, we treated each one of you as a father treats his children, exhorting and encouraging you and insisting that you conduct yourselves as worthy of the God who calls you into his kingdom and glory.

For help reflecting:

- What two analogies does St. Paul use to describe how he and his co-laborers treated the people to whom they witnessed?
- From this passage, what are St. Paul's motives for sharing the gospel?
- What do you think it means to share *oneself* with others? What types of actions and attitudes come to mind?
- What about you? With whom do you desire to share the gospel and more of your own self?
- Examine your manner of being with this person or these people. How could you be more gentle or encouraging with them? What do they need right now and what does that look like? Ask the Lord for insight into their needs and spend a few minutes in quiet prayer.

St. Paul begins this letter reminding the people of his prayers for them: "We give thanks to God always for all of you, remembering you in our prayers" (1:2). Take some time now giving thanks and interceding for whomever you've been thinking about during this prayer time.

CLOSE

Rest in God's love, letting God take and perfect your prayers for the people in your life.

I praise you, God, for your compassionate gaze and encouraging love. Lead me to recognize and respond to your call to extend that love to those I encounter today, this week, and always.

Invite Mary's intercession over those you just prayed for.

Hail Mary, full of grace, the Lord is with thee; blessed art thou among women, and blessed is the fruit of thy womb, Jesus. Holy Mary, Mother of God, pray for us sinners now and at the hour of our death. Amen.

In the name of the Father, and of the Son, and of the Holy Spirit. Amen.

Day 7. Looking Back and Forward

How can I repay the Lord
for all the great good done for me?
— Psalm 116:12

You have come to the 70th and final individual prayer time of the 10:10 Challenge—no small feat! Today in prayer, you have two goals. First, look back on your journey through the 10:10 Challenge to savor the blessings received and remember what was most important or impactful for you. Throughout Scripture, God calls his people to remember, to call to mind the lessons and blessings of the past, that they might live more faithfully in the present. For example,

> Be on your guard and be very careful not to forget the things your own eyes have seen, nor let them slip from your heart as long as you live (Deuteronomy 4:9).

> Remember the word I spoke to you (John 15:20).

> Remember then what you have received and heard (Revelation 3:3, NRSV-CE).

Secondly, look ahead: for yourself and for others. For yourself, begin making a plan to continue living out the ten *ways* covered in this book.

Next, think of others. Who else might appreciate and benefit from the 10:10 Challenge? Many people, even among Mass-going Catholics, have never had a dedicated season of personal growth and communal fellowship like the one you just experienced. "The harvest is abundant but the laborers are few" (Matthew 9:37). Consider giving one or a few others the gift of guidance and accompaniment into a deeper life with Jesus. Your second time through will further solidify your own habits of discipleship, and you'll get the added joy of passing on what you have received. You are a link in the great chain of disciple making that started with Jesus and continues throughout the world today. Though you are never "done" learning to follow Jesus yourself, you are prepared to help a few others discover the richness of a Jesus-led life. "Go, therefore, and make disciples" (Matthew 28:19)!

OPEN TO GOD

Take some deep breaths as you call to mind God's presence in a few moments of silence.

In the name of the Father, and of the Son, and of the Holy Spirit. Amen.

Come, Holy Spirit. Fill me once more with your light and your life. Give me the grace to look back in gratitude, to look forward with expectation, and to see all things through the lens of your love.

PRAY FROM THE HEART

Look Back

Prayerfully review the ten ways of a Jesus-led life covered in this book (see page 318). For each topic, what is an insight, lesson, or practice you most want to remember or repeat as you go forward from here? You might want to flip back through the book or through your journal from the last ten weeks.

Look Forward

Who in your life might appreciate and benefit from the 10:10 Challenge? Sit with this question in prayer, asking the Lord to direct your thoughts.

What do you think about inviting and accompanying this person (or these people) into the 10:10 Challenge?

317

**PRAY FROM THE
HEART**

**DWELL IN GOD'S
WORD**

**GROW
IN FREEDOM**

**WORSHIP THE
LORD**

**LOVE YOUR
NEIGHBOR**

**ENCOURAGE ONE
ANOTHER**

**FOLLOW
GOD'S LEAD**

**CALL ON MARY
AND THE SAINTS**

**ENTRUST YOUR LIFE
TO JESUS**

**SHARE THE
GOOD NEWS**

CLOSE

Close your eyes and linger in God's presence for a few moments of contemplative silence.

When you are ready, close in your own words. What do you want to say to God as you conclude these ten weeks and 70 days of prayer, study, and action?

MAKE IT A HABIT
Share the Good News

Below, find additional tips and suggested readings for continuing to grow in sharing the good news.

DEVELOP YOUR SECULAR INTERESTS

Jesus calls his followers to be the "salt of the earth" and the "light of the world" (Matthew 5:13, 14). In these analogies, location matters. Light under a bushel basket does not light up the darkness. Salt that's trampled underfoot does not season the dish. It's not enough to be bright or salty; we must also be in the places where salt and light are meant to be.

The Second Vatican Council offered some illuminating teachings about the call of the laity in the world. A big part of what distinguishes the laity vocation is their location.

> They live in the world, that is, in each and in all of the secular professions and occupations. They live in the ordinary circumstances of family and social life, from which the very web of their existence is woven. They are called there by God that by exercising their proper function and led by the spirit of the Gospel they may work for the sanctification of the world from within as a leaven.[15]

It's holy teachers, janitors, business leaders, nurses, moms, dads, first responders, baristas, school board members and motorcycle riders who will be salt and light to the places Father and Sister are not called to be. Every nook or cranny of the world needs the light, flavor, and fragrance of Christ, and the laity can bring it there.

Reflect on your place as a lay person in the world. For the moment, think beyond your involvement at church. Your interest in weight lifting, sports, local community involvement, reading books, tasting craft beers, etc., might just lead you to the nooks and crannies of the world where God wants you to be salt, light, and leaven. Who's shining the light of Christ on your neighbors if you shun the community cookout? Be in the world—not of it, but certainly in it—so that the world might encounter Christ through your unique presence and witness.

WATCH GOD USE YOUR WEAKNESS FOR HIS GLORY

One of the greatest paradoxes of the Christian life is just how mysterious and upside-down the experiences of "strength" and "weakness" can be. As the Lord said to St. Paul, "My grace is sufficient for you, for power is made perfect in weakness" (2 Corinthians 12:9).

Our efforts to evangelize are occasions to experience this counterintuitive dynamic of weakness and strength in dramatic fashion. Sometimes our best efforts and most confident plans seem to fall flat and ring hollow. Other times, when we feel utterly empty and inadequate, we see God do his most surprising and amazing work through us.

The Lord surely will call upon your gifts, strengths, and skills, but don't be surprised when he uses your weaknesses all the more. There are people who need the compassion you have in abundance because of your struggles (previous or ongoing) with particular sins, crosses, and thorns. The suffering you continue to endure will gain you credibility in someone's eyes, someone who needs to know that God won't abandon them in their pain.

LEARN THE THRESHOLDS OF DEEPENING CONVERSION

Most people in our day and age travel through semi-predictable stages of openness on their way to believing in and committing to a life of following Jesus. These are movements from distrust to trust, complacency to curiosity, being closed to being open, meandering to seeking, and being undecided to making a decision to follow Jesus. Protestant and Catholic ministry leaders have delineated helpful guidelines for recognizing and responding to each of these stages. See recommended reading for two books on the topic.

RECEIVE MISSION TRAINING

Seek further training in how to share your faith with others in ways that are loving and compelling. The Evangelical Catholic (producers of this book) partner with Catholic parishes, campus ministries, and organizations to provide mission training to lay people in communities nationwide. If your parish offers Reach More™ Mission Training from the Evangelical Catholic, talk to a staff person about taking part in the training to continue to expand and deepen your skills for sharing the good news. Also seek out training opportunities through your diocese or other local ministries.

ADDITIONAL RESOURCES

- *The Joy of the Gospel (Evangelii gaudium)*, para. 259-288 "Spirit-Filled Evangelizers," Pope Francis
- *Declaration on the Relation of the Church to Non-Christian Religions (Nostra aetate)*, Document of Vatican II
- *I Once was Lost: What Postmodern Skeptics Taught Us About Their Path to Jesus*, Don Everts and Doug Schaupp
- *Forming Intentional Disciples*, Sherry Weddell
- *Something Other than God: How I Passionately Sought Happiness and Accidentally Found It*, a memoir of an atheist's journey to the Catholic faith by Jennifer Fulwiler
- Find inspiration and ideas for how to share your faith with others by listening to the Reach More podcast from the Evangelical Catholic. Subscribe on your favorite podcast platform or on YouTube.
- The Called & Gifted™ Discernment Process from the Catherine of Siena Institute helps Christians discern the presence of charisms—spiritual gifts from the Holy Spirit—that they may have. Charisms are ways for God's goodness to bless the Church and the world through your unique gifts.

DISCIPLESHIP PRACTICES
Share the Good News

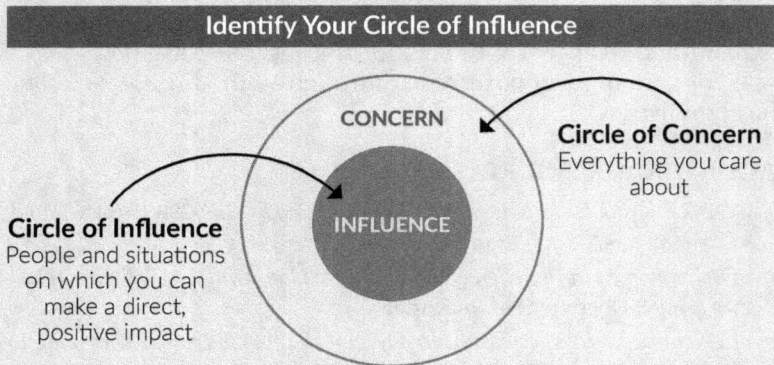

Identify Your Circle of Influence

Circle of Concern
Everything you care about

Circle of Influence
People and situations on which you can make a direct, positive impact

CONCERN

INFLUENCE

When we spend too much time focused on our circle of concern (outside our circle of influence)* we become discouraged, anxious, or bitter, and our circle of influence shrinks. For example, we might often complain about the president, global politics, or "the direction society is going." When we focus too much on concerns where we have little influence, we expend our energy in the wrong places, fewer people listen to us, and we fail to bring about positive change.

We should acknowledge and pray about our circle of concern but focus the bulk of our energy, attention, and action within our smaller circle of influence. There we can be more effective and more joyful, which causes our circle of influence to grow.

YOUR CIRCLES OF INFLUENCE AND CONCERN

From time to time, reflect and pray about your circles of influence and concern.

- What do you care deeply about, but have little direct influence over?
  - How and when do you pray for these concerns?
  - Is there an organization making an impact in this area that you can support financially or in some other way?

---

* These ideas are drawn from Stephen Covey's classic book, *The 7 Habits of Highly Effective People.*

- Who and what falls within your circle of influence?
  - First, yourself: how are *you* working to grow in character, prayer, and loving others?
  - For whom do you have a responsibility to care for, guide, or support due to family, work, or other responsibilities?
  - With whom do you have some degree of trust and influence?
  - In what settings or circumstances are you called to offer the witness of life—quietly but intentionally living as salt, light, and leaven for the Kingdom?
  - In what settings or circumstances are you called to offer the witness of word—explicitly guiding and accompanying others in faith?

Discover Your Mission

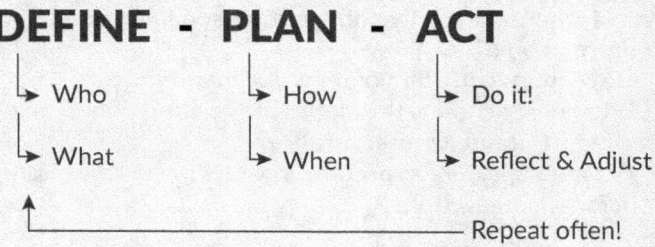

DEFINE - PLAN - ACT

↳ Who ↳ How ↳ Do it!

↳ What ↳ When ↳ Reflect & Adjust

↑—————————————————————— Repeat often!

If you're baptized, you have a unique mission to *be* and *share* the good news of God's love with the world *in a way no one else can*. If you're confirmed, you have a special anointing to be supernaturally effective in this mission. Periodically pray about who the Lord is calling you to love, serve, and guide in an intentional way. This is your unique personal apostolate (mission) in your little corner of the world.

Spend an initial 30-minute prayer time with the following prompts.

DEFINE

Who is Jesus calling you to?
- Identify your circle of influence (see page 322).

What is Jesus calling you to do?
- How can you build or strengthen relationships with the people you identified?
- What do they need at this time in their faith? (Conversation, answers to their questions, freedom to explore, new experiences that open their eyes, the steady comfort of a friend, the gentle but confident guidance of a mentor, additional help from a counselor, etc…)
- Is there anything God is calling you to stop doing to maintain spiritual health and attentiveness to your fundamental apostolic responsibilities?
- Consider the contents of the daily prayer guides in chapters 5 and 10. As you do this, do any pathways of prayer or action stand out to you as especially appropriate right now?

PLAN

How and when will you live out your personal mission to, for, and with these people?
- How and when will you pray for them?
- What next action is the Holy Spirit calling you to take to begin or continue your apostolate?
- What details do you need to consider or communicate about before taking action?

ACT

Do it!
Step out in faith and action. Of course, living your apostolate is not a one-and-done sort of action. As you put your plans into motion, you'll discover new avenues of apostolic prayer and action to pursue for your apostolate. Return to prayer frequently to discern the Lord's voice. Learn to be attentive to the Holy Spirit both in situations you planned for and in those you didn't plan for!

ENDNOTES

1. Pope Francis, *Evangelii gaudium* (Vatican City: Vatican Press, 2013), sec. 264-265.

2. Pope Paul VI, *Evangelii nuntiandi* (Vatican City: Vatican Press, 1975), sec. 21.

3. Ibid., sec. 21.

4. Ibid., sec. 22.

5. Ibid., sec. 23.

6. *Catechism*, 852.

7. *Evangelii nuntiandi*, sec. 75.

8. Bishop Donald J. Hying, *Boldly Proclaiming the Gospel*, pamphlet (Madison, WI: Diocese of Madison, 2023), 25-26.

9. St. John Paul II, *Redemptoris missio* (Vatican City: Vatican Press, 1990), sec. 42.

10. United States Conference of Catholic Bishops, *Go and Make Disciples: A National Plan and Strategy for Catholic Evangelization in the United States* (Washington, D.C.: USCCB, 2002), accessed November 10, 2023, https://www.usccb.org/beliefs-and-teachings/how-we-teach/evangelization/go-and-make-disciples, para. 6-8.

11. See Second Vatican Council, *Apostolicam actuositatem*, sec. 2.

12. St. John Paul II, *Christifideles laici* (Vatican City: Vatican Press, 1988), sec. 28.

13. Ibid., sec. 28.

14. *Evangelii gaudium*, sec. 24.

15. *Lumen gentium*, sec. 31.

FINAL CONVERSATION

LIVING A JESUS-LED LIFE

*I came so that they might have life
and have it more abundantly.*

– John 10:10

FINAL CONVERSATION
The 10:10 Challenge

INTRO AND OPENING PRAYER (5 MIN)
Read aloud.

Welcome to the final gathering of the 10:10 Challenge, and congratulations! Over the last several months you lived out a significant commitment to growing, both personally and communally, in ten transformative *ways* (practices) of discipleship. Today, take time to reflect back, not only on the final practice, Share the Good News, but also on your entire experience together. Celebrate victories and growth, and look ahead to where God is calling you to follow him next.

Select one person to open in prayer. Use the following prayer or your own words.

In the name of the Father, and of the Son, and of the Holy Spirit. Amen.

Lord God, we come to you with deep gratitude for the journey we have taken together over the last several months. Thank you for the fellowship and prayer we have shared, for constantly meeting us in our daily prayer times, and for being the author and perfecter of this beautiful faith you have bestowed upon us through the gift of the Church.

We gather today to give you thanks and reflect on the blessings we have received. And to look forward with anticipation for what you're calling each of us to next. Come and fill our time together with a generous portion of your Spirit, as you so faithfully have done.

In Jesus' name, Amen.

REVIEW SHARE THE GOOD NEWS (10 MIN)
Discuss a few of the following questions.

- Whose faith experience did you ask about in the past week?
- Summarize what is meant by the three types of witness, and how they work together. Which of these are you most and least comfortable with?
- This chapter spoke to a handful of tools and skills we can use in sharing the good news: the *kerygma*, our personal stories of God's action, our unique circles of influence, the power of relationships, and solidarity (being *with* others). What

material stretched you most this week? What prayer times did you find most meaningful?

DISCUSS YOUR EXPERIENCE OF THE 10:10 CHALLENGE (15 MIN)

In your final prayer time of Chapter 10, you took a prayerful look back over your experience of the 10:10 Challenge.

Discuss the following questions.

- What is one way you have changed for the better from this experience? Or how might you summarize what you have learned about God, discipleship, or yourself?
- What was most enjoyable or helpful about this experience?
- What was most challenging about it? (It *is* a *challenge* after all!)
- Which of the chapters did you find most memorable or impactful? Why?

  1. Pray from the Heart
  2. Dwell in God's Word
  3. Grow in Freedom
  4. Worship the Lord
  5. Love One Another
  6. Encourage One Another
  7. Follow God's Lead
  8. Call On Mary & the Saints
  9. Entrust Your Life to Jesus
  10. Share the Good News

- Which one or two of the ten ways do you want to focus on growing in currently?

YOUR FINAL CHALLENGE (10 MIN)

Read aloud.

Your final challenge is two-fold:

First, use the Discipleship Wheel on page 338 to chart a course for continuing to live and grow as a disciple of Jesus. It's a tool you can return to often to help you live out a well-rounded, concrete discipleship plan in every season of life.

Second, pay it forward. Too few people have experienced anything like the journey you just completed—a prayerful, personal, communal, experiential season of intentional growth in the heart and habits of Catholic discipleship. Yet, when people grow in discipleship and Christ-centered community, their lives, their families, and their communities are enriched and even transformed. As Sherry Weddell put it,

The presence of a significant number of disciples changes everything. We have seen it happen over and over… Disciples pray with passion. Disciples love the Church and serve her with energy and joy. Disciples give lavishly. Disciples hunger to learn more about their faith. Disciples fill every formation class in a parish or diocese. Disciples manifest charisms and discern vocations. They clamor to discern God's call because they long to live it. Disciples evangelize because they have really good news to share. Disciples share their faith with their children. Disciples care about the poor and issues of justice. Disciples take risks for the Kingdom of God.[1]

Amen!

Taking even just one or two other people through the 10:10 Challenge is a simple and enjoyable way to make disciples and change the world! More people—even many Catholics already in the pews—need to experience at greater depths the love God has for them, the freedom and joy of a Jesus-led life, and the encouraging support of intentional Christian community.

YOUR FINAL CHALLENGE:

☐ Use the Discipleship Wheel in Appendix B (page 338) to create a plan going forward.

☐ Invite one or a few others in the near future to take the 10:10 Challenge. (See Appendix A on page 335 for tips on who and how to invite.)

Discuss the following questions.

- Who do you think would enjoy going through the 10:10 Challenge as you have done?
- Would you be open to inviting them, guiding them, and accompanying them through this experience? Could this be a "risk" you are called to take for the Kingdom of God?
- If so, what is the first step toward making this happen? How and when will you do this?

CLOSING THOUGHTS (5 MINUTES)
Read aloud.

When it comes to discovering Jesus and growing in his ways, we are (happily!) never "done." St. Catherine of Siena likened God to a deep sea.

> You, Eternal Trinity, are a deep sea: the more I enter you, the more I discover, and the more I discover, the more I seek you. You are insatiable, you in whose depth the soul is sated yet remains always hungry for you, thirsty for you, Eternal Trinity.[2]

We sincerely hope this book has been a helpful guide for you in venturing a few steps deeper into the infinite ocean that God is. The adventure of living in Christ Jesus continues to unfold with new questions, new challenges, and new graces for every season of our lives. No matter where he leads, however, the ten ways (spiritual practices or disciplines) covered in this book always mark the path of discipleship. They describe the constant rhythms of all who seek and find their life in Christ, from ancient times to modern, in every corner of the world. Disciples of Jesus pray from the heart, dwell in God's Word, grow in freedom, worship the Lord, love their neighbors, encourage one another, follow God's lead, call on Mary and the saints, entrust their lives to Jesus, and share the good news.

Importantly, disciples of Jesus do all these things *imperfectly*. Because, as we said at the outset of this journey, spiritual practices are not things we do to perform for God, earning his attention or love. God gives us all the love and attention we could ever need. We engage in these timeless practices as divinely revealed ways to tune into what God is doing for us, in us, and through us. They put us into genuine, receptive contact with the living God. From there, we can say, with St. Paul, "I have the strength for everything through him who empowers me" (Philippians 4:13). We *can* grow to love our enemies better and better; to receive criticism with humility and openness; to overcome destructive habits that lead us and others to misery; to become generous givers and joyful witnesses; to get *better*, not *bitter*, as a result of suffering and loss. These are works *only God can do in us*. Our work is to keep showing up, to "believe in him whom [the Father] has sent" (John 6:29, NRSV-CE).

We, the authors, and our whole team at the Evangelical Catholic, thank you for trusting us on this journey of prayer, discussion, and action. We pray that these ten ways always mark the contours of your life, and of the lives of others through your witness and friendship.

Be sure to visit *1010challenge.org* to tell us about your experience! Together, let's change the world with Jesus, one person at a time. To Jesus be all honor and glory, both now and forever!

BONUS CHALLENGE! (5 MIN)

- Take a minute right now to tell us you completed the challenge and claim your discount code to buy the book for a friend! Visit *1010challenge.org*.
- Are there any final thoughts you wish to share before wrapping up in prayer?

CLOSING PRAYER (10 MIN)

Spend time in prayer together.

Take turns praying freely in your own words, thanking God for the graces of this journey and asking for whatever you need going forward.

After all have prayed, pray the renewal of baptismal promises aloud together, which you prayed individually in Week 9, followed by the brief litany.

Pray aloud together.

Heavenly Father, by the power of the Holy Spirit and in the name of Jesus Christ my Lord, Savior, Teacher, and Friend,

- *I renounce sin, so as to live in the freedom of the children of God.*
- *I renounce the lure of evil, so that sin may have no mastery over me.*
- *I renounce Satan, the author and prince of sin.*
- *I believe in God, the Father almighty, Creator of heaven and earth.*
- *I believe in Jesus Christ, his only Son, our Lord, who was born of the Virgin Mary, suffered death and was buried, rose again from the dead and is seated at the right hand of the Father.*
- *I believe in the Holy Spirit, the holy Catholic Church, the communion of saints, the forgiveness of sins, the resurrection of the body, and life everlasting.*

Leader:	*All:*
Mary, Mother of God,	*pray for us.*
St. Joseph,	*pray for us.*
St. Paul,	*pray for us.*
St. Teresa of Avila,	*pray for us.*
St. Ignatius of Loyola,	*pray for us.*
St. Francis de Sales,	*pray for us.*
St. Teresa of Calcutta,	*pray for us.*
St. Augustine,	*pray for us.*

Jesus, we trust in you. Lead us ever deeper into your abundant life, and help us to share this treasure of faith and Catholic discipleship with those who want and need a closer walk with you.

Hail Mary, full of grace, the Lord is with thee; blessed art thou among women, and blessed is the fruit of thy womb, Jesus. Holy Mary, Mother of God, pray for us sinners now and at the hour of our death. Amen.

ENDNOTES

1. Sherry A. Weddell, *Forming Intentional Disciples: The Path to Knowing and Following Jesus* (Huntington: Our Sunday Visitor, 2012), 81.

2. St. Catherine of Siena. *The Dialogue.* Translated by Suzanne Noffke. *The Classics of Western Spirituality* (New York: Paulist Press, 1980), 167.

APPENDIX A
Leader Resources

WHO AND HOW TO INVITE

To gather one or a few others to take the 10:10 Challenge together, first pray about who in your life might be interested in this experience. Note that it can be equally beneficial both to Catholics who are already well-established in discipleship and to those who are not.

For the less experienced disciple, the process serves to build a firm foundation for their ongoing, life-long growth in Christ. For the more seasoned disciple, the process can reinforce or deepen some aspects of their own life in Christ, and also serve as a helpful tool they can use to guide others into a life of discipleship. Finally, this book can also help interested non-Catholics explore the basics of discipleship from a Catholic perspective.

In any case, this book, and the process it represents, is for people who:

- Desire to grow closer to Jesus, guided by a Catholic understanding of discipleship;
- Are willing to put forth the effort to pray daily and faithfully discuss their progress and experiences with one or a few others; and
- Are open and teachable to Scripture, the Church, and the other person/people with whom they meet for the weekly conversations.

In short, this is for anyone who you think might respond positively to the contents of the introduction (pages 1-6). (Sign up for bonus content at *1010challenge.org* to get a shareable version). Once you've thought and prayed about who might be interested, simply

- Tell them about the 10:10 Challenge, why you're interested in it, and why you think they might like the process. Then invite them to consider joining you for these ten weeks.
- Send them to *1010challenge.org* to learn more about what the challenge entails.
- Give them some time to consider your invitation and get back to you with their thoughts, questions, or a decision.

Once you have a committed partner or small group, make sure everyone obtains a copy of the book,* schedule your first conversation (page 8), and you're off! Note that Conversation One presumes everyone has read the introduction, so remind people to do this if they haven't already.

DISCUSSION GUIDELINES

Observe these basic ground rules for fun and fruitful discussions through the 10:10 Challenge.

Purpose
We gather as believers on a common quest: to become stronger disciples of Jesus, growing in the abundant life he leads us into.

Priority
To reap the full fruit of this personal and communal experience, we will prioritize participation in the conversations and commitment to the at-home prayer times.

Promptness
We will respect people's time by starting and ending at the agreed-upon times.

Prayer
We will begin and end all discussion sessions in prayer, inviting the Holy Spirit to be present and active in our meetings. We will bring personal intentions for ourselves and others into these prayer times, sharing from the heart.

Participation
We will strive to create an environment of Spirit-filled discussion in which all are encouraged to share. To help this happen, we will observe the following guidelines:

- We strive to be attentive listeners and to encourage one another.
- We are teachable, open to learning from Scripture, the Church, and one another.
- We seek always to be respectful, humble, open, and honest in listening and sharing.

---

*   Available at *1010challenge.org*.

- We don't interrupt, respond abruptly, condemn what another says, or silently judge in our hearts.

- We keep confidential anything personal that may be shared.

- We avoid dominating the discussion, arguing, and giving unsolicited advice.

- We seek to avoid the temptation to apply what we're learning to *others* ("those…" teenagers, liberals, conservatives, Protestants, etc.), and instead focus on what the Lord is teaching *each of us* through our readings, prayer times, and conversations.

- We respect the need for occasional silence in order to reflect and process before sharing.

- While Spirit-guided tangents can happen and should be welcomed, we strive also to prioritize discussing the topics and content in the guides.

APPENDIX B
The Discipleship Wheel

DISCIPLESHIP WHEEL

A disciple seeks to live a Christ-centered life: to know Jesus, to love Jesus, and to follow Jesus. The wheel illustration below depicts seven essential elements of Catholic discipleship. Use this image to reflect on your life of discipleship and make a plan for continued growth. Which areas do you need to strengthen for a well-balanced life in Christ? Create, live, and periodically revise your discipleship plan to build holy habits for living the abundant life of Jesus.

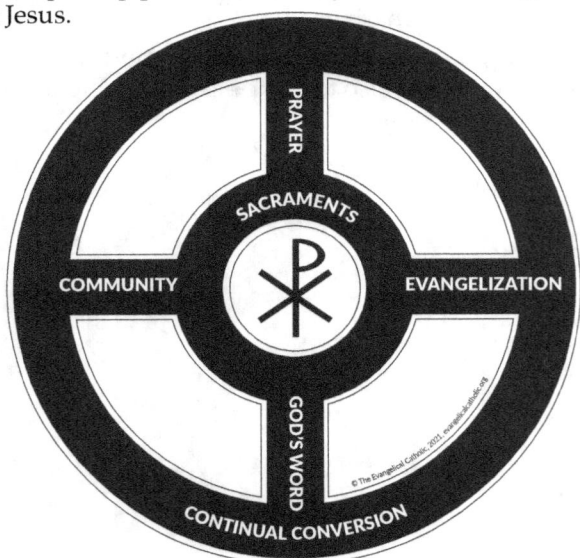

Christ the Center

The center of the Christian life is a person. In Jesus, we find our deepest identity: a beloved child of God. Jesus' words, ways, sacrifice, body, and Spirit are the infinite well we never cease to return to for unconditional love, inexhaustible power, and sure guidance from heaven.

- How well do I cling to my baptismal identity in Christ as a beloved child of God in whom the Father delights?
- How am I seeking and following the Lord's guidance in my life? (See page 225 or page 226.)

- Is there anything getting between me and God right now? How can I remedy this?
- What areas of my life do I need to entrust more completely to Jesus? (See page 291.)

Cling to the Sacraments.

The sacraments are God's chosen means of touching us most directly with his presence and saving help.

- How often will I go to Mass? When / where?
- How often will I go to confession? When / where?
- In what additional ways can I deepen my love for the Eucharist?

Pray Daily and Deeply.

Prayer is communication with God. It is essential for a fulfilling, intimate relationship with him.

- When will I pray each day?
- Where will I pray each day?
- Who am I called to intercede for in this season?

Meditate on God's Word.

We meditate on God's Word in Sacred Scripture and Tradition, letting God's truth sink deeply into our minds and hearts.

- How and when will I read and pray with Scripture?
- What other reading will I do to continue learning and growing?
- Is there a Scripture verse I'm working to memorize? (See page 67.)

Commit to Community.

Discipleship is not a solo sport. In order to remain faithful, to grow in maturity, and to accomplish God's will, we need others and others need us. We rely on the Church as a refuge and for authentic guidance into the way of Jesus.

- With whom do I have regular discipleship conversations? (See page 192.)
- How often do we get together?
- Who am I praying for and supporting in their life, growth, and mission?

Evangelize in Word and Deed.

All are called to share the good news of Jesus in words and actions; the gift expands as it is shared, to the greater glory of God.

- How am I loving my neighbor, especially the poor and the "least"?
- Who am I called to love and serve intentionally in my life right now?
- How and where is the Lord calling me to live the Works of Mercy? (See page 165.)
- What percentage of my income will I give away this year—to my parish and diocese (___%) and other charities (___%)?
- Where am I building or strengthening relationships with people who do not know the love of Jesus?
- How am I called to be salt, light, and leaven to them?
- What is my current circle of influence (see page 322) and personal mission (see page 323)?

Commit to Continual Conversion.

Discipleship is a joy-filled journey of ongoing transformation into the people God calls us to be—people who love like Jesus in all circumstances. This high calling is a grace requiring our ongoing consent, effort, and cooperation, as we grow in freedom from sin and surrender our will to God.

- Who do I admire and want to imitate (a saint or other virtuous person)?
- What habits do I want to cultivate to grow in Christian maturity?
- Which saint(s) do I want to call on for their prayers?
- Is there a particular virtue I want to concentrate on increasing in my daily life? (See page 98.)
- What crosses of pain and suffering are teaching me to depend more fully upon God?
- What specific gifts or graces do I need to ask for more of from God in order to grow?

APPENDIX C
Index of Discipleship Practices and Tips

The 10:10 Challenge includes 26 discipleship practices for prayer and action and 35 helpful tips sprinkled throughout! Return to these practices and tips often after your first pass through the book, both for yourself and to share with others. The discipleship practices are listed alphabetically below. On the following two pages, find the discipleship practices and tips organized by week.

TIPS AND PRACTICES: LISTING BY WEEK　　　　PAGE

* Tips indicated by italics.

Week 5: Love Your Neighbor

Week 6: Encourage One Another

Week 7: Follow God's Lead

Week 8: Call on Mary and the Saints

Week 9: Entrust Your Life to Jesus

Week 10: Share the Good News

ABOUT THE EVANGELICAL CATHOLIC

The Evangelical Catholic's mission is to equip Catholics to live out the Great Commission.

Since 1998, the Evangelical Catholic has trained thousands of people across the nation and the world. We envision a world where faithful lay people understand the call to be laborers (Matthew 9:37) and are equipped and empowered to bring Jesus to the world as the salt and the light of their communities.

Follow us for practical tips and inspiration to live your mission in the world.

Facebook.com/evangelicalcatholic   *Instagram: @evangelicalcatholic*
YouTube.com/evangelicalcatholic   *X: @ec_catholic*

Reach More™ Coaching Partnerships
The Evangelical Catholic also partners with parishes and campus ministries to implement the proven Reach More Mission Process that forms and trains lay people for mission in the world. The result is a growing network of missionary disciples within the community who impact their families, workplaces, schools, and neighborhoods for and with Christ.

Talk to your pastor or director of evangelization about partnering with the EC to reach more in your area.

Learn more at www.evangelicalcatholic.org.

ALSO FROM THE EVANGELICAL CATHOLIC
Small Group Discussion Guides

Small group discussion guides from the Evangelical Catholic create a transformative environment where group members can meet the real Jesus in Scripture.

Find these and more at store.evangelicalcatholic.org.

ABOUT THE AUTHORS

André Lesperance is a content creator and ministry consultant at the Evangelical Catholic. He has worked in Catholic ministry and education since 2003 and holds a master's degree in theology from Marquette University. André is passionate about learning, music, downhill skiing with his kids, helping others grow in faith, and annoying his daughter by pretending to be up on the latest tween slang. He lives near Milwaukee with his wife Jackie and their four children.

Andrea Jackson is a content creator and ministry consultant at the Evangelical Catholic. She holds a degree in English from Harvard University and a Master of Divinity from Boston College. Andrea worked in parish and campus ministry before joining the team at the Evangelical Catholic in 2018. She loves to read, knit, and bake apple pies. And, yes, she realizes how much this makes her sound like a grandma. Andrea and her husband Tom live in the Milwaukee area with their dog.